Living w̶...

hurts.

To Patty

Living without ...

Peace...

hurts.

Discovering God and Purpose in the Ordinary and Extraordinary Chaos and Joys of Life

Donna Braidic *[signature]*

Donna Braidic Publishing Greenwood SC

Published by Donna Braidic
Printed in the United States of America

Cover Art by Lauren M. Shea
Cover Design by Jeff Durham

Edited by Dr. Christine Schott, South Carolina

Scripture texts used in the work are taken from the New American Bible, Copyright 1987 by Thomas Nelson, Inc., Catholic Bible Press, Nashville.

First Edition 2022

"The world is a small place, and the miles between intersecting roads become less and less as we grow older." Donna Braidic

"You will seek me and find me when you seek me with all your heart." Jeremiah 29:13

To my mom and dad: you gave me life, you gave me love, you helped me learn to live my purpose—
God's purpose—into being.
To my husband, Scott, and my daughters, Meghan and Lauren.
To my siblings by birth and my siblings by marriage, and all of your beautiful offspring!
To Tim and David and Mary Lyn, my angels in heaven.
To my many friends.
To my families by marriage.
To my groupmates, all of them!
Thank you for supporting me.
You ALL make living wonderful.
I love you all so much.

"The chambered nautilus is one of the oldest creatures known to survive in the earth's oceans. It is a symbol of nature's grace in growth, expansion, and renewal. It is also a symbol of order amidst chaos as reflected in its spiral precision." (Beaton)

Contents

Acknowledgements

Thank you to my loving encouragers along the way. You all know who you are, and I cannot thank you enough for your kind words as I progressed through this writing process.

A.R. Charnes: you brought a very unique and empathetic view to reading my book. You were the first to say "Yes!" to reading my book, ever so humble in your reaction, yet very discerning in your critique.

Ed Devos: you gave me your invaluable time and wisdom in bringing this book to publication.

Jen Hughes: your time invaluable and friendship instantaneous. Thank you for reading this work of my heart and providing feedback that only made my words come more alive!

Liz Noe: your courage to write your story planted the seed of courage in me to write mine.

Dr. Christine Schott: Dr. Schott, you are beautiful on the inside/out and your professional articulation of critique and genuine desire to see me succeed in this endeavor is priceless.

My brother, Jeff Durham: I could not have completed this book without your amazing talent in designing my cover. Your finished product gave me courage to take this undertaking to the finish line!

My daughters, Meghan Shea and Lauren Shea: Through everything we've been through, we are better and stronger together.

My husband, Scott Braidic: you made my book better than it would have been. Thank you for your first critique; it hurt, but it was right and just.

Introduction

But now, O LORD, You are our Father,
We are the clay, and You our potter;
And all of us are the work of Your hand. Isaiah 64:8
"Abba, Father: mold us and fashion us into the image of Jesus, your son." Carey Landry

I've heard a lot of people in my lifetime—especially the older generation—say with humility and a good dose of wisdom, "I went without a lot growing up...it was a tough time, but it made me stronger! I turned out okay, so I guess it didn't hurt me too much to do without!" My dad tells stories of his childhood when the family "made do" on "Chicken-Foot Soup" (groan) and how the children were farmed out to relatives during really lean times. My ninety-six-year-old aunt by marriage has told many stories of the Great Depression when her family "barely made it through." Relatives and neighbors pulled together, but sometimes it was each family fending for themselves. One of my favorite stories that Aunt Irene tells is when, by some miracle or by an angel, she was guided to the cellar where she found a silver quarter, barely visible in the dirt floor. She picked it up, polished it off, inspected it closely and not believing her eyes, ran upstairs two at a time and gave it to her mother. That one little sparkling coin bought a dozen eggs and a few other provisions for the family—enough food to survive until her father returned from his long-distance work.

There are many stories just like these that tell of hardships that bring people together, put them down on their knees, and made them bow in surrender to God. In each story the teller often uses the tag line, "...and by the grace of God I/we made it through!" There is a valuable lesson attached to each experience that testifies to the absolute necessity of faith and community and the inner strength that comes from God. Living without and persevering is not easy, especially when it hurts so much that one would rather die than live without, but during these times of affliction, when the fire is hottest, if we can stand in faith and brace against the consuming heat, we are refined and purified (Isaiah 48:10).

Once the title **Living Without...Hurts**, came to me, I could not ignore the need to explore the blessings and struggles of my life and how they—through the grace of God—have formed me, molded me, and sustained me for my entire life. Time has been a great equalizer and it turns out, I could not have lived without my good times or bad times as they have made me the person I am today; they built my character, formed my ethics, and secured my morals, making me humbler and wiser in my actions. I have discovered God and my purpose in the ordinary and extraordinary chaos and joys of life.

The nautilus on the cover represents my development from child to adult and my experiences, good and bad, natural and forced, chaotic and joyful, each ending connecting to a new beginning, creating a wonderful spiral of unending growth. As I have written each reflection I have been guided by the spirit and have discovered how precious and wonderful life is, how good God is.

Since I opened my laptop and began writing my first reflection until the last period and final page, I have felt, like my aunt, led by something supernatural, beyond me, to write about my search for clarity and purpose in the things that have happened to me over my lifetime. My faith has been tested, I have been brought to my knees in despair, I have faced the ultimate choice: God and light; or anger, depression, and darkness—and I have found a hidden treasure.

I asked myself, could my inspired thoughts, wisdom, and stories bring hope and joy and a change of perspective to even one person's life, possibly making their life better? Could I surrender to God my thoughts, my words, my will and trust the Holy Spirit to guide the creation of this book?

At first, I felt timid and apprehensive about telling people I was writing a book. I was afraid of the variety of reactions I might receive, but gratefully, no one reacted negatively! Most were curious about what I was writing about, and some asked if they were going to be in my book. Once I spoke of my idea—like sprinkling pixie dust into the air—it became real and part of the universe. My daughter Lauren calls it "manifesting." Once the intent of my words—writing a book—became someone else's "truth," I could not go back. As my husband says, "You can't put the toothpaste back in the tube!" I went from thinking about writing a book to actually doing it, and it has become a transformational event in my life.

My courage to write comes from prayer and many years of creative writing and journaling, articulating my thoughts and inspirations through writing. Journaling has been a tremendous blessing to me because it helps me open my mind and heart to the Holy Spirit's message for me while writing my thoughts and feelings down. Journaling helps me formulate into substantive words what I am searching to know or needing to express in order to make sense of my life. Journaling gives me the space and time to express myself without judgment!

After reading each of my "living withouts," I hope you, dear reader, might write down your "living without" thoughts, your feelings, and your opinions in a journal as they relate to you, or possibly share with a trusted friend and confidant that which has been stirred within you. In my shared confidences with family and friends and sometimes even strangers, I have experienced grace and found peace, and above all, I have gained clarity of purpose. I pray that these may be found by you as well, and so much more.

It has been exciting to experience the evolution of this book. Many times, tears have welled up in my eyes and blurred my vison as I have typed my memories. I have prayed to be inspired by the Holy Spirit and through this holy collaboration, shaped and guided by something greater than myself, a book has been produced that I hope will touch minds and hearts, and there will be gladness in the reading of it.

Finally, in all times, my faith and purpose have been affirmed over and over by wonderful people who God has put into my life. Husbands, daughters, family, friends, neighbors, teachers, nuns, chaplains and pastors, directors, musicians, accompanists, choirmates, coaches, bosses, co-workers, hairdressers, massage therapists, aestheticians and bartenders, healthcare workers, law enforcement and first responders, soldiers, writers, editors, social media friends and strangers alike have all been my encouragers and faithful prayer warriors, and through our interactions and love I have been able to write this book.

May God bless us all, and may God bless you, dear reader.
Donna Braidic

Know

Spiritual Outlets

"Pray without ceasing." 1 Thessalonians 5:17

"Pain and suffering have come into your life, but remember pain, sorrow, and suffering are but the kiss of Jesus- a sign that you have come so close to him that he can kiss you." St. Mother Teresa of Calcutta

I had no idea that a simple challenge in February of 2019 to my oldest daughter and to myself to write a book would end up being such a big undertaking but also a great blessing; and best of all, it has been a marvelous spiritual outlet!

At the time of my challenge to Meghan she was unemployed, and needless to say she had a lot of time on her hands, so I said to her, "Meghan, why don't you write a book? If you write one page a day for a year, you will have 365 pages written by next year! A whole book in 365 days!" She balked at my idea; that is until I said I would write a book, too. It sounded so simple! And by the end of our conversation, she agreed to my challenge!

(I have since learned that Brad Paisley had a similar thought when he wrote, "Tomorrow is the first blank page of a 365-page book. Write a good one.")

So, Meghan and I set our date to begin writing for March 1, 2019.

I had no idea what I would write about…I thought possibly something spiritually enlightening, like a journal, perhaps…inspired by my life, by my love, by my God.

As March 1st approached, my apprehension about writing a book grew. What had I gotten myself into?! A few weeks earlier I thought writing a book was a brilliant idea, but the closer the start date came, the more my annoyance with myself grew for making the offer to match Meghan, page for page. It seemed so easy at the time, but in reality, writing a book was so much bigger than me! I didn't know what to write about, but I knew I must go through with the challenge. I could not back out! I prayed to God to inspire me and to help me write my book.

On the morning of March 1st while getting ready for work, I remembered it was the seventh anniversary of my brother's death and I was mad at myself for forgetting. I couldn't start a book with that hanging over me. It felt wrong. But my brother would not have agreed. He would have said, "Why wouldn't ya?!"

So, as I drove to work, I began talking to Jesus. The book was on my mind, but so was my brother's passing as was that of my husband, Tim, which had also occurred seven years prior. The longer I dwelled on my losses, the further my book moved to the back of my priorities for the day. The extreme sadness which I had been pressing down for so long rose up in my throat and I shattered the silence with a question, "WHY??? Why did they have to die?"

I came to a red light and stopped. While I waited for the light to change, I listened for Jesus to speak to me, but all I heard inside my head were my own words of sadness and loss coming back to me.

"David and Tim were such good men, and it is really hard to believe they are gone. I don't like living without them. I miss talking to them! I hate cancer. I hate it that cancer stole their lives. Everyone spoke so highly of them at their funerals, about how they loved their wives, their daughters and sons, their family, and working…God, country, self-discipline and respect. They were so alive in life, loving their beer and fishing and hunting and surfing the net…and music and camping…you name it, they grabbed onto it with both hands! Their deaths were so sad and random; painful to everyone who knew them!"

As I continued driving, I cried, and I talked to the empty space around me about my sadness and how much I missed them, and I cried out to Jesus in a loud voice, "It's in the living without them that hurts so much. I know they are gone. They are not coming back. But I miss them! We all miss them so much!"

I emptied my grief on the front seat of my car while squeezing my steering wheel until my fingers went numb. After a little while,

I loosened my grip, and as I quieted down I heard my inner voice speak clearly: Yes, it is in the living without so many things that hurts so much, but it is strange to admit that it is also a blessing to have experienced the hurt of loss and relationships but also the joy of so many experiences, for had I never had any of them in my life I would not be who I am today, and that would hurt me so much more.

I realized it was the "living withouts" that I had struggled through, not wanting the pain but cherishing the enrichment and fullness brought to my life. I have been blessed by wonderful people and experiences in my life, and my pain of loss has been deep, but all of it has produced a deeper faith in me. I have persevered, I have moved forward, and through living without, I have come to live in joy.

God knows how painful it was for me to lose David and Tim. Although at first it seemed wrong and inappropriate that I begin writing my book on the seventh anniversary of David's death, I realized in the silence of my car that it was right and just; I heard a voice say to me, "Seven is the biblical number for completion."

Seven is also "...the number stamped on every work of God."[1]

I prayed to God to help me with this book, and he answered me with a sign, the number seven, that I must trust him to give my words life and to see this work to completion. And he gave me the title to my book. _Living Without...Hurts_. Living without...this book...hurts.

I have wanted desperately to understand life's meaning when things have been unfair, and although I do not understand everything, I am more accepting of life's unfairness by understanding that all things in my life have made me who I am.

When my dear loved ones died and my arms were empty; when I moved away from home and had to start all over again in a new place; when I did not pass a job certification test for advancement; when I was denied a pay increase that I rightly deserved; when friends left me or I left my friends; when people lied about me behind my back and tried to ruin my reputation; when my children grew up and moved away; when I rejected God and moved spiritually to a dark, lonely space...it seemed like these were the

---

[1] "The Bible Numerology Code."

worst times to endure and my need for control was the greatest. I would look in the mirror and not know the person looking back at me. Life felt lackluster and bleak.

The longer I reflect on my "living withouts," the more I see in my development from child to adult that I am who I am as a result of living with and living without; and this is the basis for my book, that it is in the living without x, y, and z that hurts so much but also x, y, and z have played a key role in who I am, and had I not gone through the living without, or appreciated how I would have missed living without something, I would not be who I am today: a strong, faithful child of God. The more my mind and heart embrace the sum total of all my life experiences—living with and living without— the more I appreciate and accept with love my struggles, peaks, and valleys, and my outcomes. They are my life, and they make up who I am. Although it is difficult to respond positively to every adverse situation and praise every outcome, under it all there is fertile ground for growth.

I am able to look back and see when my faith was rocked by situations that weakened and disabled me, but I also see how I stretched during these times, and I experienced God's healing touch; like a surgeon reconnecting torn ligaments to bone, He reconnected my body, mind and spirit with His love, and I was able to walk stronger with my gaze fixed on the future. God healed me and strengthened me, and I have come back full circle to wholeness.

Life is exciting and exhilarating, with many twists and turns, highs and lows. Rarely do I see difficulties coming, and although sometimes it feels like everything is beyond my control, I know Jesus is riding beside me on this crazy roller coaster called life, screaming in unison with me through the dark tunnels and wild corkscrews, defying gravity, and raising our hands high above our heads and letting go to enjoy the ride!

Each of us has a different story to tell with our "living withouts"; our "living withouts" may be the same but their substance and impact are unique to each individual and should be honored. There are numerous ways to fill in the blank—"It's in the living without _____ that hurts so much"—and each is true and valid. There are no wrong answers.

One of my favorite "living withouts" is hummingbirds. I love them because they give me so much hope, knowing the challenges they encounter each year as they migrate to and from Central America on their journey of life. They remind me of one of my favorite scripture passages:

"Look at the birds of the air; they do not sow or reap or store away in barns, and yet your heavenly Father feeds them. Are you not much more valuable than they? Can any one of you by worrying add a single hour to your life?" Matthew 6:27

God's love, grace, and handprint are on every part of my life, and this knowledge has helped me accept all of my "living withouts." I marvel at how God never takes his eyes off of me. If I call to him, he hears me and he extends his hand that I might reach out. He is my help; he is my shield; he is my wisdom; he is my truth; he is my courage; he is my friend. I believe faith begets faith, love begets love, and God is love, the source of my grace-filled life.

I believe nothing happens by accident, that there is a reason for everything, and this is true regarding writing this book. Brought forth by a silly challenge born out of winter boredom this spiritual outlet has become a work of God's grace brought forth by pain and loss, as well as joy and celebration.

My life has been blessed beyond words. I miss my brother and my late husband. Living without them hurts so much, but it would hurt me so much more had I not loved them and lost them. They are in heaven and when I see them again we are going to have so much time to catch up and be together!

My prayers are being answered. While I listen. With my heart. In the silence. For inspiration and fulfilled purpose. Red light, stop. Green light, go. Listen silently. Proclaim loudly. Pray without ceasing and the answers will come.

My thoughts travel to my fingers, and I am astonished by the words that fill these pages.

Books

"The mind of the intelligent gains knowledge, and the ear of the wise seeks knowledge." Proverbs 18:15

"There must be something in books, things we can't imagine, to make a woman stay in a burning house; there must be something there." Ray Bradbury, Fahrenheit 451

I was never a big reader when I was young. In fact, I had no interest whatsoever in reading anything. Ever. Or so I thought. That is, until I became a teenager.

I was a slow reader, and it took me forever to read a book. And besides, I had better things to do with my time than "waste it" on a book. I think the only time I read anything was during "reading time" at school. Even then I didn't really read. I pretended to read, matching my page turns with my classmate's page turn. It was frustrating, but I couldn't do anything about it. I was a slow reader. Period.

Then one warm, sunny summer day, while sunbathing, I noticed my sister next to me reading a book like a speed reader and she was giggling one second and looking shocked the next, and I asked her, "Whatcha reading?" and she said, "Nothing." Well, I could tell it was more than "nothing"; it was definitely something! I asked her if I could see it, to which she retorted, "Why do you care? You don't read!"

Well, she was right...I didn't read. In fact, I had teased her many times for being a bookworm. And that was wrong. But people can change their ways, and I was about to change mine! I got up and strolled into the house, very nonchalant to avoid attracting my mother's attention, and I located her novels and chose one to read.

I was nervous "borrowing" the book, and I didn't want my sister to know I had it because she would run and tell my mom, so when I returned to my towel, I hid the book behind my back and lay down on it until my sister went into the house. Then, alone with the "forbidden fruit", I opened the book and a whole new world of reading opened up to me! I had no idea there were so many positions…to read a book! On my back, on my stomach, standing up, lying down, in the sun, under the stars, in my bed, on the floor, fully clothed, in a string bikini…in every possible position and every place imaginable, I could be found doing it…reading, that is!

At fourteen years old, I never imagined myself being hooked on reading, but I finally was, and I still am to this day!

Through the years, I have read many, many books, both fiction and non-fiction. It is true: there is nothing better than curling up with a good book! The fictional characters and imaginative plots, from here, there, and everywhere, all over the world and back, and into outer space have entertained me, frightened me, saddened me, and have at times been the highlight of my day! I have laughed out loud and cried like a baby. From epic tales, trilogies, and short stories, wartime, and peacetime, you name it, I have read it morning, noon, and night, and into the wee hours of the morning again!

I have been equally entertained and inspired by non-fiction works that have opened my mind to new ways of thinking, learning, and experiencing life. I have run the gamut, from new age to religion to saints and prayers, from self-help to cookbooks, knitting books, textbooks, and electronic gadget books…the list goes on. Thank you, authors, for your vivid imaginations and descriptive words that have taken me to so many wonderful places and have taught me so well!

By far, my best reading is the Bible and other spiritual writings. These keep me going. They provide historical context and impart knowledge about God the Father and Jesus and the Holy Spirit that I can bring into the conversation when I study and debate with others. The wisdom and personal witness–fictional and non-fiction–of many characters and people have widened my perspective and deepened my faith. The insights I have received have inspired me to believe and remain faithful.

When I read, no matter what the book, I pray my mind be open to whatever the Lord wants me to know so that when called upon to speak, I know what to say.

Recently I attended a musician's convention in Louisville, Kentucky, and in my hotel, there was a very nice men's shop that had a shirt in the window that I had my eye on. I wanted to buy it as a gift for my husband for an upcoming trip he and I had planned when I got home.

At the end of the convention, before leaving, I stopped by the shop to inquire about the shirt and found the owner with a customer; they looked to be having a serious conversation. I paused at the entrance and noticed the customer was holding a book, The Four Agreements by Miguel Ruiz, and without thinking I blurted out, "Excellent Book!" My comment startled the young man, but the owner smiled and jumped right into this new conversation without missing a beat. He asked me how I knew about the book. I responded that I had read it years ago and that the Toltec Wisdom written about had helped me grow a lot as a person. The customer asked me which agreement was my favorite, and I answered, "Be impeccable with your word." Speak truth. Think before you say. Don't hurt people with your words. You can't take it back once it is said. Be pure and holy, without stain, when you speak. Be impeccable.

The owner of the store liked this agreement very much. He quoted scripture (it always amazes me when people can do this) that was similar to the agreement and then he asked me if I was a teacher, and if I could recommend more books for his customer. I blushed at his compliment, and I recommended a few more books. When I concluded my visit to the store, I did not have a new shirt for my husband (they did not have his size), but I left with something more, something priceless. I left feeling blessed.

The power of knowledge and truth that I have acquired through reading was in me, and I received a blessing that day, the blessing of confidence. Like Cinderella being tapped on her forehead by her fairy godmother's wand, twinkling stars spiraling down her body and changing her from a maid into a princess, I was tapped on the forehead by kind, impeccable words and I felt the blessing of the Spirit swirl about me, transforming me on the inside, strengthening my confidence as a bearer of faith and truth.

"In contrast, the fruit of the Spirit is love, joy, peace, patience, kindness, generosity, faithfulness, gentleness, self-control." Galatians 5:22-23

We came together, three strangers in a men's clothing shop, and after having polite, intelligent conversation, we parted as friends. We shared a moment of grace. I know God was with us. They felt it too.

When I was young, I felt dumb because I could not read like everyone else. Books were intimidating to me. Instead of admitting I was a painfully slow reader, I hid the problem and hid from books. This hurt me, and I lost confidence in myself. For too long I watched others read about magical places and bigger-than-life characters, and I felt left out. I missed out on the adventures of Aslan, Mr. Tumnus, Mr. and Mrs. Beaver, and the children Lucy, Edmund, Susan, and Peter from C.S. Lewis's *The Lion, the Witch, and The Wardrobe*! Well, no more! The literary treasures to be found in bookstores, public libraries, basements, and attics are calling out to me, "Read me!"

I am grateful to God for inspiring people to turn their curiosities and imaginative thoughts, their life stories and their memoirs, their eyewitness accounts and doctoral research into literary treasures for all to read.

And Arthur, if you are reading this book, I hope you like it, too! May God bless you.

Goals

"Don't search for the *answers*, which could not be given to you now, because you would not be able to *live* them. And the point is to *live* everything. *Live* the questions now. Perhaps then, someday far in the future, you will gradually, without even noticing it, *live your* way *into the answer*." Rainer Maria Rilke, *Letters to a Young Poet*

I like making goals for myself because they challenge me to take an active role in my life. Call them goals, resolutions, action plans, manifestations, or heartfelt desires; by design, these aspirations have helped me improve my well-being and helped chart the course of my life for the better. Goals help me grow and change and become each day the person I am becoming.

Time goes by so fast, and the clock keeps ticking off the seconds of my life, so when I achieve a goal, it not only makes me feel really good about myself, but it makes me feel like my time is being well spent. Goals, when accomplished, become a marker, a measure, for what I have thus far accomplished; from who I was in my youth to who I have become to who I am yet to be. Most importantly, the minutes of my life and the efforts I put forth in achieving goals, when I look back over the years, reveal to me the times in my life when my faith and hope and trust in God led me into my greatest personal challenges and my most fulfilling accomplishments.

And though I have not always fulfilled a goal or met my expectations for myself, I am still glad I tried, and I have no regrets for the effort I put forth. I feel a certain amount of satisfaction in simply trying.

Goals give me direction and ambition and a passion for living.

In the early years of my life, my parents helped me set goals for myself. Simple goals, but goals nonetheless. Learn to ride a bike, go out for a sports team, keep my room clean, get along with my brothers and sister, get good grades in school, make new friends, save for the future.

My parents' resolute, uncompromising expectations for me to be successful in my life gave me the first big goal of my life: to find a job. Simply put, I had two choices as a young adult: go to college or find a full-time job. There would never be any hanging around the house watching television and eating all day long. This was never an option. I would do something productive with my life. The goal was articulated and set in motion, and I met the challenge and got my first "grown up" job at the age of eighteen as a bank teller.

I admit, I could not see myself content doing nothing at all, all day long. I enjoy my down time in the evenings and spending my weekends relaxing, but even while relaxing boredom creeps in and I become restless. I am too competitive by nature–always looking for the next challenge to prove myself–to sit around and do nothing. With that said, I do not like having every moment of my life planned out or involved in a project, either; but I do love a good challenge and am always ready to use my creativity.

It is during these times of restless agitation that I feel God whisper in my heart, telling me to assess the direction my life is taking and discern if I need to stay the course or move in another direction.

I believe somewhere in the middle of these internal conflicts–betwixt and between–God finds fertile soil to plant the seeds of good goal setting for cultivating new opportunities. By his will he helps me improve my life, bringing about great satisfaction and a sense of well-being for me.

Some of the goals of my life have been obvious needs (getting a job), while others have been a little more difficult to figure out (buying a house). Some have come along unexpectedly (finding love), while practical goals developed over time (finishing the basement). Some of my goals are silly and out of character (jumping off the high dive at age forty) and some have been impulsive and awfully expensive (buying a brand-new car). Some goals were a perfect fit (having children), and some I had to grow into, stretch or alter myself, using my imagination to readjust (being married). Some goals took a strong will (quitting smoking) while some came with ease (playing the guitar). Goals can be daunting at first, like a child's toy that comes unassembled and with lengthy directions, taking much more time and effort but bringing great joy when completed (going to college).

Sometimes I have set goals that have not felt right from the start, and I committed myself too quickly and ended up struggling to complete the task only to end up feeling full of regret. They were too difficult, uncomfortable, or out of reach at the time. Typically, this happens when my ego is stroked, and instead of letting God guide me, my pride takes control and I face an uphill climb. Consequently, in these self-serving times, I have not always achieved good results. I should have given up and admitted I was wrong, even at the risk of embarrassing myself.

But in the end, God is good, and his timing is perfect, and even lousy goals have helped me grow and change, growing in humility and making a positive change in attitude!

The goals I had in my twenties and thirties were much different than those in my forties and fifties, and now advancing into my sixties, my goals have changed again. One of the best methods I have used for goal setting is making a list at the beginning of each year, sealing it away in an envelope, and reopening it the following year to see what I was able to accomplish and what needs to be continued into the new year—or even removed entirely from the list! I started this annual tradition in my early forties, and I still have not achieved visiting the majestic Grand Canyon. The fact that this trip is still on my list makes me wonder whether this a wrong goal for me, or possibly one of the greatest goals God will gift to me in my later years!

Goals make me less fearful of the future and less anxious in my uncertainties because they are concrete and proactive, forcing me to be courageous, in charge of my destiny, and confident in my belief that all things are possible with God.

Just as my parents taught me the importance of goal setting for my life, I have passed this on to my daughters and pray they will use the gift of goal setting for their lives. I believe that if they are intentional in setting goals in their lives, as opposed to just wishing for things to occur, God will guide them to success.

What is a day, a month, a year, a lifetime, if I do not have goals to propel me forward? Had I not set the goal to quit smoking and conquer my nicotine addiction "one day at a time," my life would have taken a very different course. Goal setting helped me face my fear of change, helped me let go of my old persona, and brought me to better health and quality of life. Goal setting has sparked my creative thinking and enlightened my mind for solving difficult problems and finding ways forward, making my life purposeful and satisfying.

When I started writing this book, it was the result of a challenge, a goal I shared with another, that we each write a book. It was an unintended, unexpected goal which has clearly become a gift from God to me today, for who I am becoming. This goal has deepened my relationship with God. I have learned so much about myself, and best of all, writing has helped me see how much God loves me each and every day.

Lifelong goal: to know, love, and serve God.

Question: how can I know, love, and serve God?

Answer: by knowing, loving, and serving God.

Childhood Prayers

"But Jesus said, 'Let the children come to me, and do not prevent them; for the kingdom of heaven belongs to such as these.'" Matthew 19:14

I will never forget the first time I recited my prayers as a child without the help of others. I was in first grade at St. Mark's Catholic School in Pittsfield, Massachusetts. It was a very special day, and even though I was only six years old, I remember it like it was yesterday. Looking back now, I know it was the first step on my journey of faith with Jesus.

It started with a memorization assignment from my teacher, a Catholic nun who had for years taught young children the beautiful prayers of the rosary, the Our Father, Hail Mary, and Glory Be. She said the memorization would be very difficult but rewarding and it would make God very happy. Once we memorized the prayers we would recite them in the front of the classroom- alone-without making any mistakes and receiving no help from the teacher.

With hands folded upon my desk, I listened reverently as my teacher explained the assignment, but soon my wonder and awe faded as the full weight of the assignment settled upon me. I was excited to learn my prayers, very excited in my child-like way, but I was also scared thinking about performing in front of my classmates.

I was afraid to go to "the lavatory" by myself; I didn't know how I would find the courage to do this! But then, glancing around the classroom, I could see I was not alone in my fear; the wide-eyed expression on my classmates' faces told the story!

Sister was quick to point out that although it would be difficult to learn all three prayers, we could count on her for help, as well as our parents and older siblings. She was sure we could do it! And as an added incentive, there would be a prize for those of us who

15

successfully completed the assignment. She should have led with that! A prize changed everything!

We were all ears. We would each receive a beautiful statue of The Virgin Mary and one of The Holy Family after our prayer recitation was complete.

I was so excited! I would finally have my own statues to display in my bedroom. My big sister displayed her coveted statues prominently on her dresser, turning them to and fro to catch the light just right, letting me know how special they were. I admit I had statue envy!

As my "performance" day approached, I became more and more nervous. Memorization was really hard for me, and I felt I must be perfect on my first try, or I might never receive my statues, for we were moving to Pennsylvania the next day! I literally had one chance.

The day came, and although I was petrified, I was determined to succeed. I did not want to fail; I did not want to embarrass myself in front of my classmates; and I didn't want to let my family down.

A few of my classmates took their turns, some passing with flying colors and some "still needing a little extra practice."

Then came my turn.

Sister called me forward. I walked to the front of the classroom, stood as close to her as was permitted, and faced my classmates. My heart thumped in my chest and my hands were cold and clammy as I pressed them together, fingers pointed straight up to heaven in prayer.

Promptly, without delay, Sister commanded me to recite the Our Father. Ever so slowly I spoke each word, stumbling on one word, corrected, and continued on. I finished and Sister called for the Hail Mary, and then finally, the Glory Be. I held my breath, waiting for Sister to give me a pass or fail. And then, after stern deliberation, she declared, "Well done! You have passed!"

I could have peed my pants!

My face was beaming as I returned to my seat to await the presentation of the statues. I was so happy and proud of myself!

There was so much pomp and ceremony to receive my statues— like a graduation ceremony! My name was called, and I slid out of the safety of my desk to walk forward again, but this time was different. I was not afraid. I stood before my teacher who held out

16

to me the statue of Mary, the Mother of God and the statue of the Holy Family. My heart was so full of love. Love for my teacher, love for my classmates, love for my mom who had come to support me, love for Jesus, love for God. And I felt all of that love coming back to me, a child of God, pure and holy.

I still have my special statues, tucked away in my cedar chest. They are a treasured keepsake of my childhood that remind me of a time of pure innocence, a time never to be forgotten when I learned how to pray and believed–without question–in the divine power of prayer and the blessings prayer would bring to my life.

Lord Jesus, I pray for those who do not know how to pray, for those who do not believe in prayer, for those who do not know you are listening for their voice to call out. I pray that nothing prevents them from seeking you in prayer, and when you hear their voice, you will gather them into your arms and hold them in love and they will know you all the days of their lives.

"Jesus was praying in a certain place, and when he had finished, one of his disciples said to him,
'Lord, teach us to pray just as John taught his disciples.'
He said to them, 'When you pray, say:
Father, hallowed be your name,
your kingdom come.
Give us each day our daily bread
and forgive us our sins
for we ourselves forgive everyone in debt to us,
and do not subject us to the final test.'" Luke 11: 1-4

Glory be to the Father and to the Son and to the Holy Spirit. As it was in the beginning is now, and ever shall be, world without end! Amen!

Hail Mary, full of Grace, the Lord is with thee.
Blessed art thou among women, and blessed is the fruit of thy womb, Jesus.
Holy Mary, Mother of God, pray for us sinners, now and at the hour of our death. Amen.

Thank you, Lord Jesus, for your loving kindness and care. Amen.

Young Life

"Some friends bring ruin on us, but a true friend is more loyal than a brother." Proverbs 18:24

Let's face it. People can be mean. This can be especially true in high school.

When I was a teenager in high school, full of insecurity and ever-changing hormones, it was not uncommon to walk into the girl's bathroom in between classes and hear girls saying, "Did you *see* so and so...?", "Oh, yes, she's *so*...!" "*I know*! She thinks she's *so much* better than us!" I wish I had been brave enough to interrupt their primping and fussing over themselves to ask why they said such mean things about other girls, but I didn't. I was afraid to speak out. The last thing I wanted was to become the newest target for their criticism, ridicule, or gossip. I just steered clear, moving on as invisibly as I could, keeping my head down as I washed my hands, and pushed through the door as quickly as I could to go to my next class.

Those girls were the "mean girls" of my day, and I daresay nothing has changed. If anything, they have become more emboldened by social media. It is a shame, but they have always existed, and we all know who they are.

Are there "mean boys"? Absolutely. Mean girls, mean boys; I call them bullies.

The question is: Why did I put up with the mean girls and bullies? Fear? No confidence? Passivity? Fatigue? Inconvenience? Lack of time? All of the above and more. But mostly, I was afraid of those girls and guys in high school.

It was upsetting to see them talking behind their hands while looking straight at me, knowing full well I was the subject of their nasty comments. And the fact that they were talking behind their hands told me that whatever lies they were telling, they didn't want me to hear; they just wanted me to know they were talking about me. Their mean behavior rattled my confidence, made me sick to my stomach, and made me cry.

As an adult, I have seen these same behaviors exhibited in gatherings of people, both children and adults, at parties and at church, in parent's groups and in volunteer groups, in family gatherings, sports teams, and worst of all, at work. Yes, there is a pecking order in every social group and circumstance that dictates and perpetuates this behavior. There are some people who just don't change; they have learned that creating fear–their modus operandi–is their way of gaining power over me and over others.

But I have changed since those early days of high school. As corny as it sounds, I don't walk away from bullies anymore because I have found a friend who holds more power than all of them put together. A friend who knows well the hurt and shame of maltreatment; a friend who put his life on the line every time he spoke out against injustice in defense of the weak and unpopular, the diseased, the sinner. A friend who has my back.

I found Jesus.

When I was sixteen, I was searching within myself for understanding about who I am and why I am. I didn't know it at the time, but I was searching for purpose. I was searching for acceptance and love from others, and also from myself. I had good friends, really good friends, but my heart did not trust their friendship completely because I did not feel worthy. I did not trust love.

God knew I was lonely and in his infinite love he guided me, somehow, to attend Young Life[2], a Christian youth organization. From the first meeting I was treated warmly by those I met, and it surprised me how nice the kids and leaders were towards me. This was very different from what I was accustomed to at school. For one thing, there were no blood-thirsty mean girls huddled over in a corner, scanning the room like vampires, looking for their next victim to be afflicted with anxiety from their disdain and humiliating comments. Instead, I found nice people! Everyone smiled and

---

[2] Young Life is a mission devoted to introducing adolescents to Jesus Christ and helping them grow in their faith. They can be found at https://younglife.org.

welcomed me with non-threatening, friendly hellos. Wow. It was so lovely and different!

It was to be my first taste of what friendship could be when it is based on mutual faith and friendship in Jesus Christ. No pretense, no glamor, no who's who; just calm and relaxing friendship.

One girl in particular touched my heart that first night. I knew her only in passing at school. She was popular, and although I was not, she did not seem to mind being seen with me! She was very well known around school, and everyone liked her. When she greeted me, she smiled, and her dimples melted my heart. She was smart, and kind, and funny; she had freckles to go with her red hair, and she wore glasses and even though some might say she looked like a nerd, I thought she was so cool. She said how glad she was that I was there, and she knew my name.

She knew my name. She actually knew who I was! I almost cried!

I was someone in her eyes. Now, looking back, whenever I hear the expression "Jesus with skin on" I think of her.

I changed during those meetings. I gained confidence in myself, and I became friends with people who I might not have otherwise have ever known; popular kids, jocks, musicians, nerds, pretty people, pimply people, chubby people, skinny people, some younger and some older than me, all of us meeting together for one purpose: learning about Jesus and becoming better people, loving people, friends, and servants of Jesus Christ.

Through the many inspirational lessons given by the leaders at Young Life, I learned about Jesus and friendship and love. It was surprising to me to learn that even Jesus' friends had power struggles within their circle of twelve. They argued and fought. I learned that even the best of friends doesn't stick around during difficult times, that friends can betray confidences, lie to your face, can be unreliable, and can sell you out for fame and fortune.

I could relate to these stories because I, too, had experienced the same disloyalty, then and now, with friend and foe and even stranger. And I am ashamed to say, I have done some of these same things to people I called friends. *Please forgive me.*

Since my days at Young Life, there have been malicious, "anonymous," mean-spirited people who have enjoyed hurting me with their unjust persecutions, slapping false accusations of libel and slander on my good name, and although I wanted to walk away from their trouble, to quit, I did not. The fighter in me, the competitor, role model and leader, the Christian in me would not let their malice win; I cannot walk away without putting up a good defense! Whether dealing with horrible situations on my own or with the support of my family and friends, the spirit of the Lord is with me. I am able to "turn the other cheek," but I also stand up for myself. And even though good outcomes are never guaranteed, defending myself against wrong words, wrong treatment, and wrong deeds is the right thing to do, and it returns power back to me, and I hold my head high.

My story is not unique, and I'm not looking for pity; there are thousands of people just like me who have experienced the same troubles of life. Hearts are bruised, lessons are learned, and life goes on. There are no big winners, no great celebrations, but by the power of Jesus, despite the troubles that come my way, I know I am not alone.

At the end of the day, Young Life taught me that sometimes I have to step out of my own shadow, stop pretending I am invisible, and seek out good people to befriend. I learned that if I ask God for his protection, he will give it generously, and when I trust Jesus with my troubles and place them in his hands, the greatest power comes over me and I need not be fearful or worried anymore.

Young Life brought happiness into my life through the good people I met. They shone a light so bright on all of my false assumptions about friendship and love. I learned that Jesus loves me just as I am, and so should others. During my time in Young Life, I was able to overcome many of my high school fears and my feelings of inadequacy; I came to know that I am a child of God, deserving of friends, tried and true.

Power struggles are part of life. In high school it was all about who was prettier and richer and smarter, and about whether you had a boyfriend or not. As an adult, not much has changed. Then and now, no matter when or where, people can be mean and petty about the littlest things, and it frustrates me still when I cower and bow to this ugly behavior. I have a choice in how I respond, and I practice every day to be like Jesus, to choose love, to walk away from gossip, rumors, lies, and personal attacks, and instead give respect and cordiality to those I meet.

No more gossiping and power plays. No more mean girls and bullies.

I have found friends who are tried and true, and through them, I have found Jesus.

May God, who has blessed me with an abundance of friends, bless my friends abundantly with His love.

And let us all live to bring peace and love to one another. Stop the hate. Amen.

Spirituality

"The spirit of the LORD shall rest upon him: a spirit of wisdom and of understanding, a spirit of counsel and of strength, a spirit of knowledge and of fear of the LORD, and his delight shall be the fear of the LORD." Isaiah 11:2-3

During the early years of my life, when I was young and ignorant of God's ways, the spirit of my soul waited eagerly, deep within me to be discovered and set free, so that I might be inspired to play and sing musical masterpieces in the light of God's love.

It is difficult to describe what spirituality is and how it feels to me other than to say it is a place within me that burns with so much excitement that when I open my mind and heart to God's wisdom and direction, I want to sing, make music, and live! Spirituality is a part of me, unique and personal, and once I discovered the gift, I was set free and changed for the better. The Holy Spirit penetrates my conscious thought and whispers God's love and intentions to my longing heart.

I absolutely believe, without a doubt, that every person is born with a spiritual aspect from the moment of their conception. The spirit of the Lord is constantly enlightening my mind, helping me to fulfill my purpose for Him.

Spirituality is "a thing," but to my knowledge it has no tangible properties that I can touch or see, or taste or smell, but I know with certainty that it exists in all aspects of the universe and in me. If someone asked me to prove spirituality exists, empirically, scientifically, I could not. But in practice, yes! Through my prayer and meditation and conversations with others, I believe God and Jesus and the Holy Spirit are central to the awe and wonder I feel when new ideas and new perspectives come to light. I find clear solutions to my problems when once all I could perceive was blank thought devoid of energy in the emptiness of unknowing!

When I think of all the masterful artists from the beginning of time who have brought forth the vision of their souls through the work of their hands using all the elements of the earth, I see the power of the spirit breaking through! Captured in masterful works of art, the Spirit's essence has been articulated in rudimentary drawings on cave walls and temples of ancient cities to high rises and cathedrals in modern times.

Symbols of God's fulfilling covenant have been molded by artisan hands and fired in kilns: doves taking flight on wings of porcelain, guiding the eye towards the heavens, towards peace and hope and the New Jerusalem. Through fantastic brush strokes on silk canvas, red, orange, and white minerals reproduce a blazing bush upon the side of a mountain where a voice proclaims, "I Am Who Am." The beauty of sand from ancient beaches, melted and liquified and hardened into pieces of colorful glass, cut, and soldered together to create magnificent, stained-glass windows depicting religious themes and spiritual symbols. Musical compositions performed by voice and fine-tuned instruments, resonating with the lute and harp from ages past.

Art has profoundly inspired my soul through its timeless, unreplicable beauty, and I see and feel the Spirit's movement of love in each medium of expression. Just listening to the gentle tones of a wind chime gives me pause to wonder at the eternal wind behind each note.

Spirituality brings forth a beautiful dimension of my soul, gracious and loving. I am frequently overwhelmed when I ponder the tiny particles of my spiritual energy swirling about me and creating a conduit between me and God's universe and the spirit of all living things.

During my moments of prayer and meditation I feel something magical happen inside me. The Holy Spirit enlightens my mind and opens my heart to the intimate presence of God's wisdom, knowledge, counsel, fortitude, understanding, piety, and fear of the Lord. The seven gifts of the Holy Spirit, always so right and timely, have given me the courage to act and to make good choices at some of the most crucial times in my life. At other times, this same Spirit has clamped my mouth shut tight and distracted me from speaking impulsively or sending a terse text message at the wrong moment, helping me avoid horrible regret later!

Even when dealing with difficult people, I can hear the spirit of love calling me to reconciliation. It is for me the most difficult time to be a "true Christian." I strive toward patience and humility, which are not always my forte, and when I fail at being conciliatory, denying the spirit in me from reaching the spirit in another, the Holy Spirit is relentless, bothering my conscience, disrupting my sleep, sitting on my shoulder, and making me feel uncomfortable to the point that I want to scream, until I finally give in and seek out some sort of amicable relationship.

From the day I was born God's love has been in me and around me, whispering to my heart. As I grew up the voice became louder within me until it reached my ears and my mind, and I sought internally for answers as to its origin. I did not understand the continuous longing I felt, but I was curious and wanted to know how it came to be in me.

When I was in high school, my girlfriends invited me to join their bible study/share group, and I gladly accepted, thus taking my first steps toward understanding the longing of my soul. I was nervous and insecure at first; their knowledge of the Bible was so much greater than mine. I felt embarrassed by my ignorance of the books of the Bible, but my friends were so kind, and they did not judge me or make me feel stupid. Instead, they encircled me with their love and guided me through the lessons, helping my knowledge grow.

The trust that developed between us during our special time together brought forth unique insights and honest conversations that helped me deal with my teenage insecurities about life and purpose. My friends' warmth and acceptance were genuine, and I felt loved in a way that was new and fresh and unconditional. For the first time in my young life, I began to understand that I am a precious and beloved child of God.

The Spirit of the Lord was powerful within me as I read the Bible and wrote down my thoughts in my study journal in preparation for our meetings. This spiritual practice opened to me a new pathway to wisdom, and a lifelong quest to know God through scripture and writing.

Over time, with each level of understanding and fulfillment reached, a new level of longing for greater faith grew in me. I was coming to the realization that my connection to the Holy Spirit was strengthening, and I felt led to discern the gifts and musical talents that God had blessed me with. I sang in choirs, and occasionally performed solos, but I always hung back, safe from judgment.

And then something wonderful happened, I took to heart words of encouragement to pursue professional training in voice and guitar. As I studied and practiced and increased in performance, the years of music theory and dexterity from piano lessons and classroom instruction from my youth reawakened and I began to open up and blossom as a musician.

Gradually over time I developed a modest desire to direct music for worship. I had no idea where this inclination came from; in fact, every time I thought about it my stomach turned inside out and my heart flip-flopped! I had never sought the role of a leader, but subtly, without any fanfare, I found myself more and more in front of the choir and the congregation, leading them in song. Soon my choirmates were encouraging me to direct and I accepted the call to lead the contemporary choir at my parish.

Leadership was new to me, and I strove to be the best musician, the best liturgist, the best servant for God, and the study of scripture that I first learned in my high school share group gave me confidence in my music planning. Unbeknownst to me, even in high school the Holy Spirit had been preparing me for this time of apostolic service long before I felt called to it.

With each passing choir season, I felt a new longing within me— the desire to bring forth in others the rich experience of transformation and joy found in scripture and song and sacred liturgy. Many who served alongside me felt this same desire and they sacrificed much time and energy in service to the church.

One dear choir member in particular gave so much of herself to me and the choir. She and I met regularly to study the scripture readings to plan music for Mass. What a tremendous blessing she was to me with her wise and insightful interpretation of the Word! Our music planning was a collaborative effort that was prayerful, emotionally and intellectually stimulating, and fun! I marveled at my friend's clarity and conviction and unwavering trust in God's Word, and she led me to a deeper understanding of the readings in the Old and New Testament. Her humility kept me from feeling shallow and ill equipped for the role God had called me to. Her wisdom and depth of spirituality inspired me in every way, and her love of God and Jesus enriched my life and increased my spiritual growth. I experienced Jesus' love every time I was with my sister in Christ. I will love her and cherish her friendship forever.

Even now my spirit is renewed with fresh longing, giving rise to my "Yes!" to serve with an eagerness empowered by the Spirit. Each time I am enlightened by the Holy Spirit, my longing increases, and with every scripture I read, every song I sing, every prayer I pray, and everything I do, I feel the threads of my spiritual connection wind tighter to God so that not even death will break the bond.

Spirituality is a wonderful gift of love, and I gladly accept it with reverence and awe! I pray for God's enlightening awareness, and until He welcomes me at my heavenly homecoming, I will continue to long for his spiritual blessings every day of my life!

Music

"The aim and final end of all music should be none other than the glory of God and the refreshment of the soul." Johann Sebastian Bach

Music is a gift to me from God, that I create with my voice and instruments, for the purpose and pleasure of knowing, loving, and serving God.

I have loved music since the first time I discovered my own sweet child's voice singing lullabies to my baby dolls. It happened on a beautiful summer afternoon. I was outside, sitting by myself in the side yard of our Philadelphia home. I was wearing the prettiest light blue sundress, and I was holding my baby doll in my lap. The sky was clear, and the sun was hot, but sitting in the shade on the cool grass was sheer bliss. It felt like I was in heaven. I sat for a long time, looking into my "baby's" face, and as I rocked my baby doll in my arms, I began singing one of my many made up melodies, soothing and gentle to baby and to me. Songs of a child from a mother's love. It sounded pretty to my ears, and I felt happy and full of love and aware of myself in a new and different way.

Ever since that first musical experience, I have marveled at how the combination of words, emotion, mood, and sound can create a song that can touch the mind, heart, and soul, connecting me to others in a deep and very spiritual way. When I listen to music, I allow myself to be moved by what I am hearing, and when I sing or play my guitar, alone or with others, music is made.

Music takes me on an emotional ride from a song's first note and phrase, and oftentimes I lose myself in the moment. I am able to block out the problems of the day, the obstacles to peace, the many distractions that drain my energy and resources, and I lose myself in the beautiful sound of music. With each melody and message, I am able to push aside negativity to allow joy and happiness to take center stage for a time.

Listening to music can become a deep meditation, where the noise of the world is muted. Although never ceasing and still on the perimeter of consciousness, noise is silenced in my mind, replaced by the joy and pleasure of listening, my body absorbing the energy of the lyric, the instruments; the sound, the vibration, and beat. Music is uplifting and it changes me from the inside out. With keen awareness of sounds being created my entire being thrills and my senses become one with the music.

God has given me this gift of musical connection to help me make a difference in the world, and I know it is not by me alone, but that all of creation plays a part in my ministry.

One of my favorite places to make music is on my patio, where the beautiful sounds of nature mix with the acoustic sounds of my voice and instrument. The air is still, and all is quiet until the first strum of my guitar and first notes from my mouth. From all around me the entire natural world watches and waits in excited anticipation for me to begin, and once the tuning of my guitar is complete, all is ready to begin to make sweet music. Then, like a choir waiting for their cue to begin, the birds in the trees start singing with me, and in competing choruses we sing songs of praise to all of creation! One of the bird's favorites to sing is Beethoven's, "Hymn to Joy." I know it sounds crazy, but it is true! It is pure joy to hear the birds singing out, part of God's amazing woodland choir!

Together the birds and I find the percussive beat and rhythm of the music, and suddenly all around others join in; dogs begin barking in the distance, children laugh a little louder as they ride by on their bicycles, and the hum of traffic on a distant road amplifies the cicadas' cacophony as they too come to life in the trees and add their notes to the song. Passersby shout to one another in friendly greetings, and the music from my patio, once loud, becomes barely noticeable as all of the magnificent sounds blend together, carried on the wind to God, becoming a beautiful symphony of creation.

It so special to bring to life the many compositions written by poets and musicians, sometimes centuries old, that bless all with endless opportunities for artistic retreat. Through an unlimited inventory of compositions already written and songs soon to be scored, I am bound to past and present souls, in the natural and the supernatural realm of music. In my little organic space, the suspended creative energy and power of the music is timeless.

"Oh, how sweet the song" that unites all God's creatures–man and beast–in one breathtaking moment of melody and love!

No matter the genre or style of music, each word and tune has the ability to awaken feelings and memories that lie just beneath the surface until the moment of my hearing, and with startling clarity the music breaks open the hard shell surrounding my heart and well-protected secrets fall out. So much of life held in– sadness and joy, happiness and tears, stirred up and teased out by the complexities of music, the subtleties of song.

One such time from years ago that cracked open my heart and brought forth strong emotions was when I attended with my mom and dad the Broadway musical, *Les Miserables* (music by Claude-Michel Schönberg; book by Alain Boublil, Claude-Michel Schönberg, and Jean-Marc Natel; lyrics by Herbert Kretzmer). It was my twenty-seventh birthday and my parents wanted to do something special for me. It was to be a time for healing after the loss of my first child, a time to let go and be well again and I was looking forward to it very much.

I had never been to New York City for a Broadway show, and I was both extremely nervous and excited, all at the same time. Our seats were in the front row of the balcony, and we had a great view of the entire stage and production. I knew it was going to be a tremendous show, but I had no idea I would be moved so deeply by the music and the story. It was unforgettable.

Everything about the show was exceptional: the theater, stage, direction, and choreography; the lighting, costumes, and set design; the actors, their voices, and presence; the orchestra and conductor, the music composition, words, and story. All was perfect and beautiful and made ready for me and the audience.

The lights dimmed and the curtain rose, and it did not take long for me to forget where I was. I leaned forward in my seat, drawn by the music, listening with my whole being, barely breathing, captivated by the story of Jean Valjean and of Fantine and her tragic life. When the full, plaintive voice of Fantine began to sing,

"I Dreamed A Dream," I felt a kinship toward her as she lamented her hopes and dreams taken from her–"killed"–and her dying plea to a merciful God that her innocent child not suffer for the sins she bore.

I swayed back and forth in my seat, feeling so much emotion, as she laid bare on the stage for all to hear her plaintive song to God. What I heard was, "Why is life so unfair? Why me? What have I done to deserve this misery?"

Fantine not only sang of her hopes and joys, but she sang of my hopes and joys; she not only sang of her dreams being dashed and dying, but she sang of my dreams being dashed and dying.

When the last note played, all was still and silent for three full counts before anyone in the audience exhaled...and then the applause began...in admiration of the performance as well as thanksgiving for the gift of story that had been delivered so beautifully and received so well.

I sat frozen in my seat, unable to move. My chest felt tight, and my arms felt so heavy and empty. I began to cry quietly for many minutes well after the song ended. In that moment of music, the loss of my own dream–of my own sweet child that I would not hold or sing lullabies to–became real again and my resolve to stay strong and forge ahead crumbled, for this dream of mine was not meant to be. In that opulent Broadway theater, with all of its magical energy and continuous movement, my sorrow cracked wide open, and my tears flowed until the powerful story and music made me feel exhausted and cleansed of my sorrow. My grief, bottled up for so long, finally drained from my body and I felt relieved and renewed.

One of my greatest pleasures is bringing a piece of music to life. Whether by singing or playing my guitar or directing a choir or small group, it is so exciting to take a composition and break it down and make it sing! From the beginning stages of sight reading and rehearsal to full performance, a song becomes so much more than words and notation on a piece of paper; it becomes a living, breathing heirloom of sound for all to hear and experience.

Countless times, while performing music, I have heard the voice of God and felt the Holy Spirit penetrate my heart, my mind, my being.

It is an amazing feeling to breathe in and begin singing, allowing the music to come forth from my parted lips into the space and time of the present moment, knowing that there is an end to the song but not an end to the impression made on me and the listener.

I believe all people from every walk of life can appreciate and find pleasure and enjoyment in music; even people who cannot hear at all. Some of the most important songs I have ever performed were songs sung by my choir and members of the deaf community at my church. Side by side, in perfect pitch, the hearing and non-hearing sang together with voice and intricate sign language– lyrics written about opening our eyes, our ears, and our hearts to the love of Jesus. United by faith and bound by God's love, the messages of faith, hope and love were communicated through sign, all for the glory of God.

Music is such a beautiful gift from God to all creation, and I pray it never be silenced. God has gifted me with talent to use my voice and instruments, and with his gentle tuning of my ears and his plucking of my heartstrings he has drawn my attention to all of the musical sounds of the world, and I have become so much more than I would have been had I denied the desire to perform and allow music to be a part of my life.

I am amazed by how many rare and beautiful songs there are, created since time began and waiting to be played into life, one note, one chord, one melody at a time. Songs that have changed me, priceless wonders, gifted to me by my Creator to appreciate for as long as I live.

Truly, there is a vast library of music above and below the clouds of heaven, from simple jingles to Handel's *Messiah* and the "Hallelujah Chorus," created by gifted geniuses and ordinary people alike to be performed in God's symphonic space. I might never have noticed or given any value to music, quite possibly discarding it as useless noise, had God not touched my young heart and freed my voice to sing as only a child can sing, sweet words of comfort and pure joy.

Music is a part of me, and it is where I feel closest to God.

Within my spirit, through music, I am awake and alive, and I feel free to be me, tuning my life up to God's perfect "A."

It is where I am reshaped and made new, touched by the divine creator of all.

Fishing

The Appearance of Jesus to the Seven Disciples. John 21: 1-14

After this, Jesus revealed himself again to his disciples at the Sea of Tiberias. He revealed himself in this way. Together were Simon Peter, Thomas called Didymus, Nathanael from Cana in Galilee, Zebedee's sons, and two others of his disciples. Simon Peter said to them, "I am going fishing." They said to him, "We also will come with you." So, they went out and got into the boat, but that night they caught nothing.

When it was already dawn, Jesus was standing on the shore; but the disciples did not realize that it was Jesus. Jesus said to them, "Children, have you caught anything to eat?" They answered him, "No."

So, he said to them, "Cast the net over the right side of the boat and you will find something." So, they cast it, and were not able to pull it in because of the number of fish.

So, the disciple whom Jesus loved said to Peter, "It is the Lord." When Simon Peter heard that it was the Lord, he tucked in his garment, for he was lightly clad, and jumped into the sea.

The other disciples came in the boat, for they were not far from shore, only about a hundred yards, dragging the net with the fish. When they climbed out on shore, they saw a charcoal fire with fish on it and bread. Jesus said to them, "Bring some of the fish you just caught."

So, Simon Peter went over and dragged the net ashore full of one hundred fifty-three large fish. Even though there were so many, the net was not torn. Jesus said to them, "Come, have breakfast."

And none of the disciples dared to ask him, "Who are you?" because they realized it was the Lord.

Jesus came over and took the bread and gave it to them, and in like manner the fish.

This was now the third time Jesus was revealed to his disciples after being raised from the dead.

A Fisherman's Prayer, author unknown
I pray that I may live to fish
Until my dying day.
And when it comes to my last cast,
I then most humbly pray:
When in the Lord's great landing net
And peacefully asleep
That in his mercy I be judged
Big enough to keep.
Amen.

"I think I'll go throw a line in the water."
"The fish are biting!"
"Not one bite today…"
"You should have seen the one that got away…now that was a BIG fish!"
"Shhhhh…you'll scare the fish away."
"Oh, my gosh, I caught a fish. I caught a fish. Fish on! Fish on!"
"Easy…Don't reel in too fast or you'll break the line!"
"Get the net!!! Get the net!!!"
"I think this may be the biggest fish I've ever caught!"
"Whatda' catch that on?"
And so go the conversations of the fishermen in my life.

It is impossible to measure the overall impact the sport of fishing has had on me and my immediate and extended family. In fact, the only way I could measure its indelible mark would be to reverse time and erase it from our collective experience, and then measure the huge, empty whole in our lives, void of fun, laughter, and love that has strengthened every one of our relationships. Fishing removed from my family would be absolutely devastating and we would all be very different people had fishing not been woven into all of our lives.

Fishing unifies my family and is an essential part of our identity, extending outward into our friendships and marriages and covering more than three generations. Fishing has made us stronger, more resilient, more patient, and absolutely more prayerful in our own unique ways. Fishing is like a religion that we were baptized into, where for our entire lives we have participated in the ritual actions of planning, preparing, catching, collecting, gathering, singing, and praising, and then sharing the sacramental offering of food and fellowship with one another.

When I visit with family, our conversations move from one fishing story to another, invariably eliciting laughter and much drama about one accidental human-hooking or one near-miss tornado on the lake or one too many beers late in the evening after a successful muskie hunt, or fishing at sunset only to find out later that the water we were fishing in was infested with Great White sharks! No wonder the fish weren't biting! The time passes oh-so-quickly when we share our fishing tales, and before I know it, the emotional connections and abiding love from our shared experiences brings us ever closer together again.

Fishing is a really big deal to my family. If you ask any of the guys—my dad, brothers, husband, nephews—or gals—especially my daughters—they will tell you they are deeply passionate about fishing, some to an obsession, albeit a healthy obsession. A week does not go by when one of them is not out on the shoreline or in a fishing boat, in the ocean surf or the river's edge, "up north" on the ice, casting a line to experience the thrill of landing another keeper!

Fishing is part of our DNA and imprinted on our personalities, language, laughter, and tears; our sport, endurance, and perseverance; our living and dying; our special, unbreakable bond of love.

Fishing is like a competitive sport for the guys in my family, a serious activity that takes a lot of practice and hard work and balance no matter what size fish is on the other end of the line. There is a beautiful, intense stillness in their concentration and effort when casting their line out and steadily reeling it back, waiting for a bite, then snapping back and setting the hook at just the right time. I admire their determination and tenacity, never giving up, and I believe this is what brings them back, time and time again. They are true fishermen!

From my dad to his youngest grandson, fishing has helped build close relationships between father, sons, and grandsons. They have taken absolutely priceless fishing trips together, from the great outdoors of the Boundary Waters and Lake of the Woods; across Minnesota and parts of Canada; down to Central America and Costa Rica; to the Atlantic, the Pacific, and Gulf of Mexico...far and near, they have found secret places to throw a line out and lower their nets in to catch magnificent fish.

Although it is more of a hobby and pastime for me, I also love to fish. There is nothing finer than finding pristine waters rimmed by tall pines to cast out a line. I enjoy the elegant simplicity of lodging in a rustic cabin, frying up the catch of the day on an open fire, sipping wine and braving real conversations about health and family, country and jobs and the world we all live in. I love the peace at the end of the day; it is a perfect time to chill and just "be."

For me, there is no better place to relax and contemplate the beauty of God's creation than out by the water, under the stars and the brightness of a full moon. With country music playing distantly in the night, embers crackling on a fire, it is a luxury to sit back in an Adirondack chair and imprint on my heart good memories of fishing and fellowship with my family and friends.

As early as I can remember in our family travels, my dad made many random stops along the roadway on the pretext of "getting out to stretch our legs," when in reality it was a way to let him and my brothers investigate a newfound lake or stream. Driving with his left hand on the steering wheel and his right arm outstretched across the top of the front seat, he would give my mom's shoulder a quick squeeze while throwing a wink and a nod over his shoulder to my brothers, and before anyone knew it the car was pulled over onto the shoulder of the road and all the guys were scrambling out, leaving mom, my sister, and me choking on road dust.

We would whine and complain through the open door, but they never heard us over the noise they made grabbing the ever-present, ever-ready fishing gear from the trunk of the car. Without a glance back in our direction, we were left behind to "enjoy the fresh air and scenery" while our stomachs growled and our bladders contracted, needing relief.

A "few minutes" to the boys was like an hour to me. While mom and my sister waited in the car, I sat gingerly on the side of the gravel road, poking at ants in the dirt while watching and waiting and hoping and praying they would catch something fast so that we could continue on our way home. I had no appreciation for this thing they loved and seemed to live for...fishing. How could I when I was always left behind? As David, my then nine-year-old brother indelicately put it when I asked him why I couldn't go with him, he retorted, "You're a girl. Fishing's for boys!"

It wasn't until our summer vacation right before my thirteenth birthday–the summer I got my first bikini and the last summer I claimed to be a tomboy–that I was able to prove to the guys that I was capable of fishing–big fishing–deep-sea fishing off the coast of Myrtle Beach, South Carolina. It was not easy to persuade them that I was capable of fishing with the guys. The family had all been noticing I was "changing" and "developing," and I was constantly teetering between "tomboy" and "boy crazy," so it took time to convince my dad and brothers that I was not like other girls, and I could hold my own.

After promising over and over that I could take care of myself and I wouldn't get in the way, they finally relented and said, "Okay; you can come."

I was so excited!

We went out on a big charter fishing boat into deep water with about fifty others, and each of us lined up along the railing with a rod and reel and a gray metal bucket of slimy chopped squid, called "chum." My younger brother and I were stationed on one side of the boat, close to each other, and we had a blast! Jeff helped me figure out how to put the slimy squid on my hook, which was part of the deal if I was going fishing, and after a short time, the fish started biting, and we caught so many fish it was hard to keep up!

I also learned a valuable lesson about fishing that day. Some people get seasick, and I figured out very quickly which way the wind was blowing and to get out of their way!

The biggest excitement of the day was when we heard that on the other side of the boat David caught the biggest fish of the day: a small, mako shark! I can only imagine all the guys lining up along the railing, hovering close behind him, shouting out all their suggestions on how to land the shark!

It was quite a catch but no surprise to me, not for my brother, David, who was an exceptional fisherman!

Fishing is one of many things the guys share a passion for, and to me it is by far one of the best things they share. There is no age or ability requirement. Everyone can be part of the fishing fun as long as they carry their weight, have an appreciation for the process, and an appetite for the feast; and even though not everyone in the family is into fishing, we all love the fishing stories as we feast together on the day's catch!

Like it or not, everyone in the family has grown up with fishing and at one time or another, we have all had a fishing rod in our hands. In one single outing, I have seen boys go out in the morning with peach-fuzz on their faces and later on return as men wearing a five o'clock shadow, having learned the most important lesson of all: fishing is not for whiners!

It is probably for this reason—no whining—that I have not been accepted completely as one of them, never elevating myself into the ranks of "real fisherman."

It is true: as I have gotten older, I have whined like a girl when the guys (and my daughters, too!) have told me to "put your own bait on your hook!" and "You caught it; you take it off!"

Worms, slugs, and red worms wiggle and slip around in my fingers and I end up hooking my fingers while managing to hook only a small piece of worm that wouldn't even attract a minnow!

And when I have the good fortune of catching a fish, I am embarrassed to admit I whine then, too, because the fish are alive and slippery and they wiggle out of my hands, and they also have sharp scales and fins that cut my hands.

And probably the worst of all, bait and fish are smelly, and the stinky smell gets under my fingernails!

Pee-yew!

And that, my friends, is why I may never be fully accepted by the guys into their club, as a true fisher[wo]man!

Let's face it, helping me with the basics of fishing is a huge inconvenience for them, and I know it annoys them (it would annoy me), because I'm not carrying my own weight and they may miss out on the best fishing of the day just to stop and help me. Truthfully, if I were one of the guys, I wouldn't want to help me either!

But they are great guys (and gals!), and each of them at one time or another has helped me bait my hook and taken my fish off the hook. True sacrificial love and compassion if you ask me!

Which brings me to my husband, who surprised me with an unexpected gift: my very own fishing rod and reel, one of my best gifts ever! Not only did he want to share his love of fishing with me, but he also set my rod and reel up with a line, a sinker, and a lure! I was ready to start fishing right away and without all of the drama of worms and the like! Immediately I started casting and I felt really good, like a tomboy on the high seas again!

I was reminded that day that a couple of hours of casting out and reeling in can seem like no time at all when the fish are biting, but like an eternity if the water is still and silent, which reinforced something else I already knew about myself: it is not in my DNA to give up! It is very easy to let disappointment rule the day, so hope and optimism must be kept front and center! I never know when the next cast will be the best cast of the day followed by a tremendous, unexpected outcome.

It was just so on one hot, lazy South Carolina summer day when Scott and I were out on the lake riding around in our boat. We pulled into our favorite cove, and after a short swim, Scott lay out to dry and ended up taking a nap. I was lounging in the sun in my bikini and became bored very quickly. Looking around I noticed my fishing rod and thought about throwing a line in the water, just for fun.

I pondered for a moment, looking at it, and figured I probably wouldn't catch anything. I thought about all the times my dad had told me that the fish don't bite in the afternoon, and I could hear my mom's voice from long ago warning me as a teenager, "Donna Kay! Put some clothes on! You are not to go fishing in your bikini!" But I had no expectations of actually catching anything, and there were no other people around, so I grabbed my fishing rod, slipped on my sandals, and started leisurely passing the time throwing out a line.

After what seemed like hundreds of casts, I was ready to wake Scott up; I was bored and tired and ready to go home. But there was a little voice inside my head telling me to cast out just One.

More. Time. So, I said a little prayer back to that voice, "Jesus, help me catch a BIG one! Amen!", and I cast out one more time.

I counted to fifteen, letting the lure sink deep down into the channel, and as soon as I gave my first, quick tug to reel it back in, it snagged on the bottom; or so I thought, until the "snag" moved on its own and bent my rod in half!

My first feeling: fear! My first thought: "What do I do now? I can't catch a fish in a bikini!"

I had never hooked anything big enough to bend my rod like that, and certainly not ever, ever, ever in a bikini! The only "fish" that I had ever caught before that had bent my rod ended up being a fishing rod and reel that I snagged off the bottom of Lake Hopatcong on a cold spring day...in my parka! Talk about a surprise! (Some months later I gave that rod and reel to my dad, and he cleaned it up, good as new, and it has become one of his best setups ever.)

All of this flashed through my mind right before I shouted,

"Oh, my gosh, I caught a fish. I caught a fish. Fish on! Fish on!"

With all of my excitement and screaming, "Fish on!", Scott woke up from his nap and jumped into action. I knew the fish would get away if I tried to bring it in on my own, and I gladly handed the rod over to Scott, and he began working the catch like a pro. Yes, I know, it was a girl thing to do, but I was not going to let this big one get away! I wanted more than anything for us to land that fish so that I could take a picture of it and text it out to my family!

I especially wanted the guys to see it and weigh in on what they thought it was; how much did it weigh; what did I use to catch it with; was I going to eat it or put it back...all the good, admiring chatter that echoes into infinity with every great catch!

After about 10 minutes, Scott and I netted an estimated twenty-four-inch channel catfish (my brother, Jeff, later clarified it was a BLUE channel cat)! It was a beauty, and I felt so proud of Scott and me. I know I could not have brought it all the way onto the boat without Scott's help, so I yield the catch to Scott with an assist from me! We worked together as a team, and I felt so happy and proud of us that day!

I have learned it is the eternal hope and certainty of every fisherman and woman that even if the fish aren't biting presently, they will be at any moment. And if one fisherman is out casting a line, soon others will join in, relaying tips and advice with grunts, winks, and head nods about the right lure, bait, location, angle, stance, etc., that will ultimately land "the big one"!

I have watched this oh so familiar scene play out between Scott and my dad as they fish the banks of the pond in our backyards, and it makes me feel warm and blessed to see their love of fishing solidify their father/son bond.

Everyone has their own unique style and favorite way of casting and reeling, and there is a genuine respect among fishermen honoring their differences, even if they do raise an eyebrow in skepticism. But no matter how different they are or where they come from, they have a single-minded purpose—a universal desire—to catch the most awesome fish and in the process create the most wonderful memories for generations to come!

This love and passion for fishing, along with a small dose of luck, has been passed to each generation in my family.

My daughter, Lauren, is incredibly lucky when fishing, but unfortunately, she also gets motion sickness. Her sister, Meghan, is not as lucky but can hang out all day fishing on a rocking boat with no problem. Knowing all of this, Scott, Meghan, Lauren, and I were all in when we chartered a fishing trip in the Caymans and we all proved our worth!

True to form, Lucky Lauren caught the first fish—a trigger fish—and shortly thereafter proceeded to hang her head over the side of the boat to relieve her seasickness. Meghan, not so lucky, was frustrated as she kept reeling in empty hook after empty hook, but she was in it to the end.

The waves began getting higher and the effort to stay balanced on our feet was requiring every bit of our strength and energy. For a couple of hours Scott, Meghan and I continued fishing while Lauren waited for her sickness to pass. We were all getting frustrated when, surprise, Meghan caught a trigger fish!

Lauren lifted her head long enough to give Meghan a feeble cheer and a thumbs up.

So far, the daughters score two, Scott and me, zero.

Scott repeated more than once to anyone listening that if you start throwing up, you're done. There is no coming back from seasickness; it zaps your energy and your spirit. But not so with

Lauren! From somewhere deep within her belly a loud, roiling burp erupted, followed by another, and soon enough she was up and fishing again! And after another half an hour, no one was surprised when Lauren landed her second trigger fish! Scott's awe and amazement that Lauren overcame seasickness where many a man had been down for the count was, and still is, one of his best fishing stories! Huge respect and so much fun then and always!

It is an understatement to say my family loves fishing: it is part of our collective story. My dad could not have known in the early days if his kids and grandkids would be "hooked" on fishing, but the years have proven out that he has created a beautiful family legacy. What began many years ago in a stream by the side of the road somewhere in rural Pennsylvania has become a family tradition.

Through the adversity of bad weather and lost gear and broken lines and forgotten provisions and cut fingers we have all learned how to adapt and go with the flow. Fortunately, too, there have been many celebrations and toasts to the lucky one who landed the biggest fish of the day and a cheer for "one of the best muskie hunts ever!"

With each cast thrown out, problems and frustrations ebb away and comradery, love, and forgiveness are reeled back in. Months of loneliness and deep longing for the brotherhood of fellow fisherman is soothed as we gather and raise a toast to our beloved fishermen who are no longer with us, and the universal hope and optimism of every fisherman becomes a silent prayer in our hearts as we live to enjoy another day out and a safe return home to enjoy the abundant blessings and good fortune of a nice walleye, perch, trout, or bass dinner!

I think of fishing as a metaphor for life: you can go it alone, but it is so much better when done with others. There will be good days and bad days, so stop whining and complaining and just do what needs to be done. You may not always want to get into the stinky, slimy aspects of life, but you may have to in order to survive. Not every catch is a keeper, and there are plenty of fish in the pond. Unfortunate things will happen that are beyond your control; even so, never give up, never lose faith, show humility, and always be ready to cast out into the dark one more time, because with God's help and provision (and a little bit of luck), good things happen if you wait long enough.

"Simon said in reply, 'Master, we have worked hard all night and have caught nothing, but at your command I will lower the nets'…When they had done this, they caught a great number of fish, and their nets were tearing." Luke 5:5

Have faith and believe! Fish on!

Prayer

"Lord, I call to you; come quickly to help me; listen to my plea when I call. Let my prayer be incense before you; my uplifted hands an evening sacrifice." Psalm 141:1-2

In the name of the Father, and of the Son, and of the Holy Spirit.

Dear Lord, you know how very difficult it can be to convince people of the power of prayer, but I know first-hand how powerful prayer is, and I want everyone to experience for themselves the abundant blessings found in answered prayer. I pray for your help. Please give me words that will bear witness to your gracious love as you have helped me in my life. Thank you. Amen.

"I love the Lord, who listened to my voice in supplication, who turned an ear to me on the day I called." Psalm 116: 1-2

God hears every prayer raised to heaven, from both believers and non-believers. Wherever and whenever I pray, with family and friends, with strangers, or simply by myself, I am a part of something spiritually unifying and holy. In my communal offering or in the silence of my heart prayer makes me feel loved and protected and it is so supernatural and unexplainable that non-believers believe and the faithful are renewed in spirit.

Prayer gives me hope, even when I feel hopeless. Prayer consoles me, even when I am inconsolable. Prayer helps me feel positive, even when my thoughts and opinions turn negative. Prayer gives me confidence, even when my confidence has been stolen or withered. Prayer gives me courage when I am fearful. Prayer gives me answers when I have exhausted all options. Prayer gives me relief; prayer gives me strength, and through answered prayer I am convicted in my belief that all things are possible with God.

I know before I call out to God I will be heard, and this makes me fearless in my prayer. God accepts, he does not reject! Praying to God is like calling my very best friend on the phone, and on the first ring He answers, never sending me to voicemail. God does not put me on hold; he takes my call immediately. God never tells me he is too busy to listen, and best of all, God never interrupts me!

Prayer is sacred and mysterious. From the moment I close my eyes and bow my head I feel God's calming presence within me. His peace is my peace. Whether praying about something specific or rambling on about ideas, questions, or needs, every thought and emotion I convey is like incense swirling and wafting upward and outward from my mind and heart and spirit to God.

At an early age my mom and dad taught me to pray. With hands folded and head bowed down in reverence and humility, I learned to give thanks to God and to ask a blessing upon our meals. On Sundays and holy days, we prayed at Mass, asking for forgiveness and giving praise. And at the end of the day, when I laid my sleepy head down on my pillow, the prayer of my heart was that God watch over me and my family as we slept.

My family prayed most during the four weeks of Advent. Our home preparation and decorating for Christmas made the time extra special and sparkly, and in the early evening, when twilight was upon us, we lit our Advent wreath, and the candle flames flickered and swayed, creating an ethereal atmosphere about the room. I remember looking across the kitchen table at my sister and brothers, and my mom and dad, and I felt so small and humble in the holy presence of God.

During this prayer time the Holy Spirit surrounded my family, filling up the space with Jesus' love. As a child I could not describe what this special feeling was, but with each candle lighting and ancient prayer spoken, I felt the question rise up inside of me, "Is that you, God? Are you coming to show me the way?"

The ceremonial lighting of our Advent Wreath and reading of seasonal prayers made our family time preparing for Jesus' birth and his second coming more purposeful and deliberate, helping me grow in faith through prayer and ritual tradition, which over time led me to deeper, more personal, honest conversations with God.

One of my favorite prayers to "start the conversation" is The Lord's Prayer (Our Father), because this prayer was given directly from Jesus' to his followers:

Our Father in heaven,

Hallowed be your name,
your kingdom come,
your will be done,
On earth as in heaven.
Give us today our daily bread;
and forgive us our debts, as we forgive our debtors;
And do not subject us to the final test, but deliver us from the evil one. Matthew 6: 9-13

Although simple in nature, I know my clear expression of need and praise spoken in this prayer rings true; God knows my heart and his will shall be done.

Late one night in my teenage years my true need to be heard and understood led me to test God's existence. I was confused and depressed and I wanted proof that God was real; I was tired of "trusting and believing" in something I could not see. I was experiencing teenage rebellion, peer pressure, rejection, competition, isolation, loneliness, and I wanted proof of God. I wanted to see him.

I lay in bed and my sadness reached its climax and, crying into my pillow, I pleaded with God, "Do you even know me, God? Do you care one bit about me? Show me you love me! I want to see you!" Call it emotional exhaustion, call it imagination, call it what you will, but the calm peace that washed over me in that moment was not of me or of this world. It was gentle, loving, and kind and I knew that as impossible as I thought it to be, Jesus was with me. I saw him in the corner of my room, glowing with love and real presence for a brief moment, and then he was gone. Although my prayer was answered, I was stunned; I doubted my own eyes until, exhausted, I fell asleep. As I recalled the experience over the following days, I felt scared and I buried this supernatural experience in my memory and heart, never speaking of it out of fear of being called names and not being believed.

Proverbs 16:9 says, "In his mind man plans his course, but the Lord directs his steps."

There have been very poignant times of desperation when I have prayed, but the majority of my prayers are light and conversational, and no matter what the circumstances I feel the blessed assurance that my Lord and Savior hears my prayer. No matter the time, day or night, He is ready to answer my call.

That was the case when I decided to go back to work part-time when my daughters were in elementary school. I was restless and I knew the added income would be helpful, and although it was a tough decision, I knew it was the right one. I was not desperate, but I needed God's guidance and help in finding the right job, one that would allow me to keep my "mom time" and my involvement in my girls' school days.

I remember it like it was yesterday.

I began to pray…spontaneous and fluid…praying as I drove through town. Self-conscious, I looked to my left and then to my right to see if anyone was watching me talk "to myself" in my empty car. When I believed no one was watching, I began to talk to God, asking Him to help me find a job that best suited me:

"Dear Lord, I know I need to go back to work, but I don't know what work I should do. I don't want to miss out on my girls growing up; I want to be there for them. I know I don't want to go back to banking. I want a job that allows me to take the girls to school in the morning and pick them up in the afternoon. I only want to work part-time and please, summers off." I thought this was a pretty impossible request, but I prayed anyway, hoping by the end of the summer I would have an answer and "the perfect job."

About six weeks later, my pastor placed in my church mailbox a job description for a job at the Catholic School in town. It was a newly created position opening up and he thought I might like to take a look at the posting.

I was so grateful he thought of me!

I retrieved the piece of paper from my mailbox, unfolded it and read, "Music Coordinator; Part-time." It called for minimal hours, playing my guitar and using my musical talents, working with students grades 2-8, summers off. It was like a special delivery from God! A perfect fit! I can honestly say I was giddy with excitement! I applied for the job immediately and the following day I was called for an interview, and two weeks later the job was mine!

God is so good, and he provided a job for me that came in his perfect timing, beginning the month my youngest daughter started first grade and ending the summer she graduated from high school. God is good, all the time. All the time, God is good!

I am amazed that in receiving exactly what I asked for in prayer, God also received what He needed from me. Through my work I was able to pray openly and communally, growing in my faith and helping the young students, teachers, and staff grow in their faith, too. We became witnesses of faith in spreading the Gospel through prayer, shared study, music, and participation at Mass.

I am overcome with emotion when I marvel at how perfectly God knew what I needed, when I needed it, and for how long I needed it. The Music Coordinator job was more than I could have imagined and exactly what I hoped for, and it blessed me beyond words. It was a miracle job!

Some might call it all a big coincidence, much ado about nothing, but my faith informs me that God answered my prayers in a big way with that job!

Prayer is effortless but sometimes it takes a supreme effort to trust and believe. Not all prayers are answered as completely as my Music Coordinator job prayer. They can be answered in ways I don't want them answered. Praying can be risky. Believe me, I have been let down and disappointed plenty of times, and this is discouraging and creates doubt in my weakness. I become less inclined to pray and neglectful of my time with Jesus and when this happens, his light dims and I lose perspective. At these times, I feel shallow and empty and needy. It does not feel good or right in my soul. My pride and ego create distance until, finally, I accept that not all of my prayers are God's will. Not my will but God's will be done....

My Lord God, please listen and hear my prayer even when I am fearful and struggling to trust and believe.

At my lowest times, when I could not even lift my head to look to the heavens or move my lips to speak my prayer, God was with me. My paralysis from sadness was so great that Jesus carried the weight of my burdens without my asking. He was with me, knowing my unspoken needs and in my surrender, I knew He had all things under His control. In these weighty times, the only prayer I was able to offer was the holiest of all, His name, "Jesus...Jesus...Jesus."

The Holy Spirit gives me a vision and strength to persevere until I am ready to ask in prayer, "What next?"

I genuinely believe God rejoices when I call out his name. I imagine it to be like when my husband or my daughters call me, and I see their names in the caller ID. My heart leaps with joy; regardless of the time of day or what I might be doing. Just as I love to hear their voices and hear about the different happenings in their lives, I believe God feels the same way towards everyone. I can almost see him holding his cell phone when it buzzes and when he sees, "Donna Braidic", his eyes light up and a big smile spreads across his face. Quickly he pushes the answer button and says, "Donna, my child, how are you? What can I do for you today?"

With God, there is no pretense, no shaming, no judgment; there is only love.

When I pray–silently or out loud–no matter what I am asking for or offering to do in his name, my confidence in God's loving provisions and his desire for blessing my life is absolute. "Thy will be done" is my aim, my wish, my intent. I have nothing to lose and everything to gain if I pray for God's will, God's way, God's special, supernatural, loving direction.

Thank you, gracious and loving God, for answering all my prayers, so that come what may, thy will be done. Amen.

Donna Braidic

Christmas Star

Then God said, "Let there be lights in the dome of the sky, to separate day from night. Let them mark the fixed times, the days and years, and serve as luminaries in the dome of the sky, to shed light upon the earth." Genesis 1:14-15

As the year 2019 wound down and the crystal ball fell in Times Square, I had a good feeling about 2020. The number alone–2020–"perfect vision," boded well for seeing things clearly and making good choices for my future. Things were tracking really well for me emotionally, physically, and spiritually. Life was good! And then Covid-19 struck, and the entire world was changed forever. People were contracting the virus in my country and all across the Earth until it spread to over one hundred eighty countries. Suddenly, the future turned dark and murky, and the light of hope burned dimly for all.

People were uncertain of their safety and that of their loved ones. All "non-essential" businesses were ordered to close, children were kept home from school, wearing face masks and hand sanitizing were part of the "new normal," all in an effort to "slow the spread." In almost every country in the world human activity was shutting down. It was very eerie and equally scary.

It wasn't until my church locked its doors at the holiest time of the year that my heart completely sank, and I felt the full weight of vulnerability, loss, and fear come down on me. The coronavirus closed the House of God! On Good Friday, no one gathered silently, reverently to pay homage to Jesus or to kiss the wood of the cross on which hung the Savior of the world, or to sing "Were You There" with trembling voices filled with emotion. And on Easter Sunday, the tomb was empty but there was no Alleluia ringing throughout the church; the pews and choir loft were empty, and the church was dark.

It was a tragic, sad time for all, and worse days were ahead with no end in sight. I didn't feel very hopeful, but I pressed on.

There was not a corner of the world that the virus' impact was not felt. Hospital and emergency personnel were overwhelmed; they were our heroes on the frontline battling an enemy that struck without warning and showed no mercy. Entire families were taking ill, but the elderly were most vulnerable, and many were dying in hospital hallways and ICUs, hopeless, unconscious, alone and afraid while loved ones waited on the outside, forbidden from entering, forbidden from giving comfort for a peaceful goodbye. Sadness was exacerbated by separation, isolation, and no sacramental peace.

I prayed for a quick end to the virus. And when that did not happen, I prayed for protection and good health. I prayed to trust God. I prayed fervently, during this excruciatingly frustrating time, for a cure.

As the months passed there were some signs of hope; medicines showing positive effects against the virus, vaccines in early trials, therapeutics, but until the virus was under control, the fear of illness and death hung over everyone.

Then in November of 2020, eight months after the Easter lockdown, I heard about a "Christmas Star" coming in December, and I knew it was a sign from God, a reminder for me that God is present in all aspects of life, and to believe that he is listening to and answering my prayers, even when I don't see clear answers or hear encouraging news. The coming of a Christmas Star was a sign that renewed my hope for better days ahead.

On the Winter Solstice of December 2020, during the fourth week of Advent, the season of hope, I along with my mom and dad, my husband, my daughter, our friends, and neighbors gathered out on my driveway to view the amazing Christmas Star. We looked up into the southwestern sky, and as day turned to night, we saw in the distance Jupiter and Saturn line up to create a "great conjunction" in the crystal-clear darkness. The two large planets, orbiting in space since the beginning of time, were so close to each other and to the Earth and were in such perfect alignment that when we looked at them with our naked eyes, they appeared to be one enormous bright shining star, a Christmas Star, an astronomical miracle!

The Christmas Star was absolutely beautiful, and brighter than anything I had ever seen before in the sky. It was a light in the darkness, a sign of hope in the shadow of death, and I wondered, "Is this the same 'star' that the three Wise Men of the Orient followed for weeks until they found the baby Jesus?" Could this conjunction, so rare as to not have been seen in eight hundred years, be the same bright star that hovered over Bethlehem 2020 years ago?

This star of royal beauty bright created an excitement in us all as we looked with amazement at its impossible perfect light. For the first time in nine months, we forgot about viruses and quarantines and social distancing, and we laughed together and sang Christmas carols and toasted the Christmas Star with hot, mulled wine. We moved into a circle and bowed our heads under the light of the Christmas Star, and we gave thanks to God for one another, for our families and our health, and for the miracle of creation circling high above in the universe. We thanked God for the gift of Jesus, the gift of hope, and for the extraordinary signs of God present yesterday, today, and tomorrow.

We honored God and his Christmas Star, thanking Him for bringing family, friends, and neighbors together to share the miracle of love with one another on that special night. We paused in wonder. We, like the planets, became a conjunction of souls, closer in friendship and in perfect alignment with the God of love.

I do not know why the conjunction of Jupiter and Saturn occurred that night, that year of pandemic, but I do know it seems absolutely appropriate that it happened in the year 2020, the same number for perfect vision. The days of 2020 were fraught with anxiety, loss, pain, mourning, and uncertainty because of Covid, and on many days, the future seemed hazy, dark, and narrow. Then the blessed conjunction lit up the sky like fireworks and shined perfect light into the darkness and we could see better days ahead.

On that evening, during the celebration of the Christmas Star, I and my family and friends became part of the creation story, connected to the past, joined in the present, and looking towards the future with renewed vision and hope. Just as the three wisemen were guided by the Christmas Star to Jesus two thousand years ago, so too were we guided by a star to find love and friendship and hope on a beautiful starry night.

Solitude

"Be still and know that I am God." Psalm 46:10

Spending time in solitude is like going on a journey deep into my soul, into the still center of my being. Sometimes spontaneous and at other times planned, I escape to places where I am able to find peace and God's holy presence in my surroundings. In these lovely spaces of quietude, I leave the noise of arguments, conflicts, and mistakes; the pressure of overwhelming projects and indecision; and the burden of frustration, aggravation, and distress; and I find a balm of refreshment, renewal, and a new perspective.

Solitude is a time away where I relax my mind and body and release my grip on things that are beyond my control.

It takes effort and determination to create an opportunity to extract myself from all the things that demand "immediate" attention. To take off and decompress is necessary and worth the time for being renewed, detoxified in thought, and relaxed to receive the blessings of contemplative thought and prayer.

Once removed from my routine and the responsibilities of family, friends, work, home, church, etc., I am able to close my eyes, breathe deeply, and fill my lungs with fresh clean air, giving every cell in my body new vigor, and making me feel awake and alive again.

I inhale the comfort and peace of the Holy Spirit and exhale the stress and anxieties of my personal life that have pressed down every good thought and tightened my neck and shoulder muscles, strained my bones, and overtaxed my organs with the continuous demands life places on me.

Deep in my inmost being, I reawaken to the presence of the Holy Spirit and become more aware of the sounds in and around me, all the way down to the sound of air being drawn in and pushed back out of my nostrils with each cleansing breath I take.

My body and soul need this time away as much as I need air, food, and water to survive, and I search out places where I am able to be free for a spell.

Sometimes, my activities bring me to a serene place of solitude, unplanned and spontaneous. As I take a walk in the woods, glide through the cool water of a swimming pool, ride through the scenic hills on my bike or in my car, or a hundred other ordinary events of life, I become aware of the still quietness of God's presence in me, and I slow down and relax. His stillness and my stillness create solitude for my body and soul. It is a beautiful experience, complete, yet even so, I still find it difficult to resist the impulse to return and break the spell, knowing that just beyond the silence life continues on.

Not to be misunderstood, it is not isolation that I need or seek out, but rather a place and opportunity to turn inward for a little while and allow the presence of God to fill me up with peace for my soul.

Common and ordinary, I find peace in the stillness of a library with its calming hush all around me ("*Shhhh...*quiet, *please!*"), in bookstores, parks, and walking trails; plant nurseries and conservatories; my porch, an art gallery; and at the end of the day, in my comfy chair at home. I have also sought out sacred spaces where peace and solitude are expected and promoted, in beautiful out-of-the-way chapels and grottos where I along with loved ones and other pilgrims sit quietly in the holy presence of God, praying in the stillness of our hearts.

Early in my relationship with Scott, less than a year after Tim had passed, we were traveling to Lake Erie, when on our way, we passed a sign for the Sorrowful Mother Shrine. We turned to one another and without prior conversation about the shrine we both said at the same time how much we would like to stop in and visit the church. We looked at one another, smiled, and without another word, Scott turned the car around at the next side road and we drove back to the shrine where we entered a peaceful sanctuary.

We went into the church and found a few people who had stayed after Mass to pray. Slipping into the nearest empty pew, Scott and I snuggled in together and joined in their silent meditation. I prayed to God and to Mary about my sorrow and confusion; sorrow over the death of Tim, my husband of so many years, and confusion about how much love I already felt towards Scott in such a short amount of time. As we sat together, so young in our romance, I felt the grace of God flow over me and into my heart; I knew Scott was the one for me.

After a few minutes, the kind priest of the parish came down from the altar and saw Scott and me. He welcomed us with his sweet smile and we chatted for a few moments, and after inviting us to visit again he asked if he could bless us, thinking we were a married couple. We explained that we were not married but just starting our relationship, which surprised him, and without missing a beat, he blessed us in our new relationship!

Later when I shared with Scott how I felt towards him sitting in that holy space with me, he said he had the same feelings and thoughts about me. We felt drawn to God and to each other in that moment by the Holy Spirit and we experienced a closeness that was not physical: it was intimate and spiritual. By God's love and blessing we became one.

Although solitude implies being alone, I have felt the same peace and grace with friends and small groups while on retreat. There is a time to pull away and spend time in stillness with God, but there is also time for meditation and prayer with others. The various retreats I have attended have been life-changing because of the time I spent in solitude and stillness with others. My meditations and prayers, their meditations and prayers, all gave me perspective and wisdom, and the quiet time dedicated to journaling channeled my thoughts and continued to help me well beyond the days of retreat.

When I worked in Spiritual Care, although I was not a chaplain, the serious nature of the ministry could still take a toll on me mentally and physically, so it became my habit to take respites from my work that I called "real time," a time to step away from illness and death and go outside and remember that there is a whole world outside, beyond the suffering in the hospital, that is filled with happy and healthy people.

I could feel the sad and melancholy emotions creep in, so I would take leave of my office and go outside. As I walked along the exercise path, I could feel my body release the toxins of despair. My favorite "real time" place was at an adjoining park across the street. While sitting on the bench, tucked away from the hustle and bustle of the street, and hidden from traumas and Code Blue alerts, my awareness of squirrels, birds, and butterflies flitting about on their daily visits to oak trees, bee balm, and cone flowers instantly reconnected me to the world and to the energy of life.

In the corner of the park was a beautiful statue of Mary, the Blessed Mother of Jesus. Sometimes I would meditate on her peaceful face, her open, outstretched hands, and I would remember her joys and sorrows having Jesus as her son. My time of solitude, sitting in the park and reclaiming "real time" brought me closer to God, and I could feel my anxiety and stress melt away.

The best "real time" was when a chaplain coworker would join me on my walk, and we would sit for a few minutes on the park bench. Their presence gave me a great sense of calm and closeness to God. Their loving presence amplified the feeling of solitude and multiplied the blessings of God's grace-filled peace. Together we shared solitude, and God was all around. It was so pleasant; I did not want to leave.

When I am quiet and still, God takes away my loneliness and replaces it with peace. In His quiet space, alone in solitude, away from the bustling noise and congestion of life, I am able to calm myself for a time and become renewed in my mind, body, and spirit.

In solitude I enter into a space where I find God waiting.

In solitude I know God, whose presence is peace and whose voice is love spoken in the quiet stillness of my heart.

Donna Braidic

Peace

"Freedom from disturbance; tranquility." Oxford Languages
"I have told you these things, so that in me you may have peace. In this world you will have trouble. But take heart! I have overcome the world." John 16:33

There is a Balm in Gilead, African American spiritual

There is a balm in Gilead
to make the wounded whole.
There is a balm in Gilead
to heal the sin sick soul.

Sometimes I feel discouraged,
and think my work's in vain,
but then the Holy Spirit
revives my soul again.

Don't ever feel discouraged,
for Jesus is your friend,
who, if you ask for knowledge,
will never fail to lend.

If you cannot preach like Peter,
if you cannot pray like Paul,
you can tell the love of Jesus,
who died to save us all.

Oh, how lovely it is to feel the balm of Jesus' love poured generously over me to heal my sin-sick soul.
This is peace.
When I escape to the outdoors and enjoy the cleansing balm and simplicity of nature, I feel healed. When I watch the animals in

the wild, existing among the trees and in plain view, worrying for nothing and only clamoring and clawing for their reproductive life, I feel calm, and all is right in the world. As much as I once enjoyed the energy of city life, I now have found the less chaotic pace of nature more to my liking. Where once unending traffic and people scrambling about to meet deadlines and commitments created a rhythm and routine for me, I now find my quiet observations and the beautiful symphonic rhythm of the natural world absolutely perfect for keeping time and tempo in my life.

This is peace.

There was a time, however, when I combined the outdoors with high-energy play. One of my favorite childhood pastimes was going to the playground with my friends and riding the merry-go-round at top speed. We would run at a frenzied pace to get the merry-go-round spinning fast, then jump on and lie on our backs and look up at the sky and watch the clouds whirr by in a fluffy blur. I loved the feeling of my hair dangling over the side, slanting with the wind, and skimming the edge of the ground. It was amazing! I could have heard a pin drop in that spinning vortex of space! It was fun and dizzying and I felt so alive! And when the ride slowed to a stop and we climbed off and tried to walk, staggering to and fro, our laughter could be heard across the fields. The days were easy, the sky was an endless blue, and we were free of concerns and full of joy. Life felt so uncomplicated, and time had no beginning or end.

This is peace.

It was not until I was older, somewhere between junior prom and marriage counseling, that the chaos of day-to-day living took over and the beautiful sounds of nature became muted. And when children came along, everything began spinning like my childhood merry-go-round and work and family were loudest in my life.

It was during this time that, while quietly sitting alone at church, I heard from some distant place of consciousness the soothing melody of "There is a Balm in Gilead." It was extremely rare for me to have time alone, and as the musician played, I leaned my head back over the edge of the pew and closed my eyes. I gave my full attention to the song, listening with my ears and my heart, until a peace that is still impossible for me to describe washed over me.

It was a beautiful moment filled with love.

It was a powerful moment of relief from discouragement.

It was a holy moment of revelation.

It was as if Jesus himself was sitting in the pew next to me, and when the song ended, I turned to him and he poured the balm of healing over my head, making the sign of the cross with his thumb on my forehead and upon my heart, and I felt dizzy and at peace.

I had not realized until that sacred moment how heavy the weight of sin had been upon me. For although I believed I had been unburdening myself through apologies, confession, penitence, and reconciliation over the years, I had been fooling myself. The lingering guilt of my sins was still causing me grief and pain, and the noise of my life had muted and deadened the pain within me until that moment when I truly quieted myself, removing all distractions and allowing myself the freedom of abandonment to "let my hair dangle" over the back of the pew and be healed.

This is peace.

Peace to hear a pin drop.

Peace, free of disturbance.

Peace, free of anxiety.

Peace, free of agitation.

Peace, free of noise.

Peace, free from war.

Peace, free from sin.

Peace, found in God's presence.

Soothing, restful balm of quietude. Peace.

Oh, how lovely it is to feel the balm of Jesus' love poured generously over me to heal my sin-sick soul.

40 Days of Lent

Now the serpent was the most cunning of all the animals that the Lord God had made. The serpent asked the woman, "Did God really tell you not to eat from any of the trees in the garden?"

The woman answered the serpent, "We may eat fruit from the trees in the garden; it is only about the fruit of the tree in the middle of the garden that God said, "You shall not eat it or even touch it, lest you die."

But the serpent said to the woman, "You certainly will not die! No, God knows well that the moment you eat of it your eyes will be opened, and you will be like gods who know what is good and what is bad."

The woman saw that the tree was good for food, pleasing to the eyes, and desirable for gaining wisdom. So she took some of its fruit and ate it; and she also gave some to her husband, who was with her, and he ate it. Then the eyes of both of them were opened, and they realized that they were naked; so they sewed fig leaves together and made loincloths for themselves.

When they heard the sound of the Lord God moving about in the garden at the breezy time of the day, the man and his wife hid themselves from the Lord God among the trees of the garden. The Lord God then called to the man and asked him, "Where are you?"

He answered, "I heard you in the garden; but I was afraid, because I was naked, so I hid myself."

Then he asked, "Who told you that you were naked? You have eaten, then, from the tree of which I had forbidden you to eat!"

The man replied, "The woman whom you put here with me—she gave me fruit from the tree, and so I ate it."

The Lord God then asked the woman, "Why did you do such a thing?"

The woman answered, "The serpent tricked me into it, and I ate." Genesis 3:1-13

"You have searched me, LORD, and you know me." Psalm 139:1

"Watch and pray so that you will not fall into temptation. The spirit is willing, but the body is weak." Matthew 26:41

"No temptation has overtaken you except what is common to mankind. And God is faithful; he will not let you be tempted beyond what you can bear. But when you are tempted, he will also provide a way out so that you can endure it." 1 Corinthians 10:13

In the Catholic faith, as well as other faith denominations, the church observes forty days of Lent, beginning on Ash Wednesday and ending on Easter. As a child I did not understand or appreciate the significance of Lent or the sacrifices asked of me to bring me into a closer relationship with God. I just did them because I was an obedient child. I did not like going to confession, I did not like promising to fast from candy, or abstaining from meat on Fridays, or dropping part of my allowance into a cardboard "rice bowl" to feed children in foreign countries. But I did what I was told, and by the time Easter arrived, through these simple Lenten practices I was changed for the better.

In my early years, it felt like Lent was meant to punish me and I felt tremendous guilt for things that I had done wrong. Repentance felt forced upon me and, in some ways, didn't seem fair. I was just a kid, and I didn't understand how fighting with my brother or lying to my mom or swearing when I was mad could lead to worse behavior or worse habits, but I heard over and over they needed to be "nipped in the bud!" I was taught about venial sin and mortal sin and other offenses that were punishable by God (and the law), but these all seemed terrible compared to the little "minor things" I was doing. I saw no need to confess or acknowledge my normal misbehaving.

But the sins of childhood, left unchecked, grow into much bigger problems, and what did not seem like a big deal to me as a child or teenager later became a big deal as an adult. The bad habits associated with my sins influenced how I behaved in my family, my marriage, my relationship with my children, my relationship with my friends, my relationship with God. Bad habits, left unchecked, snowballed, and no matter how much I tried to justify them over the years, the truth is even the most insignificant of sins have hurt me and have hurt others.

My sins separate me in my relationship with God. I cannot hide my sins from God. They are inexcusable, regrettable, and I search out ways to repent. When the internal pressure of sin bubbles to the surface of my conscience and pops, I feel exposed and vulnerable, embarrassed and ashamed by the truth of my living, but also relieved by the release of toxic behaviors that have led me into darkness and caused me to sin.

I become tense in the days leading up to Lent, knowing that I am entering a time of metanoia that requires honesty with myself and my behaviors. I feel led by the spirit to the desert of my soul, a place of retreat and self-examination. I focus on self-improvement and changing my heart for love even when I do not feel love, and to become less self-reliant and controlling and more reliant on God, trusting his plan for my life. I am truthful with myself, humbler, and more contrite of heart during these times of reflection and solitude. The time to stop making excuses becomes clear, and I rethink my wayward dreams and indulgent behaviors and questionable relationships, and I ask myself what prevents me from letting these go.

For forty days I try to be more honest with God about my feelings, about my failings, examining what tempts me to sin, what keeps me from living in right relationship with him. I can be stubborn. I can be resistant. I can know it all. I resent being told I am not living my best life. I, I, I…I am not perfect. No, I am a sinner. Like Adam and Eve, I am naked in my deceptions and God sees me as I am. I still make mistakes and come up short, but I am forgiven for my imperfect actions and behaviors.

Even Jesus, God's son, who was pure and holy, was led by the spirit into the desert for forty days and was tempted by the serpent. All of the things of the world that seduce and tempt humans–fame, fortune, and power–were laid before Jesus, and in each temptation, he turned the devil down. He pushed the devil away. He scolded the devil and told him to leave. Jesus had all he ever wanted or needed in his Lord God and Father. He had need of nothing more.

Oh, to be as strong and convicted in my life as Jesus was in his!

In the same way that Jesus fully relied on God, I strive to rely on God. It is God's sustenance I need while fasting, it is God's protection I need from falling into the pit of self-absorption while standing on the precipice of greatness, and it is God's strength that I need in order to crush the temptations of the devil. Jesus' absolute reliance on God, wanting in nothing, is what I desire for myself when I am tempted to sin.

When I admit to myself and God that I am drinking too much, carousing with the wrong people, spending too much money on "stuff," caring too much about how I look and where I live and what I drive instead of caring about others, I feel ashamed. Try as I may to justify my lack of concern for the needs of others, I feel even more shallow when I expound upon my hard work and "laundry list" all of my responsibilities and claims for deserving to keep what I have earned. Dear God, from whom all blessings flow, please forgive me my selfishness in the midst of so much abundance.

During Lent and every day, in my contrition I must remind myself to live by the words of St. Teresa of Avila:

"Christ has no body now but yours. No hands, no feet on earth but yours. Yours are the eyes through which he looks compassion on this world. Yours are the feet which he walks to do good. Yours are the hands through which he blesses all the world. Yours are the hands, yours are the feet, yours are the eyes, you are the body. Christ has no body now on earth but yours."

I pray my selfishness be replaced with generosity and giving. I pray I give from my need, not from my want. I pray to be like Christ to others. I pray to share love. I pray for holy thoughts and actions to rule my mind and heart. I pray to live my life like the saints.

At the end of Jesus' forty days, he was ready for what lay ahead. He remained a good and loyal son to his mother, Mary, and his Father in heaven; he traveled the country and received what he needed from the generosity of others; he gained lifelong friends; he received admiration at the height of his ministry and was hated for his Truth; and he never swayed in his trust of his Father's plan for his life. In my days following Lent each year, I hope my prayer, fasting, and almsgiving prepare me for what lies ahead in my life, and come what may, I will be loyal, generous, loving, and forgiving in my life.

I have heard it takes forty days to form a new habit. During Lent I pray to replace bad habits with good habits and that the new, good habits stick. It is oh so easy to be persuaded by the relentless forces of evil to fall back and reclaim the bad habits of last year, last decade, last week, or even last hour. The good progress of Lent can unravel in an instant, but God is good, and I have learned that all is not lost. I know this because I have stumbled and relapsed many times in my life. One Lent is not enough for me. Truly, I need the benefits of Lent every day to stay on the right path, the path to heaven. Every day I need God's guidance, God's forgiveness, God's way for my life.

I look forward to the season of Lent each year. I look forward to changing and making things right in my life. I look forward to putting bad habits away, finding reconciliation with others, and receiving the many blessings that the Lord has waiting for me. I have learned that being an obedient child is not so bad after all, and it actually feels rather good when I correct my wayward ways and seek peace with others! I have learned that forty days is hardly any time at all, and that my sacrifices and Lenten practices have indeed brought me closer in my relationship to God, who is the same yesterday, today, and tomorrow, and his forgiveness and love are without end.

Peace, Hope and New Beginnings

"In peace I shall both lie down and sleep, for you alone, Lord, make me secure." Psalm 4:9

"Don't worry; be happy." Bob Marley

The most peaceful time of day for me is when I am on the edge of being awake, but not quite yet awake; that time when I first open my eyes and listen for the sounds of a waking house. Through half-consciousness I peek around the dimly lit room, feeling the softness of my bed, not wanting to disturb my resting body. My covers encase me like a warm cocoon, restricting my movement, while the faint memory of dreams linger until quite suddenly, poof! they vanish, and I rise.

I lower my legs over the edge of the bed and before my feet touch the floor, I check my cell phone for text messages and missed calls. Grateful for no drama at the outset of the day, I blink sleep from my eyes while putting my glasses on and the reality of a new day comes into focus. Slipping my feet into my slippers I scuff off to the bathroom. Then, once relieved, I retrieve my cell phone from the nightstand and shuffle off to the kitchen where the aroma of freshly brewed coffee wafts through the open door, enticing me to come in…ah, life is grand!

Unfortunately, my sleepy optimism for a day full of peace on earth, hope for the future, and the promise of new beginnings is short-lived. As I join my husband at the breakfast table, my café au lait becomes bitter in my mouth as my attention is drawn to the live news streaming on his laptop computer. Within minutes of watching, my optimism for wonderful new beginnings wanes, and a barrage of negative reports taunt me into believing the world is coming undone.

The same bad news every morning: storms and droughts, fires and earthquakes, COVID-19 and the latest variant, the need to vaccinate or not to vaccinate, the economy, political fighting, media bias, murder and mayhem on our city streets, and so on.

It's demoralizing; and yet, there I sit with eyes glued to the computer screen, getting my daily fix of caffeine and bad news.

I begin to worry about the physical and emotional toll so much negative stimulation is having on me.

At first, I enjoyed the news, but now before my first cup of coffee is finished, I am agitated, nervous, anxious, and angry about many things–things I have no control over and have little ability to change. Seeing all the troubles of the world and listening to the opinions of news people without being able to add my own opinion is really frustrating. Instead of arguing with the news people, I argue with my husband about what the people on the computer are arguing about, and inadvertently we have created an unhealthy love triangle! It is not good! Not mentally, emotionally, or physically, and certainly not good for my marriage!

Watching the news at the start of the day slowly crept into mine and my husband's morning routine, a little bit at a time, like a bad habit. Then one day it caught up to me. I saw how addicted I was to "Breaking News!" I knew I needed to quit filling myself up each day with bad news, but could I go cold-turkey, could I shut it down?

I asked myself, "Do I really need all this bad news first thing in the morning?" The answer was loud and clear, adamantly, "No!"

I had a problem (just like when I realized smoking a pack a day was a problem) so I decided that it would be most effective if I cut back on the news, rather than trying to eliminate it altogether. I didn't make a big announcement or start a boycott or expect anyone else to jump on the "no news" bandwagon; I just stopped watching the news as often as I was, and I tuned it out as often as I could. Let's face it, short of going completely off the grid to another planet, news is unavoidable, so it was up to me to limit how much information I was taking in each day.

It was a rude awakening to realize how much of my time was filled up with ugly, dark noise! The hardest habit to break was watching news out of boredom or when there was nothing else to watch on TV. If my husband was watching the news, I didn't ask him to turn it off; I read a book, played my guitar, went outdoors, and enjoyed the fresh air and sunshine, diverting my attention and energy to more positive input. I noticed my spirits begin to lift and my attitude changed dramatically. I stopped worrying about the many, many things that had once controlled my mood, and the world seemed brighter.

With my mind less cluttered, meditation and journaling were freer and more spontaneous, and I was more easily inspired. Things became simpler, less complicated, less frustrating; I became less short-tempered, and best of all, my rest was more sound.

In every twenty-four-hour news cycle "stuff" happens, and negative, bad news along with inspiring good news is going to be reported. I know I can't change the world nor eliminate the world's need for the news, but I can change how I live in the world and how much of the world's newsworthy events I take upon myself. I have chosen less news.

Now, instead of fretting and wringing my hands in anxiety and worry, and asking an invisible "media god," "WHY is this happening?!", I am able to relax and breath calmly while folding my hands in prayer and send up to God the troubles of the world that are for him to know and solve.

God's eye is on all things occurring in the world, including everything being reported on the news. By trusting that God is in control, my stress is lower, and I am more realistic about the impact of the news and events on me. God can manage the world and I am free to remain more hopeful for better times ahead. My attention is once again turned to the things most important to me: my husband and daughters, family, friends, home, work, church, faith, and myself.

Even on cloudy days, when the weather forecast is partly to mostly cloudy with a chance of rain, my forecast for each new day is partly to mostly sunny, because even on a cloudy day the sun is always shining, lighting the clouds from above and from within!

At the end of each day, I lay my head down upon my pillow and sigh in gratitude for the present day lived while my heart and mind are still filled with renewed hope for tomorrow and the next new beginning.

Then my dreams pull me into peaceful slumber, and I sleep.

Courage

"Be brave and steadfast; have no fear or dread of them, for it is the Lord, your God, who marches with you; he will never fail you or forsake you." Deuteronomy 31:6

"Be not afraid, I go before you always; come, follow me, and I will give you rest." Dan Schutte.

Take courage. Stand tall. Pursue peace and unity. Keep moving forward. Step up to the podium. Walk into the confessional. First day of school. New School. Look up. Say your name. Respond in the moment. Sing out loud! Speak with integrity and conviction. Be honest. Just say "NO." Overcome adversity. Charge forth. Struggle out of darkness into the light. Push. Live in sobriety. Stare down injustice. Do not blink. Leave the past behind. Pick up the pieces. Sit up. Forgive. Accept limitations. Suffer pain. Battle illness. Say goodbye....

Evolving since my infancy and progressing through adulthood, with each everchanging moment of my life–good and bad–I have learned, through trial and error, to take courage and accept God's will. I have prayed for His empowering presence, the Holy Spirit, to help me shore up my resolve when I am weak and to flood my mind and body with wisdom and strength when I hesitate; to remove fear and the obstacles that I or someone else puts in my way that prevent me from living in peace, in prosperity, in acceptance, and in love. Endeavoring to live each day of my life, come what may, takes courage.

Like the unpredictable nature of ocean waves, my life has been calm at times and then suddenly and without warning turbulent and murky, tossing me in one direction and then in another, sometimes nearly drowning me in discouragement and fear. If not for the calming presence of the Lord in my soul, I do not know where I would have washed up, or if I would have washed up at all.

At times my "shoreline" has been torn up by my own turbulent behaviors, and I have experienced the rise and fall of uncertain days. And just as natural as the moon rising and the corrective pull of gravity restoring balance and symmetry to the once turbulent waters of the sea, so too my life has been pulled back by the Holy Spirit from the chaos and destruction of my own overindulgent will. It has been roughest when I relied solely on my own understanding rather than relying on God. I have put myself in serious trouble and have fallen into troubled waters. The lessons I have learned from my failings are unforgettable and the wisdom I have gained is without end. I cannot do life all by myself; I need God to help me (Proverbs 3:5-6).

Wisdom has taught me that failure produces fear and fear produces failure. Incapacitating, paralyzing, no-way-out fear. Instead of asking God for what I need and receiving his many and varied provisions to be successful and able to rise to an occasion, I have gone it alone and left myself feeling unqualified, under-skilled, underutilized, unfulfilled, and unsuccessful. Even in the best of times, I have been shaky and anxious, wondering if I am naïve and deluding myself into thinking God hears my prayers. In those times Jesus pushes my fears away and dissolves my toxic imaginings. I trust without seeing that Jesus is leading me in the right direction, kicking over the roadblocks of uncertainty and indecision that I erect within myself.

People have been cruel and manipulative towards me, and they have lied and used false words and accusations against me to elevate themselves and have power over me. Confronting their falsehoods has taken a lot of courage. Friends and family have supported me, believed in me, and coached me in my response but it was my trust and belief that Jesus was with me in the moment of confrontation that gave me the courage to stand up for myself, stay calm, hold my head up, and rise above the malicious hostility of others in order to remain focused on the truth, which ultimately prevailed.

Still, when I think of what others go through, and the difficulties they face, my situations pale in comparison. How can I think of myself as courageous when there are people experiencing hardships so much greater than my own, situations that would tear me apart? I have not been homeless or lived in my car. I have not had bombs drop on my street or bullets rip through my home. I have not suffered a catastrophic injury or the loss of limbs or lost my sight or hearing. No one close to me has committed suicide or been murdered. These tragedies are so great. I think–No! I know– it must take tremendous courage to persevere through these hardships, and I pray for all to receive the strength and courage needed to continue forward in these times of distress. It is said, "God only gives us what we can handle," but I wonder aloud why some have so much more to handle, so many more crosses to bear.

When my crosses seem too much to bear, it is God who makes me strong, and when I am weak, He gives me the power to say, "I am able."

I have seen ordinary events quickly change and courageous actions are needed to bring order and clarity again. On any given day something may happen at home or at work, at church or at school, in my neighborhood, or literally any place I go where a situation can change and veer off course. A pleasant conversation can turn to insult, a trip to the bank can reveal a dramatic loss of funds, a road incident can cause people to raise voices in anger and profanity. In these moments, it can be challenging to find the courage to react in a level-headed way, a compassionate way, a good and holy "God-fearing" way, a Christian way.

Honesty takes courage. Telling the truth should be easy and right, no holds barred. Yet, when a lie is perpetrated or given time to grow, it takes courage to stop its progress, change course, and tell the truth. In our courts, there is a reason people go to prison for lying. It is harmful to reputations, and a lie prevents the truth from being told. It is hard to admit a lie. It is even more difficult to accuse someone of lying. It can hurt a relationship, sometimes permanently. I do not like it when people lie, and I do not like being lied to. My biggest dilemma is lying to get out of a difficult situation. It may be a small fib or half-truth, but it is still not the truth. I have a saying, "Truth always bubbles to the surface," and it is true: lies always seem to be found out. As a child I knew a lie was wrong and whenever the truth was about to be revealed my gut tightened and I was afraid. I lived with the deception burning inside of me and even if no one else knew, God knew the lie before, during, and after it was told.

Honestly, it takes courage to be honest and tell the truth, whatever the outcome.

Jesus tells me to not be afraid, to trust him and share with him my burdens. The Holy Spirit empowers and encourages me to be courageous and believe I am forgiven. It has taken courage to admit to God and to others when I have lied.

Lord, please forgive my weakness and give me courage to do what is right.

It takes courage to move beyond the safety of inaction and live in truth.

Big actions and small actions can take courage. Yes, things can seem daunting, fear can be strong, and the unknown has a power that is hard to overcome, but inaction is not always an option.

It took courage for my mom to leave the safety of her home to drive to the hospital to give birth to me while Hurricane Donna violently whipped rain and debris against the sides of the house. Mom and Dad left my sister and brother in the care of others, and they rushed to the hospital, praying my birth would be easy and the hurricane would pass over quickly, and all would remain safe. They did not know what the outcome would be, but they relied on God to see things through, and while the winds howled up to 100 mph and the seas rose along the North Carolina shoreline, I was born healthy, big, and strong.

It took courage to bring me into the world, and it took courage to let me find my way in the world, knowing injuries would occur and mistakes would be made.

When I was a baby, I learned to crawl, and when I was strong enough, I pulled myself along the edges of the furniture. I had no fear until the first time I fell and hit my head on the sharp edge of the coffee table. I learned to be more cautious, but still I did not understand all of the ways I could hurt myself. My parents did their best; they warned me to be careful, to not let go, but at some point, my cuts and bruises healed, and my fear of pain was overcome, and slowly I began to walk on my own. As a toddler I found the courage to let go of supportive hands, and once and for all, I learned to balance on my two chubby feet. I was on my own. My parents watched, holding their breath, as time moved in slow motion, and I took my first baby steps without falling.

It takes courage to let go of security and safety and move forward, step by step.

As a school-aged girl, I had courage enough to leave the security of my mother's care and shyly step into a new grade school that was filled with strangers. I saw children like myself of similar shape and size and abilities, but I also noticed some children that were set apart, who wore leg braces and were in wheelchairs, and for the first time in my young life I realized that there were people who did not experience life as I did. My child's heart expanded for these classmates. I learned these children could not run or kick a ball or skip rope or climb trees as I could. I was too young to understand how this inequity could happen, but I marveled at how courageous they were, confined and limited by their bodies' frailties.

It takes courage to accept the imperfections of one's body.

As a young teen and adult, I stretched with courage as I matured beyond the boundaries of parent and sibling relationships, making friends with people I trusted to keep my thoughts and feelings and ideas for the future a secret. In high school, I felt like one of the lucky ones to have a small group of friends. High school can be a cruel environment. I saw classmates who were teased and shunned, and I did not understand how people could be so cruel, but I did not have the courage to question the antagonism. I was afraid of experiencing the same.

My teenaged heart did not have the same boundless curiosity or courage of my childhood to step outside the box, and shamefully I admit I never mustered the courage to publicly befriend these students. Under the bright lights of the cafeteria, I looked away from their lonely glances. My fear was my failure, unlike they who had the courage to return to school day after day and endure the whispers and accusations of being ugly and unworthy of friendship. They persevered with chins thrust forward, fixing their sights squarely on graduation day and making a name for themselves.

It takes courage to believe in oneself and rise above being ostracized.

As a newlywed, courageously emboldened by love and romance and the promise of adventure, I left home to begin a new life separated from my parents' security to live in a place I did not know with a man I was excited to be with each day. A new life, a new husband, a new home. I felt blessed. While my single friends still talked about going to bars and restaurants alone, working late nights, I moved into my future, leaving the single life behind. The days of laughing and eating and retelling the events of our single days and going home alone were in the past. I prayed for my friends and for me that we would all find contentment and fulfillment in the lives we chose to live.

It takes courage to be true to oneself, independent, and free to be happy as a single or married person.

As a grieving mother and grieving wife, it was hard to continue to function day-to-day in the midst of overwhelming sadness. It was not until my mind and heart were healed enough to watch the evening news that I realized there was tragedy greater than my own being experienced in places around the world. Mothers and widows were on the evening news with their husbands' and children's lifeless bodies in their arms, their homes bombed out and in rubble. I saw their unendurable suffering in their tearful faces and my heart felt their loss. As stories of refugees filled the news, with line upon line of displaced people being herded to unknown destinations in search of shelter and a place to bury their dead, I wondered how much more courage they had than I, suffering so much loss and desolation.

Just like love cannot be measured, sadness and grief cannot be measured, nor the amount of courage it takes to endure suffering. It is impossible to measure the agony, pain, and hurt that one feels when a loved one dies. Only God knows how much we suffer. Only God knows and understands. I suppose that is why I turn to him in these times. He knows…He knows...He knows.

It takes courage to endure unimaginable loss, but with God's love and compassion, all things remain possible.

I am in awe at the tremendous courage of humanity.

I know my courage comes from the Lord. It is with trust that I ask for courage, and thus have confidence to do things that seem insurmountable or impossible. It is through God's power and strength that I am made able to do what I need to do. I was born because of an act of courage, I live with courage at the ready, and I hope to die with courage. Since the beginning of time, God has instructed his children to have courage; fear not; be stouthearted. By the power of the Holy Spirit, I am empowered to face the unknown, no matter how scary it seems.

With twenty-twenty hindsight I can see how the shoreline of my life has shifted, been corrupted, and washed away during the storms of my life, yet the balance and symmetry of my path has endured. Even when things get crazy and are turned upside down and the future is uncertain, a beautiful supernatural force brings me back to my center where God and Jesus are found, and serenity and courage prevail.

Living takes courage, but with the Lord as my strength and my shield, I believe that no matter what happens, all will be well, and peace will fill my days.

"These things I have spoken to you, so that in Me you may have peace. In the world you have tribulation but take courage; I have overcome the world." John 16:33

Seasons: Winter, Spring, Summer, Fall

There is an appointed time for everything,
    and a time for every affair under the heavens.
    A time to be born, and a time to die;
    a time to plant, and a time to uproot the plant.
    A time to kill, and a time to heal;
    a time to tear down, and a time to build.
    A time to weep, and a time to laugh;
    a time to mourn, and a time to dance.
    A time to scatter stones, and a time to gather them;
    a time to embrace, and a time to be far from embraces.
    A time to seek, and a time to lose;
    a time to keep, and a time to cast away.
    A time to rend, and a time to sew;
    a time to be silent, and a time to speak.
    A time to love, and a time to hate;
    a time of war, and a time of peace.
What advantage has the worker from his toil? I have considered the task which God has appointed for men to be busied about. He has made everything appropriate to its time, and has put the timeless into their hearts, without men's ever discovering, from beginning to end, the work which God has done. I recognized that there is nothing better than to be glad and to do well during life.

For every man, moreover, to eat and drink and enjoy the fruit of all his toil is a gift of God.

I recognized that whatever God does will endure forever; there is no adding to it, or taking from it. Thus has God done that he may be revered. What now is has already been; what is to be, already is; and God restores what would otherwise be displaced. Ecclesiastes 3: 1-15

I love the changing seasons! I consider myself truly blessed to have always lived in places where winter, spring, summer, and fall "show out" for a time each year. Winter, so pristine and elegant in its frozen stillness of dormancy and hibernation. Spring, the long-awaited thaw, with its fresh air, glistening rain, tentative sunshine, and new life budding out in every direction. Summer, so vast and unchartered, lit by daylight that seems to last forever while peaches ripen on the tree, and wild berries beg to be picked and devoured! And glorious fall, the kindest season of all, dripping with the scent of apple and pumpkin spice and s'mores over woodland bonfires...oh so fleeting, green to golden orange to brown and then no more.

I like most the seasons that flow gracefully and softly, one into the next with barely a mention. The times of greater stress prove to be seasons that sputter and jerk and whip around, vicious and cutting like sleet in March.

From one year to the next, the start and stop of the seasons has varied widely, but one thing has remained constant: it does not matter whether a groundhog or a farmer or a weather expert predicts a certain date that winter will end, the seasons change in God's good time!

As a created part of the natural world, my physical, spiritual, and emotional wellbeing is connected to both the changing seasons and the cycle of life. Consciously, subconsciously, and instinctually, from my head to my toes, every cell in my body, every strand of my DNA, every facet of my spirit responds to the dying and rebirth that takes place with the changing of the seasons. I see plants and trees, rivers and oceans, mountains and valleys, animals and people all recreate and make new, transforming the earth, evolving, and emerging again from darkness into light, rising to new life until the end of days.

Like the springtime, my early years were soft, new, and budding, filled with exploration and the constant discovery of small things. In my prime each day was like summer, bright and full of blinding-hot passion, risky and full of adventure, with plenty of time for my roots of faith to grow deeply into the fertile soil of my heart, while love of family, home, and career bloomed and overflowed to the outer limits of my being.

As I have continued to age, I feel an urgency in each new day and a greater responsibility to not waste time and, surprisingly, to show forth my true self in all of its many colors, unafraid, knowing all too well that the time of my life is finite. I have learned from fall and its quick outburst of foliage the urgency of purpose, for it is brief in its magnificence and then the winds of change quickly leave the landscape empty and bare.

Soon enough I will live into the winter of my life, slowing down and contemplating all of the amazing days contained in my memories, frozen forever in my mind. I cannot foretell when this time will come, but as I live into my final days, I hope to be filled with joyful expectation for my long-anticipated meeting with Jesus, face to face.

No matter how fast or slow I move through my days, time does not slow down or speed up; it remains constant, ticking one second into the next, one season into the next, glorious, and life-giving. I need the bright sun of summer to lift my spirit; I yearn for the quiet silence of winter to force me to slow down and take time to rest. I cherish springtime when once again I throw open the windows, ready to feel the crisp, cool breezes that blow away anxiety and reawaken my mind to endless possibilities; and in the fall I am drawn to the bright panorama of colors that set the hills and valleys on fire, matching my own spirit's fire!

Each season I will sing with the sparrow, and laugh with the baby, I will rejoice with the farmer, and cry with the widow; for to sing and laugh and rejoice and cry is a gift from God.

I praise God for the beauty of the earth and the blessing of each season, from the beginning of time to the end of the ages! Praise and glory be to God forever and ever! Amen!

The Bible

"Some will kill to have it. He will kill to protect it." The Book of Eli

"In the beginning was the Word, and the Word was with God, and the Word was God." John 1:1

I can't believe I have been using my Bible as a mouse pad while writing this reflection on the Bible! What is wrong with me?! Have I no respect for the Holy Bible and the ancient words contained within, carried forward by the people who knew and trusted and believed in God? What would Moses think, who heard and saw God in the burning bush on Mount Horeb? What is wrong with me?

Has the precious history of God's salvation been so reduced from its grandeur and glory, enthroned, protected by thousands of people who risked everything to bring this holy book to the "New World," become so ordinary that I do not see it for what it is? Do I not see the dishonor I risk to the absolute fidelity of God's chosen ones carrying forward the Word for all ages?

There must be something truly amazing and irrefutable about this book called the Bible! Only something from God could hold the short attention span of humans for so many thousands of years! It is much more than stories and folklore; the Bible contains God's perfect Truth. And sometimes…oh, how I apologize Lord…it has been inadvertently used as a mouse pad.

When I contemplate the chaos in society in the world if Bibles were removed, and if God, Jesus, and the gospel Truth were no longer spoken of, taught, or read, I am chilled to the bone with real fear for the survival and safety of the planet. I can't imagine the world without Bibles and the historical accounts therein of the earliest people who knew and believed in God. For gosh sakes, people talked to God, and he helped them out of tough spots! God gave instructions through the prophets, and people actually listened and disastrous wars were averted!

I have used my Bible for many things...oops...but also used my Bible as a guidebook for living a "God-fearing" life, a moral life, an honorable life. I would be lost without it, for within its pages I have found the secret to life! For years I have listened to and read the Old Testament and New Testament stories. I have gained wisdom and knowledge from the lessons about love and forgiveness, about knowing right from wrong, about patience and endurance through persecution and slavery, about freedom and redemption and absolute trust in God, and about the sacrificial love of Jesus and later, that of his Apostles...and I have been changed for the better.

Thank God there is no prohibition on Bibles in my country and proclaiming the Word of God is protected by the second amendment of the Constitution of the United States. I treasure my freedom to own, read, and display my Bible openly; it is my right. I am not afraid to carry my Bible into public places, and I pray Bibles are never eliminated in my country, in homes, churches, courtrooms, schools, libraries, museums, bookstores, hospitals, hotels, prisons...for I fear society, either by accident or purposefully, is losing its respect, reverence, and honor for the "Good Book."

I wonder...if Bibles ceased to exist, would faith in God and religion slowly fade away? Would hope and joy be replaced by disillusionment and lamentation? It is hard for me to believe that there are places in this world where Bibles are banned, and children have never heard the "Good News" of Jesus Christ! If the historical account of the people of God is hidden or wiped away, will the Apocalypse described in the Book of Revelation come to pass, with total mayhem, calamity, and disaster reigning until the world is destroyed?

For over five hundred years the Bible has been in print, and a wide array of institutions have kept the Bible safe and secure and still in the "public sphere." Family Bibles have maintained a significant place in the home, where for centuries family births, marriages, deaths, and other pertinent events have been recorded, by which families have traced back their roots. In the past it was not uncommon for a family to gather in the home and listen to the Word of God read by a family member. Sharing the Bible in the home, in church, and in schools has bound folks together through hardship, and the timeless stories in the Bible have given people hope and encouragement when times were tough; I know the Bible stories have strengthened me.

People of all ages and from all walks of life are searching for an historical account of how the world began and what their place is in it, for the meaning of life and its purpose, and I say to them, "Read the Bible! And quite possibly you will find your answers to these important questions and so much more!"

When I read the Bible from cover to cover for the first time it was quite an experience! The saying, "Same thing, different day!" sums it up. I had no idea there were so many stories and events replicated over and over throughout history, and this gave me hope for the world! Chapter upon chapter, humans have been building up and tearing down and building up again, maintaining power struggles and endless wars and then finding common ground and peace, healing family squabbles and honoring traditions, solving personal dilemmas with no way out except for the Lord. The people of the Bible unequivocally lived lives in defense of belief in God, belief in Jesus, belief in humanity, and belief in themselves.

It is a privilege to read the Bible, and when I approach it with humility, I feel God's love coming straight off the pages. This experience is possible for everyone, including and especially for people who think they are "unworthy" or "undeserving" of God's love. I cannot think of a better witness to this miracle of belief in oneself and belief that God is love than from men and women who in prison have been transformed by the power of the Word. I have seen with my own eyes and heard with my own ears the testimony of once angry, hate-filled people changed for the better after joining a Bible group and studying the Word with fellow incarcerated people and prison ministry teams.

When I was seven years old, I received my first New Testament, as part of a First Communion gift set from my parents. I wasn't quite sure what to do with it, but it was a neat surprise! The small book was tucked inside my First Communion purse along with a plastic rosary and a mother-of-pearl chalice pin. I was most curious about the Bible, and every so often I would pull it out and sneak a peek in it, but the words were small and hard to read, as well as difficult to understand, so I would put it away for safe keeping with my other treasures.

For a long time, I thought all Bibles were like my First Communion New Testament until my mom and dad bought a very large, very heavy New Jerusalem Bible. What a beautiful Bible! Cloth bound, gold embossed, formidable and dramatic in every way, but still very hard to read. It was not what today we call "user-friendly." Even so, its presence in our living room communicated to visitors that we were a family that believed in God and in the Gospel.

It wasn't until I was in my thirties, shortly after I attended a religious retreat that I owned my first Bible. After the talk and reflection on "Study," I felt woefully unprepared to articulate my faith and defend my beliefs as a Christian without a Bible for reference.

I went swiftly to the bookstore and looked around but could not find the Bibles, so I asked for help. For some strange reason I lowered my voice when I asked the clerk where the Bibles could be found. I guess I was still shy (er, embarrassed) and hesitant about making my faith so blatant by buying a Bible. It was no big deal to the salesclerk, though. She pointed me to the back of the store, around a corner, where the Bibles were virtually hidden and out of sight.

There were many to choose from, and after a few minutes I chose the New American Bible from Catholic Bible Press. I had a rush of excitement when I opened the protective box and smelled the "genuine" leather and *cracked* the pages apart. I had a nice surprise when I turned to the second page, marked with a bold red ribbon, and saw a picture of Pope John Paul II, who was pope at the time of publication. Realizing now the popularity of His Holiness and the love the entire world expressed for him, I still find it comforting to see his saintly eyes looking back at me when I open my Bible.

Finally, my own Bible! I completed my statement of ownership by writing my name in it, claiming unapologetically that this Bible belonged to me. Once it was "signed, sealed, and delivered," I commenced reading. With slow deliberation, scanning through the "Introduction" and "How to Use this Book" sections, I started reading the greatest best seller of all time: "In the beginning when

God created the heavens and the earth..." (Genesis 1:1–yes, it really starts that way!).

As I progressed through the Old Testament, I began to know Abraham, Noah, Jeremiah, and Ruth: people who put their absolute faith and trust in God's hands. Their stories revealed a reverence and reliance on God, fear–i.e., respect–of God that through the ages compelled generation after generation to believe in God's divine, supernatural power and providence.

Reading about Sarah (Genesis 21:1) and Elizabeth (Luke 1:36), women who were barren and then conceived, made me feel less singled out in my own struggle with infertility and conception. I read about Passover and the Feast of the Dedication (Hanukkah) and I understood more deeply how important and ancient are the traditions of my Jewish relatives; their God is my God, and my God is their God (Ruth 1:16). As each chapter ended, my knowledge of God grew and I could say, "I know God as never before!"

It amazes me every time I think that within the Old Testament, the sacred Word of God, are the same Hebrew writings that Jesus memorized as a young boy and recited at his Bar Mitzvah. As a grown man embarking on his ministry, Jesus unrolled the Torah and taught with authority in the temple, reading the same covenant stories that are told today. Remarkably, those same words of long ago that passed through the lips of Jesus are still proclaimed today in synagogues and churches around the world!

As a Christian, reading the New Testament helped me gain a new perspective of Jesus as a real human being. He had a life like no other. As I read the four Gospels, the truth of his human nature became undeniable. Jesus was smart and funny and quick-witted. He expressed his feelings and did not withhold his emotions. He did not shy away from challenging questions from religious hierarchy, and he was quick to forgive. He loved people and creation as no other human being will ever love again. Jesus is why I am Christian.

I could relate to Jesus' story.

Jesus *disappointed his parents* when he ventured off without telling them where he was going, and after three days, Mary and Joseph, worried sick, found Jesus in the temple "with his Father" (Luke 2: 41-52).

Jesus *honored his mother and accepted her guidance* when it was time for him to enter into his ministry, performing his first miracle by turning water into wine at the wedding at Cana (John 2:1-11).

Jesus *became annoyed* with his friends when they squabbled about who was most important, showing their lack of understanding about the Kingdom of God (Mark 10: 35-40).

And Jesus *mourned*, shedding real tears when Lazarus, his friend whom he loved, died (John 11: 5, 32-36).

Jesus became physically tired, overwhelmed, and angry at times and would go to a deserted place to pray. Jesus *prayed to God*, whom he relied on for his help and direction (Luke 5:15-16).

Jesus *showed weakness*, questioning his Father about his divine mission when his anxiety grew, and *sadness* when his friends betrayed and abandoned him (Luke 22:39-46).

Jesus *went alone* on the long, painful journey to the crucifixion. His face was bloodied and bruised from the violent blows of the Roman centurions, and his body bled from head to toe from the forty lashes inflicted upon him. Jesus' skin tore when pierced by the crown of thorns, and his blood dripped and stung in his swollen eyes. And like any man who is half dead, Jesus was not strong enough to carry the large wooden cross up the hill to Golgotha. Jesus *received help* from another, Simon of Cyrene (Matthew 27:27-32).

Jesus was like all humans; he bled, his breathing stopped, his heart stopped, his brain stopped, and he died (Matthew 27:45-50).

Yet Jesus was divine in every way, and he rose from the dead to new life as he promised (Matthew 27:57-28:10)!

Each of the Gospels brings me into the life of Jesus: a biographical account of Jesus, the son of Mary, the Son of God, followed by the compelling stories of the resurrected Christ and the apostolic stories of the new Christian church.

I would be lost without the guidance of the inspired words found in the Bible. The wisdom I have received has changed me, improved my attitude, empowered me to make my life better, and brought forth from me a more charitable love towards others. God's message is Truth and as I apply his lessons in my life, my faith and acceptance of life's events increases exponentially and his Word makes my music ministry, my calling, a sublime work.

"All scripture is inspired by God and is useful for teaching, for refutation, for correction, and for training in righteousness, so that one who belongs to God may be competent, equipped for every good work" (2 Timothy 3:16).

Without studying the Bible, I would still be living in a haze of faith.

When I received my first New Testament for my First Communion, I did not understand the precious treasure given to me and I tucked it away as a keepsake. When later I learned that the key to knowing God was reading His Word, I gave myself his guidebook, his road atlas, for my spiritual journey of faith. I have used (and sometimes abused) my Bible. The binding is well-worn, the gilded pages have dulled, and the end of the red satin ribbon is frayed from marking my place, and I love it!

Through the ages the Bible has been preserved and protected by the faithful, transported across continents by pilgrims, so that from generation to generation people will have answers to "Who is God?" and "Why do I believe?" Scholars and plain folk like me have researched and referenced Bibles; memorized passages and marked up pages; and reported on the miracles and deeds of Moses, Elijah, and King David; of Saints Peter, Barnabas, and Bartholomew, all for the glory of God.

Thank you, ancestral people of Abraham, Isaac, and Jacob, for carrying forward through all adversity the sacred Word of God. I am filled with hope for future generations that people who believe in religious freedom will preserve every chapter and verse within the Bible so that whether read privately or proclaimed out loud in the public square, hearts will be changed, and all will know the Lord God and peace will reign.

Oh, the miles God's Word has traveled! If only those Bibles could talk! What stories of faith they could tell!

Donna Braidic

Love

Home

"By wisdom is a house built, by understanding is it made firm; and by knowledge are its rooms filled with every precious and pleasing possession." Proverbs 24:3-4

The first time I heard the phrase, "Home is where the heart is," it struck a strong emotional chord in me. I had always thought of home as the house I grew up in with my family, but when I replaced house with heart, I realized home was more than a place or a town or a "house with a picket fence"; it is the place in my heart where togetherness with family and friends is held close. Home is warm, safe, inviting, accepting, and restful. Home is stability, rooted in love.

Home is more than a building. Home is the lovely soft place on my husband's shoulder where I can rest my head after a difficult day, where I am able to close my eyes and forget my business woe and strife. Home is a state of mind, where peace and contentment are my primary concern. Home is within me, where love and security and safety mix with God's will for my life, and no matter where I find myself at the end of the day, I am home.

Hollywood gave us great TV shows like *Leave It to Beaver* and *Father Knows Best* and *Happy Days* to model what a happy home looks like, but they were fiction, and Wally and Jim and Richie were actors. Unfortunately, when I was young, I didn't know the difference between real life and fiction, and these shows and others like them influenced my perception of what home is. They led me to believe that everyone has a perfect house on a perfect street in a perfect neighborhood where all the neighbors know each other and call out to one another with a smile and a wave, "Hey, Mr. and Mrs. So-and-So, nice day!"

However sweet and idyllic these shows were, they did not represent real life; they did not represent what home was for me or for most people. It was a relief for me to learn that not all children always play nicely together or ride their bicycles in pairs or sit side by side at the soda fountain at the corner drugstore enjoying a root beer float from the same straw. Yes, these overly sentimental portrayals of hometown were a good representation of what home is when people love and care about one another, but it wasn't real, and I needed the real deal: I needed to find my family's Mayberry, I needed to find home.

Television convinced me that everyone had two parents and four grandparents, all living close by (that is, until *The Courtship of Eddie's Father*). It took a while to figure out not all families are white (hello, *Fresh Prince of Bel-Air*). And guess what? Most high school sweethearts don't stay together after graduating from high school. They find their own careers and live independent lives. The "happily ever after" is rarely what it seems, and there is nothing wrong with that!

However, my parents are the exception. They were like a made-for-TV couple! They met as young teenagers and fell in love almost immediately. They married when Mom was nineteen and Dad was twenty, and soon after, my siblings and I started coming along. My dad worked for a major electrical supply company, and although it was a great job, the downside was the upheaval to my family; whenever Dad earned a promotion, we had to move! But Mom and Dad always kept love in their marriage and love in our home and I never questioned where my home was; it was with them.

So it surprised me and put me off a little when people asked me, "Where are you from? Where is home for you?" I didn't know what they were asking. Wasn't it obvious? "I live here, with my family." Family was my home.

Now, as an adult, I understand those were loaded questions about who I am, where I was born, where I grew up, where "my roots" are.

From the moment I came into the world, home was wherever my parents and my sister and brothers were. The entire time my mom was in labor and even after I was born, Hurricane Donna, a Category 3 hurricane, was making landfall in the Carolinas, and no matter how hard the winds blew or the rain fell, as long as I was with my parents in the hospital maternity ward, newly born and being watched over with tender loving care, I was home. It comes as no surprise to me that after such a historic hurricane, my name stuck: Donna after my dad, Donald, and Kay after my mom, Kathleen!

While growing up, Mom and Dad took us back to their Kentucky home and I met my relatives and bonded as family. I always felt sad when it was time to leave but happy that I had spent time with all of them. From these trips I learned so much about my mom and dad's home: the streets they grew up on, the houses they lived in and the schools they attended, all of their favorite hangouts, and where they courted. Most importantly, these visits brought me back to my roots and the people and places that influenced and formed my mom and dad into my parents.

The short time with my grandparents and great-grandparents was unforgettable, and the holidays with my aunts and uncles and cousins were fun and informative. As we would bounce from one family reunion to the next, many stories surfaced about my mom and dad and what they were like as kids, what life was like for them in Louisville, and a few stories about my grandparents, including the one about my grandfather, "Vince" Klein, playing baseball for the famed Louisville Colonels baseball team! I was so proud of my family and our home! They were the real deal!

Every house smelled of baked ham and sugar cookies and tobacco and bourbon, and conversations about the old days were told and retold in colorful language thick with southern accents. My parents would quickly slide back into the ease of conversation and laughter with their brothers and sisters, and it was neat to see them forget for a while that they were parents and just be themselves.

Sometimes a serious mood shrouded the dining table or living room, usually when someone passed away. I remember when my grandma, Dottie, died. I was only six years old, and my family had to travel from Massachusetts to Louisville very quickly. It was December, and Christmastime was shrouded in extreme sadness. Dottie was in her early fifties, and her death was completely unexpected. I heard words like "blood clot" and "stroke" and "aneurysm" as I sat snuggled up close to my mom in the funeral parlor. I was so sad for my mom, and I cried. It was the first time I

91

understood people could go away forever, and it scared me. Home changed for my mom, but her love for her family was still strong, and this gave me comfort.

Some of the best and most honest stories shared at our family reunions were of their struggles to make a living. Although sparse, there were still family gatherings to spread warmth during difficult times. From endless seasons of planting, canning, cleaning, laundering, preparing meals, and rolling out dough for noodles and dumplings, entire lifetimes were lived to provide for the family. My relatives gave their all to make a living, and in one way or another—in the military, church, community, government—each served to keep America and our family safe and free, and these values were held in high regard by my parents.

One story that my dad tells is how his mom, "Mother," made "Chicken Foot Soup." Without going into details, let us just say things could be pretty meager when Dad was a boy and Mother would make a chicken broth from the little bit of chicken fat found under the ankle skin of a chicken foot! I can't help turning my nose up when he tells this story, imagining the skin on the spiky chicken foot being peeled back to the ankle and a drop of fat and a sliver of bone being thrown into a pot of boiling water to make an entire meal. Dad acknowledges it might not have been much, but no one starved, especially when Mother added her delicious homemade dumplings!

I think this story exemplifies the ethics that were impressed upon me, and upon my parents, and upon their parents, that during lean times and prosperity one should share as much as one can, providing hospitality and giving generously; be strong, work hard, persevere, forgiving one another and having faith in God, and remembering always you are home as long as you have love. My relatives loved me the same way they loved my parents, and I know through our family visits we were part of something bigger and more permanent than a physical house: we were part of a home.

Because my family moved so often, we learned quickly that sports, school activities, and church helped us meet and make friends quickly. Ice hockey was in our blood, starting with my dad from his days playing for a league in Louisville, so we usually found our way to the ice rink fairly quickly. As my dad would say, "The family that skates together stays together!"

This was certainly true for us! Ice skating was something everyone in my family enjoyed doing, and we did it together.

Dad loved ice hockey, so it was an easy fit for him to coach the boys throughout their youth, from pee wees into adulthood. When I was fourteen, I played on a girls' ice hockey team, and Dad, always the coach, sometimes gave me pointers on improving my game. From Massachusetts to Philadelphia to Columbus to Minnesota, the ice rink always felt like home to me.

No matter where we lived, Mom and Dad always made sure there was a church within easy driving distance from our house. On Sundays and other church occasions, Dad could be heard saying as we complained about going, "The family that goes to church together stays together!"

Church was a big part of my family's life, and sometimes it was as cozy and friendly as our living room at home. One of my favorite memories of church was when my parents hosted a Seder meal in our home with church friends and our parish priest. I didn't quite understand what was going on, but it was exciting to see my parents and their friends strengthen their bond of faith while seeking greater knowledge about the history of the Jewish faith and its traditions. My mom and dad welcomed the Jewish faith into our home, broadening our religious experience and creating acceptance that would be important to our family ties later in life when my brother and his Jewish wife had two sons, sons they would raise in their Jewish faith.

Mom and Dad integrated rituals and traditions of Judaism into our Catholic home throughout the years, so that when my nephews made their Bar Mitzvahs, the occasions were much more special to us all. It was an unbelievable privilege and joy to pray together and sing the same ancient psalms in synagogue that we had sung at Mass. Our Christian and Jewish faiths are connected by God who is the tie that binds us together. Learning about Judaism seemed so exotic and radical and beautiful when I was young, but now I see clearly how God was working then in ways that would keep my family close in faith, keep love in our family, and keep peace in our homes.

93

It wasn't easy moving as often as my family did, but all of our colorful experiences which might not have happened otherwise kept us growing together in whatever home we found ourselves in. It took strength to keep recreating home. It took hard work. It took perseverance. It took forgiveness. It took love. And most of all, it took my parents' faith in God that he would always lead us to the best house to make our home in.

Home is agape love: giving and self-sacrifice, which are the brick and mortar that holds home together- from the past and present generations to the future ones yet to be born. Home is my place of belonging and my place of accepting who I am. Wherever I live, near or far, no matter what my circumstances, in successes, or failures, yet-to-be reconciled hurts, or quarrels, love is what binds the heart of my family together.

North Carolina was my birthplace, but home is my loving family and all the places we have lived and all the life experiences we have shared. Home is my mom and dad and their "Old Kentucky Home." Home is my sister and brothers, my many in-laws, my nieces and nephews, my cousins, and my friends. Home is my daughters. Home is my husband. Home is where I live. Home is stability and safety. Home is church and spirit and ritual and sacrament. Home is faith in God.

Home is where I live, in my house, with my husband.
Home is family.
Home is where my heart is.
Home is Love.

Family Time

"This is what I have observed to be good: that it is appropriate for a person to eat, to drink and to find satisfaction in their toilsome labor under the sun during the few days of life God has given them—for this is their lot. Moreover, when God gives someone wealth and possessions, and the ability to enjoy them, to accept their lot and be happy in their toil—this is a gift of God. They seldom reflect on the days of their life because God keeps them occupied with gladness of heart." Ecclesiastes 5:18-20

Family time is one of the greatest blessings of my childhood and my life.

My family is very close-knit. Our bond is strong and resilient, proven so by many ups and downs over the years, and it will last forever. The love that my mom and dad discovered as teenagers is still unbroken to this day; it is a bright and vibrant thread woven into every experience that we have had as a family, and it holds us tightly together even as each of us has grown up and begun our own lives apart from one another.

By today's standards, my mom and dad were very young–too young–when they got married and started their family. They were still very inexperienced in the ways of the world and hadn't yet grown up completely, but they were in love, and they wanted very badly to be together as husband and wife. I think that in some ways my parents and my siblings and I all grew up together.

Mom and Dad liked to have fun, and I think it was for this reason that they created "family time." Even with five kids in tow, it was a way for them to still go out and have a good time together! I think it was time well spent, whether we had fun or not, because we learned how to be a family. No matter where we went, at any given time we could be found laughing, crying, poking, jabbing, fighting, celebrating, belonging to each other, journeying together to exciting destinations.

We were adventurers traveling to places unknown, driving along backroads and busy city streets, guided by well-worn maps and my dad's internal compass. We learned to share our snacks and get along, compromising one day and getting our way the next, and we relied on the generosity of people, locals who knew their way around town, providing secret shortcuts around a traffic jam, helping us reset our course when dad or mom took a wrong turn.

Mom and Dad were married in November of 1956, and soon after, they started their family. Lisa, my big sister, was the first child to come along and my baby brother, Chris, was the last born, with David, me, and Jeff coming in between. I can't imagine having five kids today, but for young couples like my mom and dad, raised Catholic in the post-World War II era, "popping babies out" was pretty common. And believe it or not, it was a real blessing being raised in a big family.

Dad worked for a major electrical manufacturer, and as his work began to impress the higher ups, promotions and relocations became a regular event. I think it must have been hard for my mom and dad, being barely out of their teens, married with two children by their third wedding anniversary, and being relocated from Kentucky to Massachusetts. Moving so many miles away from the security of their loving families and beginning a life and career together, I think it must have been very hard, and I know they missed their Kentucky home very much.

I often think of mom and dad as the pioneers of a more transient and mobile society, birthing their "baby boomers" on the go, leaving everything they loved behind to follow their dreams. Thank goodness Mom and Dad had a good foundation of faith in God during these times of constant change. Church was a place where they could always find relief from homesickness and built-up stress, and it was a place to find friends, support, and babysitters!

Needless to say, Mom and Dad did not have the luxury of a lot of "down time" with a growing family, and when our many relocations from state to state were added in, we all felt pretty stressed out, tired, and homesick. Mom and dad needed a break. We all needed a break. We needed a vacation!

There was no question about who needed it the most or the least: we all needed it the same! My mom, who was always up by six and in bed by ten, go-go-going with no stops in between, needed a break. My dad, always up and out working hard, making sales, marketing products, managing people, and when not traveling for business was home giving every spare minute to meet family obligations and bring home the paycheck, needed a break. And my siblings and me, always needing something for school or sports teams or after-school groups, competing for our parents' attention and their help in every way, doing our chores to save a little money, we all needed some time off!

Occasionally, even a vacation, with all of its preparations and nickel-and-dime saving, could produce more stress, making me wonder if the vacation would even be worth it! But in the end, short tempers aside, when all was packed and everyone was buckled in the car, we all breathed a sigh of relief as Dad backed the car down the driveway and shifted into drive, taking us away to a great destination.

I loved riding in the "way back" seat of the station wagon with my brother. It faced backwards and it felt so weird to look at the drivers coming up from behind. We all tried to avoid looking at each other, but it was impossible! We would wave to the driver or passenger behind us, and sometimes they were friendly enough to wave back. That made my brother and me giggle, like we had a secret, and of course this only encouraged us to wave again and again. We would play games and sing songs along with the radio. No matter how old I get, whenever I hear "I Shot the Sheriff" or "American Pie," I smile with a pang of nostalgia, remembering our family trip to Myrtle Beach and all the great memories we made there.

My earliest memory of a family vacation is our trip to the World's Fair when I was just four years old. We traveled many hours in our small car, stuck in bumper-to-bumper traffic with no air conditioning, and the constant smell of fresh tar coming in through the open windows made us all a little lightheaded. David, Lisa, and I rode in the back seat, pressed up against each other with barely a wisp of air moving between us. Needless to say, there was a lot of whining and complaining from the back seat!

Nobody knew at the time that my sister was prone to car sickness, but we would soon find out! The combination of fast, slow, accelerating, braking, along with the heat, humidity, fumes, and close quarters simply overcame Lisa, and before anyone knew what was happening, Lisa leaned her head onto my shoulder and threw up on my head! Talk about a "bonding" experience!

David yelled, "Eww! Lisa threw up on Donna's head!"

As much as my dad wanted to keep going, he pulled the car over onto the shoulder of the road, and we all climbed out of the car. Lisa was crying, I just stood in shock, afraid to move my head, and David made frowny faces at all of us. My mom took one look at me and even though she tried to make me feel better, there was nothing she could say that would help. I had my sister's breakfast dripping down the side of my face!

Mom wiped off what she could, but there was nothing else she could do for me until we were in the park!

In the end, the one vivid, happy memory I have from The World's Fair is of the fountain sink in the ladies' room where my mom was finally able to wash the nasty vomit out of my hair. Unforgettable day, unforgettable family time, unforgettable memories!

From that trip forward there was never a dull moment on our family vacations. Lisa became known as the "puker," and most of our cars gave witness to this name at trade-in, evidenced by the purple and pink Hi-C beverage splatters staining the ceiling above the backseat windows! Jeff, Chris, and I were pretty easy-going travelers, and David was the adventurer with very little fear or impulse control, though somehow he managed to avoid the law. Most of the time.

Every family vacation David led the way to adventure, catching fish and snakes, frogs and crawdads, any number of slimy, gross things that could slither their way out of his pocket and onto the car floor! My mom even found a long-forgotten, dried up, very dead frog in my brother's pocket! Some of David's famous sayings may very well have been born out of his early years of mischief: "Why wouldn't ya?"; "That dog don't hunt"; "Livin' large and in charge!"; "I'm five days ahead!"; "Don't get ahead of it!"

Yes, David was very creative with his phrases! *"Why wouldn't ya?"* Why wouldn't you do something; what do you have to lose?

"That dog don't hunt." This idea won't work; it's just not going to happen. *"Livin' large and in charge!"* By definition, how David lived! Bigger than life and ruling the day! *"I'm five days ahead!"* As a very successful salesman, David was always looking five days ahead, planning his next move; like chess, always thinking five moves ahead. *"Don't get ahead of it!"* Stay in the moment; work the problem.

On our first trip to Martha's Vineyard, we stopped for a gasoline fill-up and bathroom break, and everyone but David took the time to use the facilities. David wasn't about to waste his time waiting in line for the bathroom when he had the woods to conceal his business and hunt for critters, all at the same time! I mean, "why wouldn't ya?" So, off he went into the wooded ravine behind the gas station while the rest of us waited for our turn in line!

After about twenty minutes we were back in the car, heading down the highway when my mom asked in a somewhat panicked voice, "Where is David?!" She did a quick head count and realized David was missing; he had been left behind!

Without a second to spare, my dad made a U-turn right in the middle of the highway, tires squealing, grinding up the gravel on both sides of the road, and raced back to the gas station. Everyone piled out of the car–again–and alerted the gas station attendant that David was missing. We all started calling out David's name, following a path down the ravine where we of course found my brother, fearless and grinning ear to ear, holding up the frogs he had caught in the creek.

After tremendous sighs of relief, tussles of hair, and hugs of gratitude, David, along with the rest of us, counted off as we climbed back in the car for the rest of the trip. Unfortunately, the elation wore off quickly and we had to listen to my parents lecture us the rest of the way on the dangers of separating from the group without permission and the major groundings we could expect if we ever did anything like that again!

I loved our family vacations to Martha's Vineyard, staying in the quaint town of Oak Bluffs, and the colorful, gingerbread cottages. I loved the ferry that took us to the island and the excitement that my siblings and I felt as we leaned over the front seat, watching with amazement as my dad parked our car on a boat!

The crossing to Oak Bluffs across the Martha's Vineyard Sound seemed to take forever to a child (it was only about forty-five minutes in "adult time"), but I did not complain! I took in everything: sea air, seagulls, bellowing horns signaling our departure, people milling about on the upper deck, cigarette smoke and popcorn and diesel fuel, body odor and fresh painted latrines and ocean spray heavy with the smell of fish. The ride to the island was just the beginning of a week of vacation fun, family time, and bonding!

After the ferry docked and we disembarked the first thing I saw was the Flying Horses Carousel. It was like a carnival, so colorful and noisy, and magical. I knew I was in a very special place.

My family had so much fun together, and this has never changed. Sure, we had arguments about what we would do first or which beach was the best to swim at or how long it would take to catch a fish, but all of this banter taught us to listen to one another and be less selfish and more flexible, and most of all that crying doesn't always get one's way. I didn't always get to go to the chocolate shop first, and that was okay, because when I finally did and I bought my milk chocolate sailboat lollipop and bit into it, it was even better than I remembered!

At the beach, I enjoyed the white noise of the pounding surf and the children and adults calling out to one another as laughter rose above the crash of waves from people body surfing and tumbling onto the beach. I discovered how relaxing it was to collect shells, but as a child I was not content to just admire their beauty; I glued them together and made little shell people, giving them the names of my family. I loved those shells.

As my family and I settled into the slower pace of the island, we relaxed and enjoyed talking and eating and laughing together, telling stories about our day's adventures.

Each vacation was a blessing, melding us as family again, from Canada to Myrtle Beach to Duluth, and even though islands and ocean ferries and foreign countries and southern beaches sound exotic, we were just as happy traveling back and forth to the towns we had moved from, visiting neighbors and relatives, seeing that with each passing year we were getting a little older, a little bigger, and a little closer to being on our own. Time did not stand still, and I learned to enjoy every minute of each day and the blessings that flowed into that day.

With this wisdom I began to appreciate the constancy of my sister and my brothers' companionship along my life journey.

Our last family vacation before I graduated from high school was to Duluth, Minnesota, to go skiing. Nothing says "spring break" like Duluth, Minnesota! It sounds strange now, living as I do in the south, that a vacation even in the coldest climate wasn't so bad when spent with my family! It was a weird vacation, too, because it was to be the last trip I would have as a kid with my entire family.

My parents did everything to make that trip special for us. We stayed in a really cool, oval-shaped house on the mountain where we could ski right out the front door and onto the slopes. That was really awesome! I loved being able to strap on my skis and glide off like a professional skier! It never ceased to amaze me how soft and shiny the snow was after a fresh fall overnight, never having been touched, and how cold the air was the first thing in the morning.

We each skied at different degrees of difficulty, so it was difficult to spend time together as a group on that trip. The house was empty most of the day until dinnertime, so I had a lot of time to reflect on my life and ponder my future. I found myself talking to God and listening for his answers in the silent, cold wind. There were so many questions I needed answers to: about who I was and where I was going, and I really wanted God to help me understand.

I was insecure and scared about growing up and leaving my family. I felt so melancholy. And then I understood very well what God wanted me to know. I was growing up and moving into a new part of my life, separate from them, and I needed to begin making decisions for myself. No one was overly pressuring me for answers about where I was going to college or what I wanted to do with my life, but it had been hanging in the air for a while.

It was at this most isolated and distant place that I realized, more than ever, that I loved my family, and I loved our time together. We had bonded over the years without my realizing it and despite our sibling rivalry I knew we would do anything for each other, anywhere, anytime; we had each other's backs. Even with all of our squabbles and tussles in the back seat of the family station wagon, I would not change one minute of our travels together, puke and all! We are family and we are forever bonded by all of our wonderful, and horrible, shared experiences. This is a gift.

As adults, my siblings and I have continued the beautiful tradition of vacationing with our own families, but we have also made family reunions with our parents a priority, celebrating together over the years holidays, birthdays, christenings, sporting events, new homes, church gatherings, weddings, picnics, graduations, the funeral of my late husband, and sadly, the funeral for my big brother, David—who is now and forever always five days ahead of us all, catching frogs and fish and holding a reservation for us all in some heavenly, family-time vacation spot!

From our family time together, my mom and dad fostered in me and my sibs a sense of family and belonging that began when they first set eyes on each other. It was hard work knitting our family together. It took commitment, sacrifice, patience, forgiveness, love, and so much more. I am in awe of my mom and dad and the love that they have kept vibrantly alive in their marriage for over sixty-five years, and my siblings and I are so blessed to have been included on their journey.

Holidays

"Jesus spoke to them again, saying, "I am the light of the world. Whoever follows me will not walk in darkness, but will have the light of life." John 8:12

The holidays are my favorite time of year! I love everything about them! House decorating; Christmas lights; family and friends gathering for food, fun, gifts; reminiscing about the good old days; football; and all of the delicious smells from Thanksgiving to New Year's! The holidays–especially Christmas–are set apart from all other times of the year by their unique sights, sounds, and smells that stir up my nostalgic feelings and memories. Most Christmases from my childhood to now have been wonderful, for which I am very grateful. Sure, there have been a few that were not as pleasant as others, but the abundance of joy that I carry in my heart brought forth by the many holiday traditions of my childhood recreate Christmas Magic for me and mine year after year.

Thanksgiving kicked off the holiday season, but it wasn't until the first candle on the Advent wreath was lit that I felt the season come alive with expectation. With each passing week my excitement built as we prepared our home for Christmas, and the hope, peace, and joy of my heart came just in time for Jesus, the light of the world, to be born again.

As a child, I couldn't wait to go downtown to see the Christmas lights and the tall storefront windows with toys and Christmas villages on display! It wouldn't surprise me to learn that Santa's elves snuck into town the night before Thanksgiving and worked all night long until morning to transform the streets and business fronts for the holidays! It was fantastic to see ordinary stores become Santa's Workshop! Children and adults alike lined up in front of the windows to see the animated displays of miniature elves and toy shops and miniature trains circling the North Pole. I could have spent all day looking into those windows, but my mom had to hurry me along. She was a little busier than usual at Christmastime and there was much to accomplish on our Christmas shopping adventure.

Once inside, there were more decorations to marvel at as we made our way up the store escalator to the *Men's Department*. Each year my mom would help me buy a gift for my dad, a bottle of Old Spice Cologne, "because it was his favorite." Once my purchase was made, we returned to the main floor where it was impossible to pass the candy and nut counter without buying a sweet treat for the ride home! It was me and mom's little secret, which made my treats taste all the sweeter!

During my teenage years, a fun family tradition was making "buckeyes," a candy we made as gifts at the holidays. It started as a fundraiser for my brother David's hockey team in Ohio, but when we moved to Minnesota it became a favorite novelty of our friends and neighbors. To this day, the smell of peanut butter and confectioners' sugar and warm chocolate remind me of those sticky, gooey, happy times in our Minnesota kitchen!

The one gift I wish Santa could bring to all at the holidays that would never break or be used up is joy, but unfortunately, the holidays can be sad for people. I have found myself feeling depressed at times as I recall simple Christmastimes of my youth juxtaposed against the complicated, busy Christmases now. It confounds me that through the months of November and December my emotions flip flop back and forth–like an entire month of crazy hormones–between joy and sadness! I cannot stop myself from welling up with emotion when I see little children standing next to Santa on his golden throne, asking for their hearts' desire. Every twinkling light and evergreen bough transports me back to past holidays, and in a flash of memory the happiest and saddest times rush into my thoughts, and I am frozen in the middle of my shopping spree, somewhere between Teavana joy and overspending-on-credit sorrow.

Soon I am pulled out of my funk with the distant sound of bells ringing. Ring...ring...ringing at department store entrances and exits draw my attention to shoppers absently dropping their loose change and dollar bills into a bucket. During one of the holiest times of the year, the care and generosity of others lifts my spirits again, and my Christmas gloom turns back to Christmas cheer! In the giving and receiving from what we have, the essence of Christmas resonates in every corner of the world.

One of my favorite places to shop during the holidays is the bookstore. There is literally something there for everyone! Love is the smell of a bookstore at Christmastime, where the scent of fresh balsam and cinnamon linger in the air, and the aroma of coffee mixed with caramel and cream clings to shoppers as they pass by. So subtle, yet so strongly enticing I forget which direction I am going until finally I remember–BOOKS–and begin to peruse the smorgasbord of literature, sneaking a peek under the covers as I go.

The best Christmas tradition instilled in me by my parents was going to church, "no ifs, ands, or buts about it!" There were no excuses for missing Mass. No weather, no distance, no lack of transportation, no moving in between homes, no illness, or threat of illness (don't even think about it, Covid), no nothing could prevent our attendance at Christmas Mass. Regardless of how stubborn and ornery five children could be, Mom and Dad made sure we were at church on either Christmas Eve or Christmas Day. There was much ado about what we would wear, but Mom always had a new outfit prepared for each of us. We would don our coats and hats and drive off to Mass in the family station wagon.

During my teenage years, my family attended midnight Mass at the cathedral downtown, and try as we might to be on time, we were always late! There were never any seats left, so we ended up standing along the wall like comps at an overbooked Broadway show. It was embarrassing and uncomfortable; my feet were pinched and cold in my impractical high-heeled shoes, while at the same time I became overheated by the layers of scratchy wool clothing under my winter coat, and by midway through Mass I felt like a mangy sheep being herded to worship the newborn king.

Even so, no matter how unpleasant things seemed, some of my fondest memories of Christmas were created in church. I remember it like it was yesterday: the cold, crunchy snow, the blast of warm air and bright lights upon entering the church, and the hundreds and hundreds of people standing shoulder to shoulder in every pew! The air was filled with ladies' perfume mingling with the scents of pungent incense and beeswax candles. We always seemed to enter right as the grand organ began to play and the choir raised their voices in heavenly praise, "Gloria in excelsis deo!" And, oh, how the beautiful nativity scene, brightly lit from behind, beckoned me to believe as I approached the altar for communion.

In the midst of all of these wonderful remembrances I am humbled by the amount of effort my parents put forth to raise my siblings and me in the Christian faith, just as I am humbled by the scene of Mary and Joseph with the stable animals in the creche looking at Jesus with so much love. It has been at church every Christmas of my life that I have seen and heard multitudes of people proclaim their belief and faith that Jesus is the Son of God, born on Christmas day in a stable in Bethlehem, and although it was not a usual place of lodging, on that night, it was a good and holy place for God's son to be born.

I celebrate Jesus, a welcome sign of love for all. He is the reason for my holy traditions. I am drawn into the darkness of winter, and from Advent until Christmas I rejoice in the magic of Christmas while I await Jesus, the light of the world, coming into the world. On Christmas day each year my faith is affirmed, my belief is strong, and I receive the gift of love, Jesus, born in a manger, the Savior of the world.

I cannot imagine the wonder and awe that Mary and Joseph must have felt when they birthed Jesus into the world, wrapped him in swaddling clothes, and laid him in a manger. To gaze upon Jesus' holy countenance, the unadorned, innocent face of God, is a gift beyond words. Simply priceless.

The baby Jesus.
Unadorned and innocent.
Illuminated love.
The light of the world.

Church

"And so I say to you, you are Peter, and upon this rock I will build my church, and the gates of the netherworld shall not prevail against it." Matthew 16:18

I wonder how Peter felt when Jesus put the entire future of the Christian movement on his shoulders. Peter, you are the Rock...Peter, you are the fisher of men...Peter, you are the betrayer...Peter, you are the denier...Peter, you are Ecclesiastes: gatherer, teacher, preacher. Peter, you are church, the bearer of the Word, of Jesus Christ's Gospel. Peter, you are mission and miracle worker. Peter, you are protector and builder of the first church of the "New Jerusalem." No matter how Peter might have felt when he was given the task to build the Church, I believe he took his assignment to heart and he was successful.

In two thousand years the Church has changed considerably from its inception, but one thing remains: Jesus Christ is still present in the Church, in the community, in the sacraments, prayers, and in worship. The church is the house of the Lord God where all are welcome to come and be led to a deeper relationship with God; the God who is and always will be, love.

As a kid I would have never admitted I loved church, but as an adult I not only admit I love church, but I also encourage others to come and join me! It is impossible to remove the indelible mark that worshipping at church with my family as a child made on my heart. When I was a kid, the seven of us usually had to squeeze together to fit into a pew that only had enough room for a family of five! Even though my brothers and sister and I poked and prodded one another from behind my mom and dad's backs, we knew we must be respectful when the Bible readings were being proclaimed and when it was time for communion. We listened and learned about God and Jesus and the Holy Spirit, written about in the Old and New Testament readings, and it was good.

It wasn't until I was older that I saw the cracks in the Church's walls, cracks not of a physical nature but of a metaphorical nature. The Church has been crumbling on the edges and, in some instances, completely cracked open with its fair share of problems and scandals.

Just like Peter, today's churches are filled with flawed, imperfect people who have been weak in their human and divine call and, unfortunately, some of them have caused me to second guess my commitment and membership in any church. I have seen my fair share of hypocrisy among the members and abuse by clergy and worship leaders, and it makes me angry every time I recall them, yet I still belong. It is hard to find the right words to justify this allegiance to the Church when I meet people who have denounced God and faith once and for all as a result of these corrupt, amoral behaviors and policies. I understand completely; they feel betrayed, as do I.

I see and hear their pain and all I can say is God is love and He implores all people on earth, "Come back to me, with all your heart, don't let fear keep us apart. Trees do bend, though straight and tall, so must we to others call. Long have I waited for your coming home to me and living deeply our new life" (Norbet).

The Church is not perfect, but as a community we are strong. We keep love and peace alive, and this has been crucial in times of war, civil unrest, natural disasters, and unprecedented tragedies.

When Scott and I moved to South Carolina it was a surprise to both of us how open folks are about faith and church and Jesus Christ. Just like our church friends in the North, they are "all in" for the Lord, but in the South, I find people are much more vocal about faith and Jesus Christ in their evangelization and their commitment to church attendance. And when we met our new neighbors, their welcome was heartfelt, followed up by two questions: (1) "Where do y'all go to church?" and (2) "Tigers or Gamecocks?" We were a little stunned at first, especially because it seemed church and college football were equal in priority, but we got used to it, and it actually made us feel more at home knowing we were in "God's country"!

And what better place to experience God in all of His glory than in the country? I have had some wonderful church experiences in the great outdoors over the years that are unforgettable: Camping With Christ, Marmon Valley Cowgirl Church, 7th Grade Camp Friendship Church, Camp Akita, and boating on the lake with my husband on a glorious summer morning! At each place I felt taken back in time to what I think the earliest church must have been like for Peter and the apostles and their early followers, when people met "al fresco" and shared the Gospel stories and broke bread with one another in remembrance of Jesus. I imagine them, like me, sitting side-by-side on a log by a campfire or walking into a clearing and with the sun rising on the horizon and people joining together in a song of praise to God. I have friends who have shared their experiences of church by a lake, church at the beach, church in an outdoor pavilion, and they speak of these experiences with indescribable reverence and awe. Something special happens when people gather outside to worship God.

I have imagined my church out in the country standing without walls or a roof or a door to push through. There are cars and trucks going by and when they see the people standing together in the pews, they slow down to see what is going on, and they realize it is church. They are drawn by the power and energy of the faithful congregation and by their own deep need for belonging and need to know the love of Jesus Christ. They turn into the church driveway and pile out of their cars, walking into the community unencumbered, joining in the celebration and worship. It is a perfect day.

It is my hope for all to see church not as a building, confining and private, but as a place where one can *be* church and also be one with God at the same time, with or without roof or walls or doors. A place enclosed but that is as natural as a lake or a mountaintop, the seashore or one's own backyard.

When Jesus spoke to Peter about the future Church, I'm sure Peter was "all in," too, just as I and many others are today. For hundreds of years after Peter and the first evangelists departed from their homes to spread the Gospel far and wide, from the east to the west, people still believed the Earth was flat and the Word could be passed from believer to believer laterally to the edge of the world. If only Peter could have known that the world was round, and that from top to bottom, sideways, and diagonally, Christianity would spread throughout the entire world until today when over two billion people profess faith in Jesus Christ. What a tremendous accomplishment by such a small but mighty group of believers, brought forth by the power of the Holy Spirit, set on a course of evangelization for the Lord, taking upon themselves Jesus' Great Commission:

"All power in heaven and on earth has been given to me. Go, therefore, and make disciples of all nations, baptizing them in the name of the Father, and of the Son, and of the Holy Spirit, teaching them to observe all that I have commanded you. And behold, I am with you always, until the end of the age" (Matthew 28:18-20).

Jesus knew there would be difficulties ahead for the early Christians. Through his own human life, death, and resurrection, he knew the road would not be easy, and for some it would prove to be impossible. But as some fell away others came forward and filled the gap, and Jesus' commandment continues to be fulfilled to this day. Peter preached the Gospel whenever and wherever he could, converting to Christianity hundreds, thousands, until his death. Through his work, his ekklesia, the Church of Jesus Christ, was founded. Peter, the rock, laid the foundation for a worldwide movement that continues moving forward today and for the times to come. Today I, along with fellow Christians everywhere, am filling the gap, keeping faith and Jesus Christ alive in the church, in our families and homes, in our communities, in our countries, and in our hearts.

With every Easter, the people's "Alleluia" is lifted to the rafters of the church, and new servants join in the work of Christ, but there are many more needed!

Come! Rejoice! Believe!

Big Sister, Big Brother, Little Brother, Little Brother

"Each friend represents a world in us, a world possibly not born until they arrive, and it is only by this meeting that a new world is born." Anais Nin

Growing up in a family of seven, with one sister and three brothers was pretty awesome!

I can say that now; I am grown and out of the house...but at the time...whew, did we fight and complain and compete against one another! It was not that we didn't 'love' each other, we just didn't understand what being siblings was all about.

There were times I didn't feel like I knew them as I should. Who were my sister and my brothers, and how did I end up in the middle?! Sometimes I would look at us in a photo taken at the holidays and wonder, "Why am I always squished in between? Who do I look like? Do I really belong to this family?" I felt like an outsider watching my family be a family while I kept a low profile, avoiding being bopped by my brother or pushed to the side by my sister! At one period I actually had convinced myself that I was adopted, and I just hadn't been told yet.

As a kid growing up, I didn't know or appreciate how much I needed my sister and brothers. My parents gave us what all kids need: love and a roof over our heads, three meals a day, education, church on Sundays, etc., etc., but my siblings gave me the secret sauce to developing my personality and my drive to succeed and not fail. They were the buffer and friction that I needed in order to become me, not an imitation of one of them.

Being the middle child is not the most popular place in the family; at least that is what I was always told. But for me it was exactly where I needed to be. My siblings surrounded me and gave

111

me a place in the family to be born into, to grow into, to cocoon in for a while, and to emerge from, fully grown and ready to take all that they had taught me through the years—good and bad—so that I could survive on my own.

Like a butterfly, my family was my place of metamorphosis—my place to transform into a wholly unique and beautiful individual. I was cute and roly-poly as a baby crawling along the floor; prickly and squirmy as a youth running here, there, and everywhere and eating us out house and home; indecisive, lost, and withdrawn during my teenage years, searching from within for my place and purpose; finally, emerging as an adult, hesitant but ready to spread my wings and fly.

My sister and brothers are why I am who I am, and I am why they are who they are.

When we were young, our age differences seemed so great; eleven years between the oldest and youngest was an enormous gap developmentally and socially, but now I don't even think about our age differences. The rivalries of my youth that made me angry and resentful and hurt so much at the time have disappeared and my siblings are now my closest friends, my life-long companions who know more about me than my parents or my husband or my friends! The arguing over who sits where at the dinner table or in the front seat of the car; who gets to use the shower first and the finger pointing when all the hot water was used up; who did the best job cleaning their room or who raked the most leaves, and on and on have lost their significance in the grand scheme of things. There were hundreds of things that we competed for and disagreed about, and there were times when we had a hard time finding a reason to like each other, but surely as I know now, deep down, we knew then that we could never stay mad forever. We were family.

My siblings and I have been like five rocks gathered and carried for years in a small drawstring bag, constantly grinding, bumping, rolling, chafing, and shifting against one another. Our sharp edges were chipped away, our grooves and crevices smoothed over, yet we have each retained our original interior veins and shimmering cracks. Each of us is a precious, glistening gemstone brought to light by the refining abrasion of one another. We still rub each other the wrong way sometimes and sparks fly, but never so much so that we set the entire bag on fire!

Sometime between my teens and twenties, it hit me hard how much I love my siblings and how proud I am of them. It was at that time that I began to make the connection between who I was and how each of them had influenced who I was becoming. Each of us so different in our manners, talents, and gifts; our temperaments and personalities ground against the others in ways that made us become better people. Our insults and tussles, sometimes very painful, brought forth the interior beauty and strength of the other so that we might shine in our own God-given way!

My sister, Lisa, the oldest sibling, was always the smartest; she is super smart, but when we were growing up this grated on my nerves. "Why couldn't I be the smartest?" I would ask myself. Now I know this was not my gift to have; it was not what God gave me to fulfill my life and purpose. To this day, Lisa is the smartest and I am so proud of her and how she has used her amazing intellect and gift to bring life to the creative genius of playwrights and screenwriters in her acting.

David, my slightly older brother, was a handful, and he was very active as a child–so I am told–and his birth a month early and quick physical development put Lisa's safety more than a few times in jeopardy and one such mishap left an indelible mark on both Lisa's forehead and her memory! David was a natural born disruptor because no matter where he went or what he did, he disrupted everyone and everything in his path! Although he was in trouble *all the time*, and sometimes punishment was warranted, it was his trouble that attracted so many to him. He had a charisma that was like a magnet; he could convince people that they could do anything, including jumping their ten-speed bikes over barrels in a driveway like Evil Knievel!

David was smart and devious, but also kind, and compassionate, and generous. When he was diagnosed with cancer, his God-given gift of grit and fire helped him live for seventeen years, knowing he was dying. He took the bull by the horns and rode that beast to the end, bucking and hanging on until he couldn't hold on any longer. I admire David so much, and he inspires me still to go for it and to not be afraid. David is why I am

113

writing this book, because like David, once I said I would do it, I was not going to give up!

My younger brother, Jeff, joined Lisa, David, and me two and a half years after I was born.

Jeff was adorable, imaginative, and oh so funny. His mind, so full of comedy, romance, and tragedy, has produced a world of creativity born of risk and reward. His art and expression through graphics and media give the world but a glimpse of all the things Jeff imagines while soaring in his dreams. Jeff is the beating heart that the family has needed in order to persevere, and he brings forth laughter and joy in the tragic moments of our family's lives. I remember the first time I laughed after Tim died; it was with my brother, Jeff, while watching the movie *Bridesmaids*. There was something that he said while watching the ladies at the bridal shop evacuate their bodies of everything they had eaten at lunch that cracked me up, in spite of my grief, and I laughed, and I laughed, and I laughed! I remember feeling so alive again yet guilty for feeling happy, but with Jeff laughing right along with me, it was okay and glorious!

Chris, my youngest brother, came along shortly after my eighth birthday.

Before Chris came home from the hospital everything seemed equal, fair, and balanced to my eight-year-old mind: girl, boy, girl, boy. But after the reality hit me that another person would be competing with me for Mom and Dad's attention, I felt out of sync, out of place, and insecure. It was a seismic shift for me. My mom and dad saw my insecurity as I withdrew in fear and uncertainty, and they invited me to be the first to hold Chris.

I remember so clearly walking into the master bedroom and feeling very shy and small. My dad led me to a big, comfy chair where I sat down, and my mom placed Chris gently in my arms. I was so afraid to hold him, sure that I would do something wrong and hurt him. I barely breathed as I looked into his sweet face. I had never held a baby before, and when I looked at him, I felt instant love for him; we bonded immediately. I changed in that moment, holding this new life in my arms.

Until that moment Chris had been a nebulous bump in my mother's belly, but holding him, feeling his warmth and his weight, he became a real human being. I was given a gift that day. Being specially chosen to hold him first gave me a feeling of belonging in my family again. Suddenly my heart knew love as never before, new and fresh, born in the moment I held my brother. This new, permanent member of my family was the living embodiment of love, and I beheld it in his beautiful face. I discovered what love is. I gave my love to Chris, and it came back to me. Love came back to me. That experience enlarged my world and expanded my heart.

I had not known this feeling of love before. As the second daughter, it was natural for my sister and me to compete for my mom and dad's attention. We both sought their approval and affirmation, which took some of the fun out of being sisters. Instead of building one another up, we tore each other down.

Lisa and I were complete opposites, and we didn't have a lot in common. Lisa loved ballet; I hated ballet. Lisa loved play-acting; I hated the spotlight. Lisa was a good girl; I was a rebellious girl. Lisa was super smart, and she could read really fast; I was average in my grades and it took me forever to read one page of a book! Lisa was super pretty, and she wore pre-teen girl clothes; I was tall and skinny and I wore boys' extra-slim blue jeans. Lisa was haughty and I was shy. Lisa was older and I was too young to fit in.

There was a day, though, that I saw a different side of my sister, a kind, sweet side of Lisa that gave me a glimpse of the woman she would become. Lisa had been a pen pal with an American soldier serving in Vietnam. In her letter she wrote that she collected dolls. The soldier took this to heart, and upon his return to the States he came to our home and presented Lisa with a doll from Vietnam. She blushed and there was not a scintilla of bravado in Lisa's demeanor. She told him how grateful she was for the gift. Lisa's kind acceptance let me see her gracious inner beauty and vulnerability, and the soldier, a man fresh from the war, brought joy to our home that day.

Lisa and I weren't always at odds. I loved it when she played her records and didn't shoo me away. I was really good at memorizing the words and music, which impressed Lisa, and this made me super happy. We played "Leavin' On A Jet Plane" over and over until I knew every word. I still remember singing it out on the playground during recess as my friends tried to sing along! Another favorite time was playing our made-up music game. Sitting in our bedroom, Lisa and I would take turns humming a song and she or I would guess the familiar pop song, nursery song, or showtune. We didn't keep score or win a prize, but I felt love develop between us as we shared some fun times.

I was a natural athlete, so sports gave me a step up in getting attention in the winner's circle. I loved to run, and the faster the better. I loved jumping across puddles and leaping from one sidewalk crack to the next. I played softball and kickball, tetherball and tag. I loved the President's Physical Fitness Award and climbing to the ceiling of the gym on the knotted rope. I could do sit-ups and pullups faster and longer than any other girl in the fifth grade! I was fearless. I had as much energy as my brothers and the same amount of natural curiosity about the limits to which I could push my body. Unfortunately for me, girls were not supposed to behave like boys; they were supposed to be more like my sister, interested in "girl things."

It was impossible to hang out with my brother David. He was all boy and much too rough for me. Even when I was allowed entry into his boys' club it did not take long for them to send me off on some distracting errand and ditch me. It hurt my feelings but it did not surprise me; I was a girl and I just didn't fit in.

Jeff and I had a lot of fun together, and I thoroughly enjoyed our comfortable friendship. Jeff was always up for taking risks and finding adventure, and he seldom questioned my authority. In hindsight, I think he must have looked up to me as a Big Sis. I was just enough older than him that he trusted me when we broke rules, and he believed I could get us out of trouble (or would take the fall) if we were caught by Mom and Dad in one of our antics!

One morning when we were six and eight years old, we ate an entire loaf of Wonder bread, one piece at a time, and no one ever knew! We discovered how butter, when softened and spread on hot toasted bread, melts evenly, perfectly, without crushing the toasted surface, and when sprinkled with cinnamon and sugar, it is a taste of heaven! It was so much fun and it was our secret for a long time!

But Jeff soon found friends his own age around the neighborhood, and I lost my partner in crime.

Due to our age difference, Chris and I didn't have childhood playtime together, but we did have some great times. I have never felt sibling rivalry with Chris, just proud of him and his accomplishments, and protective of him. Especially protective. I never forgot the first time I held Chris, and I carried in my heart the need to watch over him the best I could, but one winter day in Minnesota, a rare "snow day," an accident happened that was so terrible. All the neighborhood kids were sledding down the hill onto Melody Lake, and Chris was too small to go down alone. I took him down the hill, holding on tightly to the flying saucer with Chris sitting securely in my lap...until we crossed the lip of the lake, and we flew apart, falling head over heels onto the ice.

Chris's head slammed onto the ice, and he lay there bleeding. His skull was fractured. I was so afraid; it was my fault. I know now God sent angels to surround Chris to stabilize his body until help arrived. Out of all the days that a neurologist could be driving by the lake and see the accident at this critical moment of need, that was the day! The doctor ran to my brother's aid and I believe he saved his life. After this accident, I felt another seismic shift in my place in the family. In my mind I became the one who nearly killed Chris. I hid in shame to avoid accusatory looks, but Chris? He never held the accident against me. I apologized to Chris a few years ago and he looked at me, surprised, and then he put his arm on my shoulder and shrugged it off. He said he never saw the need for an apology, but he forgave me.

I do not know what to say when people tell me about their relationship with a sibling being broken. I feel their pain and wish I could help. I pray for them to not wait too long to mend their relationship, to find it in their heart to apologize or forgive a stale disagreement or altercation that produced the original anger and hurt. I realize not everyone can abide by or agree with the views or choices of their sibling, and unfortunately, sometimes the only solution is to go their separate ways. I pray for them when this is the only way to peace.

Certainly, my siblings and I have disagreed, been frustrated and angry with one another, but our love and acceptance of the others' right to choose their own path and have their own opinions is honored. In some ways, being related has afforded a certain

117

amount of grace and forgiveness when our conversations have gone sideways. I have overstepped at times giving my opinion, thinking I knew best, and I have been wrong. I needed to listen more and hear myself talk less. It takes time to make things right and a lot of humility on my part helps move reconciliation along. We still get annoyed with each other, but we cut each other a break and forgive, and we stick together.

I pray for all brothers and sisters who have gone their separate ways. Rejection hurts, but not trying hurts even more. I feel especially bad for the parents who feel unable to make things right between their younger and older children, because their loyalties are split in two. But I know that with the power of the Holy Spirit miracles happen, hearts open, and forgiveness can be found.

"Therefore, as God's chosen people, holy and dearly loved, clothe yourselves with compassion, kindness, humility, gentleness, and patience. Bear with each other and forgive one another if any of you has a grievance against someone. Forgive as the Lord forgave you. And over all these virtues put on love, which binds them all together in perfect unity" (Colossians 3:12-14).

Mine and my sibling's childhood memories differ because we experienced things differently. After leaving home, I missed them all terribly. I was the center, the middle, the round hole in the donut (see, Jeff? Now my nickname makes sense!) and I felt extremely alone. We kept in touch through long distance telephone calls. We never ran out of things to say, and it was during these phone calls that I really got to know my sister and brothers. The last call I had with David was unforgettable; it was the night before his final surgery. We talked for a little while, but he was tired; he had been fighting for a long time. He said he loved me, and I told him I loved him. As I hung up the phone, I knew it was our last good-bye, and I cried.

As the years go by, we will have many goodbyes. I miss my brother, and when David passed, a light went out in all of our lives, and I was changed. I am not the same as I would be if he were still here enriching my life. I treasure the part of me that is David, and a remnant of him remains in all of us.

We are family, and we are blessed. My siblings know me best, and I know them best in certain ways. We have secrets we'll never tell and confidences that are private to our family.

I am amazed at the uniqueness of each of us, and also by the similarities we share. We have never looked identical, but when we introduce each other to our friends for the first time, they always say, "Oh, yeah...I definitely see the resemblance!" We may not have been best friends or "two peas in a pod" or "like twins" growing up, but we are who we are as a result of the trials and celebrations that refined us and molded us during our years growing up.

When each of us married, we brought to the family new sisters and new brothers to love and beautiful grandchildren for my parents, and our circle of incredible people expanded. Just like Chris did when I held him for the first time so many years ago, my new family members have enriched my life, expanded my heart, reciprocated my love, and they have added to who I am becoming.

I am forever grateful to God for creating my family exactly as it is and for his divine wisdom in placing me in the middle of my amazing sister and brothers, surrounded from every angle by love!

Donna Braidic

Parents

"Children, obey your parents [in the Lord], for this is right. 'Honor your father and mother.' This is the First Commandment with a promise, 'that it may go well with you and that you may have a long life on earth.'" Ephesians 6:1-3

The love that my parents have for one another is the glue that has held them together when they first set eyes on each other as teens over seventy years ago. When they married, they not only joined together the love they had for each other, but they joined the love from their families and the experiences that had formed them. The love their parents had given them doubled in my parents, expanding and spreading outward into the family they created. Their strong and unbreakable love, given to me and my sister and my brothers as we grew and formed into adults, has now been passed on through each of us to our spouses and children. I am a better parent to my daughters than I might have been due to this legacy of love so generously given to me.

When I was a little girl, my parents were my world, and our circle of love had no beginning or end.

I depended on my parents for everything, and I trusted them implicitly. They loved me and took care of me, and I felt secure no matter where we called home! At night they tucked me into bed and, brushing my hair from my forehead, they kissed me goodnight, and I slept soundly knowing they would be waiting for me in the morning. When my grandmother died, I was afraid that my parents would die, too, and they would not be waiting for me in the morning anymore. Mom and Dad understood my fears and they reassured me until I believed they would never, ever leave me. *Our circle of love was unbroken.*

When I was sick or injured, my mom nursed me back to health more times than I can count. She was a busy wife, mother, and homemaker, but somehow, when she was caring for me, no one else seemed to matter. I'm sure mom still made certain everyone

120

had what they needed for the day, but my dad and siblings worked together and cared for each other while she attended to my needs. They may have worn the same clothes every day and eaten macaroni and cheese every night for dinner, but they survived! *Our circle of love was compassionate.*

As I grew from childhood into a teenager my relationship with my parents went through many changes. For years I was quiet, sweet, "no trouble at all Donna," but then overnight, it seemed, I changed into Donna who was in constant trouble! Of course, my parents got mad at me and sent me to my room, and they often resorted to threatening me with spankings and groundings. Of course, they did what they learned from their parents; they loved me, and they were teaching me to respect them, to follow their rules, and to behave so that things would go well in my life. But I did not like their discipline, and it made me wonder if they loved me at all. Oh, I had so much to learn about love and discipline. *Our circle of love valued obedience.*

I was a handful, and I tested my parents' love and patience, and despite my rebellion, the challenges I presented on a daily basis did not break their resolve or commitment to raising me. Oh, they definitely threatened sending me off to a camp for undisciplined children when they had reached the end of their rope, but Mom and Dad never gave up on me. They gritted their teeth and kept loving me just as much as they had when I was a baby and dirtied my diaper. They pinched their noses during my tough teenage years and kept wiping the slate clean. *Our circle of love was undaunted.*

It seemed my parents' resilience and strength had no bounds. They carried on with their lives and over time, their steady influence of discipline and love began to gnaw at my heart and my conscience. All of the right and good behaviors I had been taught over the years, and all that I had been given with an abundance of generosity, were rising above my perceived injustices, my anger and resentments, forcing me to examine who I was and who I was becoming. I realized I was on the wrong path and I was destroying all that was good in my life while disrespecting my parents in the process. Increasingly I felt ashamed of my behavior. I felt guilty for my words that were mean and filthy. I knew I must change and get back on the right track and stop causing so much pain to those I loved and needed most. It was my choice to make; the right and proper course could not be forced upon me. It was up to me to choose. *Our circle of love was transformational.*

I prayed to God to help me change my heart and my attitude, and to protect me from falling back into my old ways. I prayed that my parents would forgive me. Yes, in the midst of my misbehavior and dishonor of my parents for the care they gave me, I turned to God. To whom else could I go? My good friends did not like the person I had become; they didn't want to be with me. I believed God was with me, and just like my parents, God had not given up on me and he would help me get my life back. I went to bed each night hoping for better days ahead for all of us.

Once I made the decision to change my ways, I slept soundly knowing my parents would still be waiting for me in the morning. They never, ever left me. It was scary to face their scowls of disapproval and consternation, and it hurt to hear their heavy sighs that had become the norm when I walked into the room. I was a disappointment. It would take time to heal. *Our circle of love called for a reckoning.*

Up until then I took my parents' love for granted. Love is what parents do; they love their kids. Right? I expected to be loved by my parents, and they did. But they were hurt and disappointed and angry with me. With my decision to live right, I had to prove myself worthy of my parents' trust and forgiveness again, and I worked hard to make them proud of me. *Our circle of love sought repentance.*

I never had the hardship of unhappy, divorcing parents; or terminally ill parents; or parents who abused their children; or parents who abused drugs or alcohol; or absent parents. I was blessed beyond words and didn't even know it. I was well taken care of, and I took it completely for granted, and that was wrong.

I did not realize in my youth that my positive experience of parents' love was not shared by all, and I felt guilty for being so wretched towards Mom and Dad, and oh, so grateful for the chance to turn my life around. My parents never lost hope that their quiet, sweet, "no trouble at all Donna" would return to them. And deep down inside, in a place where only God knows my true feelings, I wanted to return, too.

I know my parents, like most parents, did their absolute best in raising their five children. Certainly, they made mistakes, and so did their parents and so have I with my daughters. Sometimes parents are wrong, sometimes children are wrong, sometimes everyone is wrong, and no one is right. I ended up in a family where everyone gets to be right some of the time, and not everyone is wrong all of the time. Sometimes my parents were stubborn in their rules and sometimes they relented, and many, many times, they met me where I was, but ultimately it was up to me to return with all my heart to the life and purpose I was born to live. *Our circle of love was very humbling.*

Mom and Dad's devotion to God and their Catholic faith kept them morally grounded, which in turn kept me morally grounded and tethered to my Catholic faith and devotion to God. After I made the choice to become who I was born to be, Mom and Dad gave me the time and space needed to prove myself worthy of their love again, and I appreciated them all the more for this grace. *Our circle of love was redemptive.*

My mom and dad have been wonderful parents.

Their example of faith and commitment to God and church has been their greatest gift to me.

Their commitment to friendships has shown me that no matter how many years may pass between visits with friends, the bond of true friendship is timeless and eternal.

Their work ethic has taught me responsibility and accountability in earning a living and contributing to society.

Their commitment to their physical health and well-being has taught me to take care of myself in body, mind, and spirit so that I might enjoy my life to the fullest.

Most of all, their commitment to family sets them apart. There is nothing they will not do for their family and no distance too great to travel when need arises. Mom and Dad's love for each other, for their children, and their children's children is for all time, a circle of love that has no end.

Looking back over my life as their daughter, I am able to see very clearly where my need for independence collided with my parents' need to raise a child with good judgment and wisdom. I am "all grown up now," but every so often, they will look up at me with a certain smile or a twinkle in their eye and for a moment the years roll back, and I see myself, quiet, sweet, "no trouble at all Donna" waking in the morning to the smell of fresh coffee and pancakes and sausage, throwing back the covers and running down the stairs knowing I will find my parents waiting for me with a welcome smile and love in their heart.

Thank you, God, for my amazing mom and dad.

Tough Love

"We have come to know and to believe in the love God has for us. God is love, and whoever remains in love remains in God and God in him." 1 John 4:16

When I hit puberty, I made a 180-degree change from quiet, sweet, "no trouble at all Donna," athletic and cooperative, to belligerent, sullen, moody, and obstinate "pain-in-the butt-Donna" who was in constant trouble. The only part of the old Donna that I retained was the athletic part. I loved sports, I was good at them, and I clicked with my teammates more than any other group of people I was associated with.

At first, people who knew the nice Donna said I was just acting like a teenager. But it was much more than that. I was rebelling and angry, sad, and lost.

At thirteen, my peers said it was "cool" to "hate your parents." It was very "uncool" to love your parents or show any hint of acceptance of parental involvement in anything. At first, I didn't like this notion because I loved my parents. I wanted them around. I felt secure and safe with them around. They gave me everything I needed, a lovely home, clothes and food, church and school, and they celebrated me with birthday presents on my birthday and Christmas presents on Christmas. They didn't ask for anything in return; I knew that I should love and respect them.

But in order to "fit in" I accepted this new view that parents were the enemy to all things teenager, and along with it, I started misbehaving and acting out in ways I had never done before. And when Mom or Dad caught me doing things I had no business doing, they punished me, which made it a lot easier to view my parents as very uncool! In fact, they became so uncool to me that it became easier to go along with my friends, to be cool and hate my parents and to believe they hated me.

Each time I was sent to my room, I was more convinced than ever that my parents did not love me and being grounded only caused my anger and dislike of my parents to fester and grow. My bedroom became a place for me to throw one big pity party after another for myself. I would lie on my bed, looking up at the ceiling and rant on and on to no one in particular about the unfairness of life. I started questioning why this sibling got this and that sibling got that, and why I didn't get anything. Were they loved more? Was I loved less? It was depressing and lonely and I didn't like it.

I began asking myself, "What is love?" Not romantic love, but the love that you see when a new mom holds her baby, the love that a team has for each other when they win a state championship or the Super Bowl, the love a person feels for their pet, the love that the song "Jesus Loves Me" talks about.

I wondered what exactly that feeling of love is and where it came from, and more to the point, how it happened. I was too young in my limited life experience to articulate in words what the feeling was, but I knew it was special. I felt it when I was younger, but somehow it had faded. I felt it when I babysat, and when I found a new friend in the neighborhood. I felt it for my dog, Mickey. I loved that dog so much; we had a special bond of reciprocal need and acceptance and dependence. As a child I wish I had figured out what I learned later in life, that the word "dog" is "God" spelled backwards. Man's best friend. Coincidence? God is love…

After pondering the subject at length, I was not able to come up with a satisfactory answer to "what love is," but the fact that I was questioning it in the first place caused me to presume that I was not loved as I needed to be, by others or myself.

And so, I filled in the cracks and crevices of my emptiness with unhealthy lifestyle and relationship choices. I started smoking cigarettes and drinking to get drunk. I experimented with other things, too. I snuck out of the house when I was supposed to be at home, and I hung out with the "wrong crowd." I was doing all the wrong things to validate my assumption that I was not loved by making myself unlovable by misbehaving.

I was having fairly good success, too. I acted out and misbehaved and guess what? My parents and my siblings and even some of my friends stopped liking me. I fought with them all, I was constantly grounded, and I lost my freedom. Even today it sounds really harsh, but my parents had no choice. They were losing the battle against the evil that had taken hold of me and they were losing their child, I can tell you that. They would not, could not give up on me, they would not abandon me, but they had to take drastic actions. I was in serious trouble. My mom and dad had to be strong and resilient and forceful and consistent in their treatment of me.

What free time I had was restricted, I was given additional chores, and I was treated like the juvenile delinquent I was turning into. The last straw: I was given a curfew! And when all these things failed to change me and my behavior, my mom's frustration and hurt boiled over at dinner one evening and she threatened the entire family with going to counseling. It turns out I wasn't the only one acting out! We all needed some tough love.

I had heard about counseling on a made-for-TV-movie I had recently watched, *Go Ask Alice*, which to this day I refer to as the *Scared Straight* of TV programming for me. The movie scared me because I saw in Alice the girl I was becoming and the trouble I was heading for if I did not change. For whatever reason, the movie represented what "tough love" meant to me and if I didn't change, I would be "sent away," which to me at that time meant people were giving up on me–or worse, I could possibly die.

Looking back, I think the straw that broke the camel's back for my mom was when she and I were in her bathroom having yet another argument, and I told her very meanly and with intent to hurt, "I hate you." She did not miss a beat, and her hand came up and slapped me across the face, something she had never done before, ever, and something she has not done since. Needless to say, I was surprised and shocked and really hurt that she hit me. But I deserved it. I was equally shocked that those words of hate had come out of my mouth. They were not true. I felt awful and my eyes stung with tears.

That realization was enough for me. I was not going to be Alice. I was not going to die. I was going to change. I had to make a change. Little by little, without my parents knowing it, I found my own counseling that I went to after school with some new friends, and I started going to Young Life, and over two years I righted my ship and reset my rudder to turn back the 180-degrees that I had steered off course.

I turned a big corner in my behavior and began restoring my relationship with my parents, my siblings, and my friends. It was a critical juncture in my life. It was the first time as a young adult that I asked the question, "What is love?", and unbeknownst to me, God was listening. He showed me what love is through the love of my parents and their unfailing love for me. Was it all cuddly, cozy, sweet, and adoring? No. It was better. Their love was steady, deliberate, decisive, and correcting. It was tough and it was cold. It was sacrificial. It was love in its rawest form.

Their love is agape love. Unconditional, godly love. Not a feeling but an action. Tough love. A love that looks into the eyes of hate and does not blink, does not look away but is determined to love anyway. A forgiving love that never gives up or gives in and believes the best is still in me. That's what my mom and dad gave to me. Agape love.

"God is love, and all who live in love live in God, and God lives in them" (1 John 4:16).

Sorrow

"Pray without ceasing. In all circumstances give thanks: for this is the will of God for you in Christ." 1 Thessalonians 5:17-18

> I love the Lord, who listened
> to my voice in supplication,
> Who turned an ear to me on the day I called.
> I was caught by the cords of death;
> the snares of Sheol had seized me;
> I felt agony and dread.
> Then I called on the name of the Lord,
> "O Lord, save my life!"
>
> Gracious is the Lord and just;
> yes, our God is merciful.
> The Lord protects the simple;
> I was helpless, but God saved me.
> Return, my soul, to your rest;
> the Lord has been good to you.
> For my soul has been freed from death,
> My eyes from tears, my feet from stumbling.
> I shall walk before the Lord
> In the land of the living. Psalm 116:1-9

During our thirty-one years of marriage, my late husband, Tim, and I changed and matured as we dealt with disappointment and loss. Sometimes our love faltered as we struggled to adjust to who we were becoming, but we withstood the inclination to give up. We were committed to our marriage and to each other, as well as to our family, and as impossible as it seemed from time to time, by our love we grew to accept one another and found peace in the many stages of our married life.

One of our biggest challenges early in our marriage was infertility, which sometimes can destroy even the strongest marriage. It's hard not to blame the other for the inability to get pregnant; neither of us wanted the infertility to be "my fault." It was demoralizing to go through with all the treatments my doctors recommended. We dreaded all the medical procedures and taking all the medications, and it was a joke when they told us to "relax"; especially when at the end of my cycle I was not pregnant for the twentieth or thirtieth time. It was painful, embarrassing, and financially draining. It tested Tim's and my will to continue trying, to be patient with one another, and it especially tested our faith in God.

When we finally did become pregnant, we were ecstatic! People said it was a miracle, "a gift from God!" All of our faith and perseverance was rewarded, and we were finally going to have a baby!

As the weeks of my pregnancy passed and Thanksgiving, Christmas, and Easter came and went, my ever-expanding belly revealed to all who noticed that a new life was growing within me, waiting to be born. I was already deeply in love with this baby, and I couldn't wait for her to be born.

And then the devastating news came. No heartbeat. No movement. No life.

Our baby girl was stillborn. Our beautiful little Mary Lyn died, and our empty arms ached with the weight of our loss. She was everything to me. We were childless again.

Through my anguish and tears, I cried out to God, "Why? How could this happen? How could you let my baby die?!"

I felt so empty inside and very alone, torn apart from my baby, from Tim, and from God. Death broke me, and I did not want to keep living.

Tim wanted to put our loss behind us, to move forward and stop grieving, but I could not. His sorrow was real, but he did not want to feel it. He was in terrible pain, but privately. I was in terrible pain, too, but I needed him to comfort me, and he could not. So I grieved silently and kept my loss deep inside my breaking heart.

My sorrow weighed heavily on me until the following spring, when during a Lenten retreat at my church, I found some closure and peace.

One of the retreat presenters was a nun who was as:
the reconciliation part of the retreat. The sister and I me
away from others, and I confessed to her my anger with God. I told
her I could barely pray or talk to God. I was so mad at him for
putting me through so much disappointment and pain. I blamed
him for not saving my baby. I told her I hated God.

Her eyes were so kind, and her voice was so gentle as she said,
"It is very sad what has happened to you. I understand why you
are so angry with God. But he loves you. He knows how hurt you
are, and he is with you. I want you to try something. As impossible
as this may sound right now, I would ask you to pray to love your
loss. By loving the loss of your baby, you will hopefully find
acceptance and peace. It will take time; this will not happen
overnight. But some day, unexpectedly, you may love this loss,
and you will have found acceptance and peace."

She saw in my expression I thought this was a crazy idea, and
truthfully, I felt extremely let down and utterly deflated. I wanted
her to tell me she could take my sadness away, that there would
be more babies, and instead she was asking me to fix myself and
accept my baby's death and love it.

This made no sense.

She took my hands in hers and, looking into my eyes, asked,
"Do you believe in God, and that through him, all things are
possible?"

I said I did.

She then explained that when we are angry and holding onto
hate, we have no peace or acceptance, and it eats away at our
soul and hurts our relationship with God, who loves us so much
and who hurts when we are hurting. When we love something, it
is quite easy to accept it and find peace with it. Initially, we need
to choose to love the thing that is causing us pain—in my case, to
say, "I love my loss."

She then asked if I would try to begin praying to love my loss,
and I said I would.

She gently smiled, and squeezing my hands a little tighter,
assured me she would be praying for me, too, to find acceptance
and peace.

And so, I did what I believed at the time to be the most absurd thing in the world: I committed my mind, heart, and soul to loving my loss. I truly did.

I prayed and prayed myself into loving not only the loss of my baby, but to love the loss of my hopes and dreams for more children.

I can't exactly say when my sorrow ended or when I began to feel acceptance and peace with my loss, but it started after the births of my two daughters, years later.

This prayerful prescription for loving, accepting, and finding peace became a powerful intercessory prayer for me on behalf of myself to help me come to terms with the disappointments, challenges, and setbacks that would come throughout the years. It became as natural to pray for loving my hardships as it was to pray for a sunny day.

And then the devastating news came. Again. Stage four lung cancer. Metastasized to the brain. Radiation. Chemo. Suffering. No heartbeat. A beautiful life ended.

My husband, Tim, died, and I was a widow.

Suddenly, overnight, I was no longer married, no longer part of someone else's life. I was single, alone, and afraid, and once again crying out to God, "Why? How could this happen? Why did Tim have to die?"

I had not felt such deep sadness and depression since our baby girl, Mary Lyn, had died, but this time my grieving was different; I did not hold onto my sorrow as a private cross to bear, nor did I pray in the night in anger and rage at God, but rather I cried as one held in her Father's loving care, and I felt at peace.

I have changed over the years since meeting my special nun on retreat. I have taken to heart the practice of praying to love that which seems impossible to love, and in the most difficult times I have found acceptance and peace. I am no longer mad at God, nor do I blame him for the difficulties of my life. I know he loves me; I know he loved Tim; I know he loved Mary Lyn, and I am grateful for my faith, knowing Tim and Mary Lyn are together in heaven, living eternally with God.

I love that Mary Lyn and Jesus greeted Tim when he arrived in heaven. I am so happy that Tim is able to feel the weight of Mary Lyn in his arms again, and I feel joy knowing that they will greet me when I come to be in heaven when my time on earth is at an end.

This gives me peace and acceptance for the end of my life, whenever it may come.

Through my ongoing prayer to love that which seems impossible to love, I will continue to find acceptance and peace in all circumstances; and I believe that God, who is love, is in all circumstances bringing His love to me as I pray for acceptance and peace.

Sorrow will come to me again, as it does in all times and all seasons, and I pray that when that time comes, I will love and accept that which I cannot change, and in so doing, find peace again.

Daughters

"Can a mother forget her infant, be without tenderness for the child of her womb? Even should she forget, I will never forget you." Isaiah 49:15

I cannot imagine my life without my daughters. The vibrancy and light that they bring to my life is without question a gift from God. To be childless and then receive not one but two miracles of life overwhelm me. I love my daughters more than anything. Nothing can break my love for them. Nothing. I will protect them with my life if need be. As long as I live my daughters live in my heart as if still a physical presence within me. Now and forever.

They are beautiful, smart, funny, and on their way to being successful, independent, and self-reliant. They are sweet girls. Most of all, they love each other, and they love their family and their friends. They are connected to good people in their relationships, and I am happy they have learned how to find good people, honest people, truthful people, kind people to share their time with.

They are grown now, into their thirties, and beginning to fulfill their dreams and aspirations. I have raised them to believe in themselves and to call upon God to help them find all they are looking for in life. They have the world and all of its opportunities right out in front of them. It's up to them; they need only ask for direction and go for it!

In the minutes after they were born, I knew my beautiful baby girls were to be the greatest joy of my life and at the same time the greatest concern of my life. I never felt so vulnerable and ill-prepared for anything as I did motherhood! But thankfully, the girls were healthy and ready to instruct me on the ways of taking care of them. Through their loud crying I learned quickly when to feed, clean, powder, and warmly swaddle them.

As with all adorable children, it was hard to get enough of them when they were little. Both girls were happy and animated from a very early age. Meghan could speak in complete sentences by two years old and Lauren imitated her sister in every way possible. It was clear to me that Lauren, although a year and a half younger than her sister, thought she could do everything her big sister could do, and most of the time, when she smiled and looked at me with her twinkling, blue eyes, I was convinced, too!

The girls never seemed afraid to try new things, and I was delighted when they both wanted to take piano lessons. I had benefited so much from my own piano lessons growing up, and I hoped they would, too. I discovered their musical talents extended well beyond the keyboard when for the first time I heard them sing, and the school and church choirs were blessed by their voices, so full of tone and resonant beauty!

Our home became much noisier (a joyful noise to my ears) when Meghan began playing the clarinet and Lauren the double bass, starting in fifth grade, and extending through their high school years. One of Meghan's crowning achievements was as a senior in the marching band when she was chosen to march with a sousaphone and dot the "i" in the word "Lions" during the Senior Night football game. And Lauren, not to be out-done, was chosen in her senior year to play her double-bass for Handel's *Messiah* with the Columbus Symphony Orchestra! Both accomplishments absolutely brilliant!

As the girl's natural talents emerged, there was something that was uniquely Meghan and something that was uniquely Lauren that revealed the special gifts God had blessed them with.

Meghan's extreme intellect, memory, and recall is impressive beyond words, and I knew she would be able to out-debate me by the end of middle school with all the information she was storing up! Her ability to take standardized tests and topic-specific tests amazed me. Her physical speed in track and field set records in the high hurdles in high school, and although she doesn't boast about it, I know this is something that she takes great pride in, as well she should. Meghan's loving heart and helpful nature, when channeled in the right directions, make her an unforgettable friend.

Lauren has art oozing from every pore and hair follicle of her being and her talent shows! Before she could walk, she could draw a happy face, imitating her sister as Meghan produced dozens of smiling self-portraits at the kitchen table with her "Poppop." By second grade Lauren's style was emerging, her talent was undeniable, and her art teacher encouraged her to take classes at the Arts College in our town. Lauren, too, has a high intellect and this is reflected in her creative ability to transfer thoughts and ideas to paper and canvas. Her studio, like her, is very minimal and elegant in its simplicity, and the art she produces is emotionally provocative and moving. With her extraordinary ability, Lauren brings each piece to life with the life-like gaze and light and color of the eyes of each of her subjects, and her style, form, and palette create air and sound and movement in each work of art.

Lauren has always leaned more towards fun and games, so her quirky side comes out naturally when she puts on a flowing skirt and tank-top and twirls, swoops, and soars barefooted in the grass under the moonlight like a gypsy moth, carefree, fully embodying her adventurous, artistic spirit while her flaming hula hoop spins around her body.

As I brag on about my daughters like the proud parent I am, I ponder anew what God might say about all of his children, his created ones, his Adams, and Eves, what he says about me. Sometimes I picture him like a jolly Santa Claus, looking over his "naughty and nice" list, glowing with happiness over some names and frowning with a deep consternation and furrowed brow at the behavior of others. His blessings and praises flow for some, and his reprimands and scolding fall upon others. But unique only to God–even greater than a mother's love–is the love of God, for he came to protect, teach, and save all from perishing eternally. He forgives even the most difficult, problem child: he has forgiven me.

As a mom, as a human, I am limited to this time and space to express my undying love for my children, but God is not limited, and his love knows no bounds. He loves us all and his grace is for all, no matter what side of the "naughty and nice" list one finds oneself on. This is the greatest lesson I can teach my children, the greatest gift for living life to the fullest, that I can give to my daughters.

God cannot imagine the world without me and my daughters. The vibrancy and light that we bring to life is without question a gift from God. He is overwhelmed with joy at our being created. He loves me and my daughters as if there is no other. Now and forever. Nothing can break his love for us. Nothing. He will protect us with his life. From the beginning to the end of time, we live in God's heart forever.

There are days I still can't wrap my head around how wonderful my life has been because of Meghan and Lauren. They are miracles of life; they are gifts from God. I will never stop thanking God for them. I am grateful beyond words.

Thank you, Lord God. Thank you, Lord God. Thank you, Lord God.

Donna Braidic

$\mathcal{F}ootball$

"Amen, amen, I say to you, you will weep and mourn, while the world rejoices; you will grieve but your grief will become joy." John 16:20

Okay, ladies, I have to do it. Yes, I have to...but you'll like it. Like a Hallmark movie, it has a happy ending! It's in the living without FOOTBALL that hurts so much. Please, hear me out...this is romantic!

After my husband Tim and my brother David died, I was very full of grief and anguish. I was so sad. They were so big in my life, and then they were dead, three months apart; it was too much all at once. I went through my days in a kind of stupor, knowing they were gone. I was never going to see them, touch them, hug them, or hear their voices again.

Tim and David were not coming back, and I must move forward.

I was going through the motions, chugging along. Thankfully, I was still very involved in music ministry and directing my choir, and this was a saving grace for me. I forced myself to prepare for rehearsals and Mass, and I forced myself to engage in ministry in a lively, spiritual way. No excuses: God was with me, Tim and David were with me in spirit, and I must not let anyone down.

I guess you could say I was doing okay, but not great. I was balancing a new full-time job and keeping a close tab on my daughters who had a few weeks left in their academic years at college.

Time was marching on. Tim died in November, David died in March, and Easter had come and gone. The music ministry spring concert was quickly approaching, and I had my head deeply focused on preparing the choir for the concert. At the same time, we were also preparing music for a wedding, a beautiful occasion to celebrate and be joyful. My bucket was full. I did not have time to grieve.

And then I was blindsided. In the midst of everything, I came up against a hard stop. I would have to push through Mary Lyn's date of death, April 30. I dreaded the day, because although it had been twenty-five years, I knew in my emotional state, it was going to be as if she had died that year. All of my emotions were raw, I was feeling my losses acutely, and I was vulnerable.

Yes, I was weak, and in an attempt to forget everything for a while, I drank too much one evening, and when my friend dropped me off at home, I staggered up my front door stoop, walked into the house, closed the door behind me, and started bawling my eyes out. I lay prostrate on the stairs to Tim's office and cried and cried and cried, and I complained and yelled and pounded the floor in frustration and pain. I had a total meltdown. In my tirade I told Tim and David, "You have to find someone for me; I do not want to be alone!" I was not doing life by myself! And then my eldest daughter was there, climbing onto the floor beside me, and she asked me what I was doing. All I could do was lie there and cry and accept her loving presence.

Less than a week later I was standing in front of my choir at rehearsal, trying to hold it together and not break down: I did not want them to know it was the date of my stillborn baby's death. That evening it was difficult to press forward, but I was strong, and the Lord was with me. I just kept thinking, "One more song, one more song, and then I can go home."

But unbeknownst to me, the men in the bass section had other plans for me that evening. They asked me to come along with them and some other choir members after rehearsal to a local restaurant hangout. I really wasn't feeling up to it; they could see it. So, they turned the screws a little tighter and told me the new guy, Scott, was also coming and it would be a nice way for all of us to welcome him and get to know each other a little better. And as an added incentive, they highlighted the rare warm spring evening in central Ohio and how nice it would be to sit out on the patio…"no pressure, of course."

I hemmed and hawed and then relented and agreed to meet them. I arrived last and everyone had already chosen seats, and the only one left was the one next to the new guy, Scott. Great, I couldn't just sit there and drink my beer…I was going to have to engage in polite conversation.

After introductions and pleasantries, the guys dominated much of the conversation with talk about the Buckeyes and the spring game the team had just played. Each gave their own opinion of how the team was shaping up, statistics, prospects, height and weight of each player, blah, blah, blah. Well, I was a little less patient than usual with sports talk, and I couldn't resist a little antagonistic barb and asked,

"What is the big deal about the Buckeyes?"

The table went stone cold silent. I could see in the facial expressions the questions running through their minds: Has she lost her mind? No, she's just not herself. She is tired. She doesn't know what she is saying.

Scott, the most stunned of all by my ignorance, turned and looked straight at me and said, "They are the best college football team around!"

I said, "I just don't see what the big deal is…it's just football."

I may have just crossed a line with that last comment that I might not ever come back from.

Suddenly, as if splashed with water, everyone came out of their shock and all at once jumped into the conversation, explaining quite vehemently what I had never understood: Ohio State football is not *just* football. It is friendship, family, fun, tailgating, comradery, "The Shoe." Woody Hayes, Brutus Buckeye, fans, rivalries, players, coaches, national titles, Carmen Ohio…. It is not just football: it is TRADITION!

There was a pause in the back and forth, as if the group was going into a huddle to set up their next play.

Then something happened, something so charming and sweet and gallant and heart stopping (this is the Hallmark moment)…

Scott turned to me again and this time more calmly asked, "Have you ever been to a game?"

"No."

"Well then, I shall take you to a game this season and then you will know what is so great about football, Ohio State football!"

I was speechless. I didn't know what to say. Everyone was looking at me. Would I say, "Okay?" Was this a future date? Was this even appropriate, was it allowed, did it fall under Grieving and

Loss 101: First date after losing husband? I still wore my wedding band. Was I being unfaithful to Tim? So much ran through my mind, and I wondered as I looked at Scott, was this an answer to my request and prayer to not to be alone?

Scott quickly added, "Everyone should see a game at least once in their lifetime."

Okay, so it wasn't a date. It was a friendly outing, a sympathy invitation. I couldn't hold off answering; I either had to accept or make an excuse about washing my hair on game day or something…

I responded, "Okay, thank you. I would like to go!"

Scott smiled and said, "Great. I will get tickets and let you know when we're going!"

From that day on, our relationship was a whirlwind. We went from, "So, what's your story?" and friendship to romance and love. It moved so fast I felt breathless, young, and alive again. My youngest daughter could see IT and warned me I had a crush on "that man"; my sister saw IT and warned me to take it slow and not get hurt; my mom saw IT and said I looked radiant and if I was happy, she was happy; my eldest daughter saw IT and told me to be responsible. The basses in the choir saw IT and with a very satisfied look on their faces, feigned ignorance about how IT had happened!

I would like to think Tim and David saw that Scott and I found IT and were very pleased, especially when they saw our seats were not just any old sympathy seats. No! Scott bought tickets for us on A-deck on the fifty-yard line!

Scott took me to my first Ohio State football game in The Shoe on September 15, 2012. Before the game, we went to the tailgate brunch at the Faculty Club where we had game day Bloody Mary's and eggs Benedict and pastries galore! Scott thought of everything, and he arranged for the Ohio State Men's Glee Club to serenade me and wish me a happy birthday, and I blushed scarlet–yes, I did! The game was so much more than I thought it could be; the size of the stadium was beyond my imagination, and the Buckeyes won the game against the Golden Bears 35-28. It was a perfect day, and it was the beginning of my excitement and passion for football!

Love is...football on a Saturday afternoon "with my baby."
I love you, Scott. With you, I shall never be alone.
"Oh, Come let's sing Ohio's praise
And songs to Alma Mater raise
While our hearts rebounding thrill
With joy which death alone can still
Summer's heat or winter's cold
The seasons pass the years will roll
Time and change will surely show
How firm the friendship...
O-HI-O!"

Hummingbirds

"All things bright and beautiful, All creatures great and small, All things wise and wonderful, the Lord God made them all." Cecil Francis Alexander

"Lord, your love reaches to the heavens; your fidelity, to the clouds. Your justice is like the highest mountains; your judgments, like the mighty deep; all living creatures you sustain, Lord. How precious is your love, O God! We take refuge in the shadow of your wings." Psalm 36:6-7

I love hummingbirds.

I think hummingbirds are one of God's most amazing creatures. No matter where I am or what I am doing, when I see a hummingbird's red throat flash in front of me or hear a group of females chattering, my spirits are lifted and I smile in remembrance of Mary Lyn.

I became fascinated with hummingbirds the summer after Meghan was born. She and I would spend many hours a day playing outside and working in the garden, discovering together all of the marvelous plants and creatures in our yard. On perfect summer days, when the wind was calm and the shade was deep, I would lay Meghan down for her nap in her Pack 'n Play and the fresh air and sounds of nature would quickly lull her to sleep.

One day while I was feeding Meghan, I heard birds singing all around us just outside the gazebo, but there was one bit of chatter I did not recognize. Birds have always fascinated me, and I have learned to recognize and mimic some of their songs, but this bird was completely different from those. There was no "song."

My curiosity was piqued, but when I looked around, I did not see any new birds flying by.

Until, out of the corner of my eye, I noticed little flickers of motion, flying near the fuchsia plants hanging above my head. The movement was quick and flashy, but my six-month-old daughter noticed the motion and she smiled. I looked around with a mother's fierce protective love, worried it was a bumble bee, but quick as it had arrived, it departed.

I heard this same buzzing the next day while I was kneeling in Mary Lyn's Garden, the special garden my brother planted in memory of my first baby girl. I was tidying up the bee balm that I had planted earlier in the summer, pulling out weeds between mature plant stalks and making room for an abundance of bright crimson flowers showing out.

I kept sensing something whirring around within range of my head, so I stopped weeding and without moving my body, I looked to my left and then to my right, and I came eye to eye with a female hummingbird hovering just next to my shoulder. I froze at first, holding my breath, and then slowly I sat back on my heels, staying as motionless as I could, hoping not to scare her away.

It was so quiet there in the garden, and every chirp of pleasure and whirr of her wings was amplified in the stillness. I couldn't believe how close we were to each other; I felt like time had stopped and she and I were connected spiritually, blessed by a fantastical moment of vulnerability and trust.

Then all of a sudden, she broke the spell, gave me a little chirp and wiggle of her tail feathers, and flew above my head as if I were not even there and then back down in a little dancing arc to the nearest flower, where she began sucking the nectar out of the thin trumpet-shaped blossoms.

I was given a lovely gift of insight about my life that day from one of God's most remarkable creatures.

The little hummingbird taught me that there are wonders and miracles all around me, and it is up to me to take notice and appreciate them. I learned that once I slow down and change my orientation to the world, I see it with the eyes of a newborn, capturing in my sight many splendid and small, less visible marvels of God's creation.

I don't know how I possibly missed hummingbirds flying around my yard for so many years, but I did! My only defense is I was not looking for them; I was not paying attention. I thought hummingbirds were only found in southern states and the tropical islands, when in fact they migrate every year all the way up into the northern United States and Canadian provinces! I never expected to see such a small and exotic bird flying anywhere close to me except possibly in an aviary, or in a controlled habitat at the zoo.

Once I became attuned to their comings and goings, I saw how marvelous they are. Their high-speed flying, along with their sudden stops, vertical hovering, and directional changes–backward and forward–all made in a single instant, are impressive! I am in awe of their biannual migration to and from my home, flying hundreds to thousands of miles, and overcoming every kind of weather obstacle along their way. They seem never to rest, visiting flower after flower and feeder after feeder the whole day long.

And they are so cute with little "feet" tucked up under their full bellies as they hover at flower blossoms, sipping sweet nectar for their nourishment.

After watching them in my backyard for many years, I have noticed that they are not all business all the time. I see them rest in nearby trees and play among the leaves, and it is amusing to see their mischief, as they sit quietly camouflaged, ready to dive-bomb hummers that sneak in the yard to take a little sip from "their" feeder. Their silent stealth attacks on other hummingbirds entering the yard are well planned and executed, swooping down to show interlopers who reigns supreme in the yard. I have watched them as two form an alliance and team up, zooming down on a feeder and drawing a big sip before they are discovered by the "owner" and run off with accusatory "*#@!*##$@#!" chirps.

I used to think their tiny size made them vulnerable to predators and too small to harm anything, but I have seen even the smallest hummer hold its own when aggressively defending its territory against encroaching hummingbirds, flying insects, squirrels, and people, too. The males are especially impressive when their ruby throats flash like brilliant fire while they perform their steep v-shaped mating dance.

Hummingbirds are funny, too, seeming to share with each other the latest gossip from the neighborhood with their chirps and chatter. Sometimes when I listen closely, it almost sounds like Morse Code!

I am sad when fall approaches because I know they will begin their migration back to Mexico and my feeder will be abandoned through the winter. Steadily through the month of September I see their numbers dwindle until the last one leaves in early October.

So, imagine my elation and surprise when in the last days of October, my neighbors and I catch sight of a late migrator in our yards foraging for sustenance among dwindling flower blossoms! You would have thought it was the return of the Prodigal Son the way I ran around my house looking for my feeder to fill! Knowing this was an anomalous occurrence, I felt very blessed that this little bird found its way to our yards. I quickly prepared sugar water and set it out, and it did not take long for our latecomer to start sipping from the feeder, uninterrupted, replenishing much-needed calories and strength for the last leg of his journey home.

Needless to say, as winter ends and April is just weeks away, I begin the preparation for the hummingbirds' return and set out my feeder filled with fresh sugar water, ready to provide a welcome meal for early migrators, hoping some might stay in my yard and enjoy the summer with me and my family once again.

About a month after they return, I usually count about a dozen or so ruby-throated hummingbirds visiting my feeder, both male and female, and no two birds are exactly alike. Each one has a different personality and up close I can see little markings, blemishes, or scars that help me tell them apart. There are some that are only a year or so old and have not filled out completely yet, and there are others who are mature and regal looking, flashing their emerald, white and ruby-red tones as the light strikes the edges of their feathers, dazzling in every way.

I think my little hummingbird visitors are brave ambassadors from God, sent to bring good cheer and lightheartedness to me and to all who see them; to remind us to spend a part of each day discovering the marvelous creatures in God's earthly garden and appreciating the priceless beauty all around.

I am so grateful for the gift of the hummingbird and the hope and faith they inspire in me.

They remind me that I am blessed, I am loved.

And as long as there are hummingbirds visiting me each year, I will never forget Mary Lyn or the brief time she and I had together so many years ago.

Birthday Wishes

"This is the day the Lord has made; let us rejoice in it and be glad!" Psalm 118:24

Birthdays are really important to me; just ask my daughters! When I was growing up my mom always made sure that birthdays were a little more special than any other day of the year. She always made sure my dad knew he was expected to be home for our celebrations, and as far as I can remember, he was always there for mine (which wasn't always easy as a traveling salesman)! My mom always made our favorite meal for dinner—mine was fried chicken—and she would bake our favorite cake—mine was chocolate.

Every birthday, my family and sometimes friends, too, would give me birthday cards and presents and then sing a rollicking rendition of "Happy Birthday," followed by my favorite part of all: blowing out the candles on my birthday cake and making a wish for anything my heart desired. On that one day each year I felt like a princess—the most important, appreciated, and loved person in the world.

After I married and moved away from my home and family, I naively assumed celebrating my birthday and other special occasions would continue with Tim, but this was not the case. After our wedding day, Tim downplayed the importance of special days; in his words, "they were just another day." I felt confused. Wait, what? This was news to me! He had always celebrated my birthday before, when we were dating and engaged to be married, with gifts and cards and candle-lit dinners with violin trios serenading us…. What changed? Only he and God knew.

I was really frustrated with this change in birthday status! He knew birthdays were THE day of the year that I was allowed to be the center of attention, a day set apart from any other because it was the day the Lord made for me to be born. It was an "I love you" day like no other. Tim's lack of celebration really hurt me and instead of feeling special and joyful on my birthdays, I felt sad and dejected–for me and for him. I couldn't fathom the depth of disappointment and hurt that he harbored inside that made him hold on to this lousy attitude.

Nevertheless, my mom taught me well, so I baked my own birthday cake and prepared my own favorite meal and sang happy birthday to myself and blew out my one candle, wishing for next year to be different. As I opened my birthday cards sent from near and far, wishing me love and happiness, tears welled up in my eyes and spilled over onto my empty plate. I did not feel special, I did not feel loved. I felt alone and sad on what had always been one of the happiest days of the year.

But thank God, as time went by, Tim began to understand the joy of birthdays, in part because I still made his birthday special for him, but more so because he loved his daughters, and he could not deny them a birthday celebration! He was all in for the girls, seeing their smiles and hearing their giggles of delight, and their love and joy moved his heart. I mean, come on, who doesn't love watching a baby eat their first birthday cake! Soon enough, the three amigos–Tim, Meghan, and Lauren–were secretly planning my birthdays, and this was the miracle, the gift of love returned, to Tim and to me. I rejoice that before he died Tim came to understand that celebrating the ones you love is a priceless gift to both giver and receiver.

Scott was a different story! He has made each and every birthday special, from the first after I started dating him to my most recent! He plans surprises and writes little notes and leaves them like rose petals under my pillow and in my drawers, knowing they will be discovered throughout the day. My favorite surprise was being serenaded by the University Glee Club! Boy could those guys harmonize! Oh, so dreamy! Everything Scott does for me shouts, "I love you!"

Since their childhoods, my girls have remembered me on my birthday with cards and gifts to express their love for me. When they are busy in their lives, they give me a few minutes on the phone, which for some may not sound like much, but for me, to hear their voices singing "Happy Birthday" and saying, "I miss you" and "I love you, Mom," there is no greater gift I wish to receive from them!

My mom and dad have devised a new way to continue making birthdays special for their family by sending group email messages on our birthdays. They have creatively involved the entire family in sending well-wishes to us all in a timely, inexpensive way. On each birthday my parents send a group email titled "Birthday Wishes" that contains a personalized message straight from the heart, filled with love and encouragement wishes that we will fulfill all of our hopes and dreams.

Each message begins, "This is the day the Lord has made; let us rejoice in it and be glad!" (Psalm 118:24), followed by funny recollections about us, and a little sage advice and wisdom for living a good life each and every year. Photos are included from different milestones in our lives that make me laugh and cry. Their message is a message of love that no matter how we have been or what direction we have been going in, good things are wished for our life and future.

Once the message hits all of our inboxes, a steady stream of silly and serious messages are sent out for the birthday boy or girl for all to read and enjoy. It is wonderful to read all of the honest, open, heartfelt messages...it is easy for me to imagine all of us together again at the dining room table licking fried chicken grease off of our fingers and diving into a chocolate cake!

The birthday wishes do not cost a thing, but they bring more joy and love and comfort than diamonds and gold. Through this very simple act of love, Mom and Dad, my siblings and in-laws, nieces, nephews, friends, and relatives have stayed connected even when we are apart. Each email message lifts my spirits and tells me I am loved and valued and not forgotten.

Even years after my brother's passing, my mom and dad still send a birthday email in remembrance of David, reminding us all how lucky we were to have shared our lives with him, and to say that no matter what our circumstances, each of us will always be in their hearts.

Most of all, it is nice to hear my mom and dad's hopes and dreams for me, no matter how old I get. In a powerful way it reveals to me how much God blessed me on the day I was born with parents who rejoice with gladness in my being born.

Mom and Dad have created a wonderful tradition of communicating love that will be easily carried on from generation to generation. They have made their expectations known and they are very clear: do not miss each other's birthdays! Love one another.

God sends us to earth to do amazing work for an extraordinary purpose! Sometimes the simplest act is by far the most genuine and sincere for making a loved one feel important, for reconnecting with family, for setting aside differences, for sending joy across the miles.

It is wonderful to know that on my birthday each year I will find in my inbox celebratory messages of love, and on that one blessed, perfect day each year, my heart is filled with joy and gladness!

Compliments

"I praise you, so wonderfully you made me; wonderful are your works!" Psalm 139:14

"If you don't have anything nice to say, don't say anything at all!"

At the same time, if you have something nice to say, say it!

Say something nice. It feels good. For the giver and the receiver.

Compliments are like a gentle hug around my heart. They are kindness wrapped in nice words. Civility, graciousness, and love that make me feel like I am valued and am making a difference in someone else's life.

God knows me so well, and He knows when I am getting down on myself or when I need a boost of confidence, and he also knows when I am succeeding, and my spirits are high. In either case, he knows that in order to keep me fighting and winning for myself and for Him, I need encouragement. And so he sends an "angel" to praise me and bolster my resolve in staying the course. God speaks to me through people, saying the nicest things about me, and in so doing, he cancels out all the negative thoughts and feelings of unworthiness that I may be feeling, reinforcing positivity so that I can continue my work in his name.

Say something nice. It feels good. For the giver and the receiver.

It is hard for me to accept compliments; they tend to throw me off and I fumble around with how to respond. Instead of saying, "Thank you!" I deflect or deny a compliment. After nullifying an act of kindness from another I blush in embarrassment and fumble awkwardly for words to express my true gratitude. It is my insecurities about myself, my abilities, my appearance, that make it hard for me to believe the kind things that others say about me, especially if they are positive and complimentary. I can be very frustrating to myself!

I groan inside and clinch my fists.

Just say, "Thank you!"

How hard is it? Apparently, for me, very hard.

But I am getting better...

Say something nice. It feels good. For the giver and the receiver.

Compliments are like gifts wrapped in colorful paper and tied with a beautiful yellow bow of sunshine. My parents brought me up right and they taught me from a very young age that when receiving a gift, always say, "Thank you!"

Once I began thinking of compliments as gifts, I could no longer deny them or refuse to accept them; that would be impolite, as well as ungrateful.

Say something nice. It feels good. For the giver and the receiver.

Compliments are precious and rare, and they make me sparkle and shine like gemstones.

The most amazing compliments are the ones that come spontaneously and unexpectedly. Whether they are about my appearance or the way I have performed in my work, they make a difference. And when my brother, who had not seen me in a couple of years, said to me, "Donna, you never age!" Well, that made my day! His compliment was genuine and sincere, spontaneous, and true, a gift from the heart!

Say something nice. It feels good. For the giver and the receiver.

Compliments are humbling, especially in a public setting.

Whether on stage, in church, or on the field of sport, the one thing I have consistently worked towards is being my best. Yet when praise and recognition are given from my peers, I stiffen up as if poked in the middle of my back and I hide my face as if a bright light is shining on me. Even still, I stand as tall as I can, give a shy princess wave, and receive their praise, because as time goes by, I realize how fortunate I am to receive such praises, and my gratefulness and joyful acceptance is a gift back to the giver.

Say something nice. It feels good. For the giver and the receiver.

Compliments are powerful and they have changed me in a powerful way. Looking at myself in a mirror now, when before I saw wrinkles and flaws and imperfections, I now see Donna, who is respected and loved, and the imperfections melt away.

Say something nice. It feels good. For the giver and the receiver.

Compliments have been a pathway to loving myself, paved with assurances that who I am and things I do are good and true. My eyes, my ears, my heart have been opened and I see the same Donna others see, someone who has allowed love to enter into my way of thinking about myself. My perception of who I am is right and just.

From my newfound love of myself I feel worthy of compliments, and I am truly humbled to receive them. I still feel awkward when I am paid a compliment, but that does not keep me from thanking the giver, and in turn, thanking God for the gift giver.

Say something nice. It feels good. For the giver and the receiver.

Compliments have the power to change a lifetime of negativity. There is no expiration date on a compliment and no age limit on giving or receiving them. In fact, the most beautiful thing to behold is the joy on the face of a person, young or old, who has heard something wonderful said about them, possibly for the first time in their life.

Don't wait until a person is gone to sing their praises; the opportunity may not present itself again in this lifetime. Don't say I shoulda, woulda, coulda in paying a compliment to a loved one or friend. Instead, imagine all the joy a person will feel in this life knowing how much they are valued and appreciated and loved.

Say something nice. It feels good. For the giver and the receiver.

Compliments are to me gentle, kind, and loving, the touch of an angel, straight from heaven above.

Say something nice. It feels good. For the giver and the receiver.

Donna Braidic

Group Reunion

"For where two or three are gathered together in my name, there am I in the midst of them." Matthew 18:20

Come Holy Spirit, fill the hearts of your faithful and kindle in them the fire of your love. Send forth your Spirit and they shall be created. And You shall renew the face of the earth.

O, God, who by the light of the Holy Spirit, did instruct the hearts of the faithful, grant that by the same Holy Spirit we may be truly wise and ever enjoy His consolations, Through Christ Our Lord, Amen.

Leader: Christ is counting on you…
Me: And I on him!

But what does this mean and how is "Christ counting on me"? Christ is counting on *me*? Why me? I'm not comfortable or qualified to be an evangelist, a disciple of Christ. I don't have influence over people. I have no power, and I'm too quiet. Everyone says so. And besides, my life is very busy; I have enough to do. He demands too much of me. Love my enemies? Christ? Counting on me? No, I don't think so. You must be mistaken.

When my three-day Cursillo/Cum Christo weekend retreat was coming to an end, all of my old excuses for not following Jesus Christ began creeping back in my mind, and the devil was doing a happy jig on the top of my head! But at the same time, I felt more convicted in my faith than ever before, and the love of Christ was hugging me from the inside out. It was a strange and wonderful feeling, exhilarating and dramatic. But feelings–good and bad– slowly fade over time, and I was worried I would soon return to my old self.

A battle of wills played out in my mind, and it wasn't until I was standing on the stage at the closing ceremony with my table group, looking out over the entire, supportive Cum Christo community, that I knew who would win the battle for my will. I stood there, as if

154

on a precipice, knowing the challenges ahead, yet when my name was called, I stepped forward, my legs steady and my feet on solid ground. I looked into the eyes of each spiritual leader and received a blessing. They read my name from my commitment card and when the leader handed my card back to me, she said,

"Christ is counting on you."

I took the card in my hand, looked at it for but a brief second, and answered back,

"And I on him."

Silence...and then applause rang out both in heaven and on earth, exuberant and loud, cheering and whistling, and when I turned back to the audience, faces of loved ones were beaming back at me with joy, and with that triumph, my fourth day of the three-day weekend had begun...

Looking back over the experience of my weekend it took many people praying and sacrificing in my name to knock down the fortress I had built up around my heart. I had been building my wall up for years and it was highly fortified, protecting me from being hurt and feeling pain. I was constantly on guard, remaining cool and reserved. To move me to accept Jesus Christ's call to serve him without reservation—no ifs, ands, or buts—would take a miracle.

Learning how to follow Jesus and commit myself to him was a three-day battle of wills, and honestly, it still continues to this day. I did not want to be moved at all in my thoughts about God or my feelings for Jesus; I was quite comfortable with the way things were. In fact, I decided going into the weekend that no one and nothing would make me feel vulnerable or emotionally broken: I would not cry or loosen up when they hugged me! I was in control. I was there to learn and to take some time off, to have a little vacation!

From the outset I was determined to withhold myself and keep my sharing about my life to a minimum, yet even before I arrived at the Cum Christo Center, I had a strong feeling that I was supposed to be on the weekend, that God was calling me to attend, and so I went in with a positive attitude. I would discover that I was not alone in how I felt when I was dropped off for the retreat. Throughout the weekend other women expressed their feelings of trepidation when they arrived, and how at the same time they felt an inexplicable need to be there.

God was working on each of us, breaking down our resistance and walls of protection, as well as enlightening our hearts and minds to new ideas and endless possibilities for ministry.

Come Holy Spirit, fill the hearts of your faithful and kindle in them the fire of your love...

Throughout the weekend, I met many wonderful women from different walks of life who were at different stages in their lives. There were young women, unencumbered, open to learning about the incredible plans God had for them; and older women, empty nesters, who bestowed their wisdom with loving kindness, sharing incredible stories of patience and perseverance, loss, and success. I took it all in, preferring to listen to everyone else's story, and sharing as little about myself as I could get away with. I wanted time away from home and an opportunity to be with God, not share time. I did not realize it then, but the entire weekend Jesus was with me, speaking to me through the women who were strangers at the beginning of the weekend and who became some of my most intimate friends by the end.

...Send forth your Spirit and they shall be created...

All weekend long we laughed and cried, sang, and prayed, and we had a lot of fun together, too, expressing our ideas in various creative ways! At our mealtimes, some of the less restrained ladies made me laugh out loud with their corny, silly, pun-filled jokes. Our lighthearted conversations helped me relax and created an atmosphere conducive to letting down my guard and immersing myself in the life sharing and faith sharing with my table group. The ladies were like a living, breathing profession of faith. I was blessed to be trusted with their private stories, some of which were painful for them to recount, yet which they courageously shared for the benefit of all.

During the chapel visits, I retreated into myself, contemplating who I was and what my purpose was in the world. I was restless in my spirit. I wanted God's love and forgiveness...I wanted to know and feel God in the same way others said they felt God in their lives...I wanted to unlock and open the impenetrable door to my heart, and I knew I held the key. It was my choice, my free will, to allow the Lord in. He was knocking: I could feel his spirit moving strongly within me…and my heart softened, and I let him in. I was vulnerable and I knew I needed to confess my sins to him, to pour out all that I had hidden away. I needed to surrender my heart, with its hurt and pain and anger and resentment and bitterness that I had carried within me since being molested as a child. I needed to speak, to say the words out loud to my confessor and to my God that I hated the pedophile who hurt me and used me for his perverted pleasure and stole my innocence with his filthy actions. I did not want to hurt anymore. I did not want to feel responsible for keeping his sin secret anymore. I hated feeling guilty for someone else's shameful deeds against me. I wanted to be clean, I wanted the guilt to go away. I didn't want to carry hate in my heart anymore.

I wanted love to heal me, I wanted God to forgive me and to cleanse my soul and make me new again.

And so, I gathered my courage and sat before the priest with my head bowed and my hands tucked into my lap, and when he laid his hand gently upon my head, like a loving father would do to his child, I felt safe to confess my secret childhood trauma. It was excruciatingly painful to bring forth, like bile burning in my throat, but once done, my feelings of being dirty and bad completely left me. I then confessed to lying to my mom on that horrible day of lost innocence out of fear of being punished, afraid I would be blamed for the shameful act and for not running away. Father pressed down a little more firmly on my head, not in discipline but in compassion, reassurance, and comfort. He felt my sadness and all that I had endured, and when he released his sigh of compassionate understanding, it seemed not to be coming from him but from Jesus, whose spirit was present with us in that dimly lit chapel. And I knew I was forgiven.

Once I opened the door and confessed the wretched truth, the wall that I had built up between God and me came down, and the agonizing pain and self-loathing of years rose up and came out of my chest and I felt a rush of love. For the first time in my life, I knew God's healing energy and power, and it consumed my sin. I cried and laughed all at once, finding it hard to breathe, and suddenly I felt like "me," but reborn, like a new creation with a clean slate.

The priest blessed me then and told me to go forth and sin no more. Thanks be to God.

...And You shall renew the face of the earth...

I was transformed and my attitude going forth was profoundly changed; it was my metanoia. I was no longer the victim: *I was the victor!*

From that moment to the end of the weekend, I was convinced more than ever that "nothing can separate [me] from the love of God." Jesus was with me, and Jesus loves me. I felt secure in his forgiveness. I felt free and I had a new perspective on everything.

I carried this tremendous feeling to the end of the weekend and shared my excitement and "cloud nine" experience with my family and friends at the closing ceremony. That evening, some of my church friends invited me to join their permanent table group, and thus began my newfound commitment to Christ, my journey of faith with others.

...O, God, who by the light of the Holy Spirit, did instruct the hearts of the faithful...

Group Reunion, "Group," as it is called, has without a doubt been the most important thing I have done for myself to sustain my journey of faith with Jesus Christ since my weekend. My group mates have helped me stay on track as I have lived out my life of faith, and they have kept me strong and resilient in staying the course and avoiding sin.

To "let go and let God" was scary, and my Group gave me the support and encouragement that I needed to be less controlling and more accepting of God's will. They are my prayer group, my share group, my confidants, my friends in Christ whom I can tell anything. Through our sharing of faith, praying together, worshiping together, and serving together, we have progressed significantly in our faith journey as a Group and as individuals. I have served with these ladies in charitable endeavors, and I have witnessed their love and generosity towards others. My group mates have encouraged my music ministry for years, since the very beginning, and their support has not faltered. They are why I believe so strongly in myself.

...Grant that by the same Holy Spirit we may be truly wise and ever enjoy His consolations...

Needless to say, it was extremely painful and sad when I moved to South Carolina and left my Group behind. They are my best friends, my confidants, my most trusted allies, and I love them so much. I need their wisdom and humor, and their honesty. I was absolutely delighted when we met for a time on live stream during Covid; it was surely needed by all, and it gave me an anchor of stability and hope to endure the isolation from family and friends near and far! Each time we met was a gift, a time to treasure.

Group reunion created an invisible link of sisterhood between me and my friends, and I know that no matter the distance, if I need them, they are there for me.

I continue with my study and prayer, my worship and service. That will never change. To stop would undo all my good work with my Group and my Cum Christo table group and Jesus Christ himself. Group reunion brought Christ into every aspect of my life, and my Group helped me to live for Christ in every aspect of my life.

I miss my group. They are Jesus with skin on: they are love. Near or far, nothing can separate us as long as we love.

We started a great thing years ago when we formed our Group. We are family, and these beautiful women will be a part of my life until the day I die.

Christ is counting on me. He is counting on all of us.

And I on him.

...through Jesus Christ Our Lord, Amen.

INFJ: Knowing Who I Am

I am "created in the image and likeness of God." Genesis 1:27

According to the results of my Myers-Briggs personality type assessment, I am an INFJ: Introverted, Intuitive, Feeling, Judging personality type. You may say, "So what?" or "Really! Well hot dog! I'm an ESTP!", in response to which I would wonder which famous criminal (Al Capone–yikes!) or actor (Lucille Ball) or politician (George W. Bush) you are and whether I can have your autograph (Kristenson)!

Of course, as an INFJ I would probably never be able to wiggle my way through a crowd to get your autograph, as all the ESFJ fans would have already positioned themselves perfectly along the stage, three rows deep, ready to swoon and faint as soon as you took the stage.

Their excitement and energy would have overpowered me an hour before and by the time the headlining act was announced and you appeared, I would be wilting in the background, trying to stay awake (no offense)!

Now, that is, of course, unless I have my husband, Scott, with me: he is my game changer! With him by my side I would definitely get your autograph, or at least a finger-tip handshake, as I did when presidential candidate Ben Carson was campaigning! With Scott, I had an ESTJ on my side and with his tactical, supply-chain "Lean Six Sigma" brain, he saw the weak spot, where a suspected INFJ lagged from over-thinking their next move, and at just the right moment Scott was able to push me forward in that split-second and there I was, face to face with the famous politician, touching fingertips and having my picture taken for all to see! I finally knew what it felt like to be an ESFP!

And then in true INFJ fashion, I left the rally, got in the car, buckled up, tried to understand what just happened, and went fast to sleep!

When I returned to college in my early forties–once and for all–to complete my bachelor's degree, one of the signature courses in the first six weeks was Personality Typing. The objective of the assignment was for the cohort of students to personality type themselves in order to help us see how our personalities would impact our learning and our interaction in the classroom and study groups. Typing ourselves proved to be an invaluable tool in helping me blend with the stronger adult personalities and helping them blend with my very methodical way of approaching assignments. We were from many different walks of life and our personalities had played a part in where we found ourselves at this juncture of our lives. We were adult learners, and we were set in our ways. Typing ourselves was the key to the success of the program (although the ESTP in my group thought it was a waste of time!).

I was not a very enthusiastic student the first time around, but this time I was ready to jump into my classwork. I was excited to continue growing as a person and personality typing fit the bill right away.

The coursework was based on the book *Type Talk At Work*, by Janet M. Thuesen and Otto Kroeger, experts in the field of personality typing, utilizing Carl Jung's psychological typology.

The subject of personality typing was brand new to me, and I thought it was really interesting.

Learning about the sixteen different personality type combinations described in the book was an eye-opener, and after taking my own self-assessment for classwork, I finally began to understand myself.

Truly, it was the first time in my life that I understood why I am the way I am! It was a fresh beginning for me! Knowing this one thing changed how I interacted with everyone, from my classmates to family to my coworkers, friends, and strangers, too.

At first, I was disappointed to be an INFJ. I didn't want to be classified as introverted! It sounded so sedate and tiresome and BORING. I wanted to be an ESFP: I wanted to party and laugh out loud and have spontaneous FUN! But the more I studied my personality type and learned how each part of it influenced who I am and why I am the way I am, the more I grew to accept myself with happiness, which was a life changer for me.

My new knowledge about personalities gave me confidence to be myself, knowing that although my different perspective or ideas might have conflicted with others, it did not mean I was wrong in what I said and believed. I began standing my ground when before I might have backed down to avoid what I thought might turn into an argument. I found my voice and it felt so good to be heard.

For the first time in my life, I stopped thinking I was dull; I realized my unusual deep thinking has merit and I began to shine! As much as I rejected it at first, being an INFJ became pretty cool to me!

As an INFJ, I am in a group of about two percent of the population, including some pretty famous people. Gandhi, Mother Teresa, Nelson Mandela, and yes, even Jesus are INFJ personality types! Unfortunately, some of the worst, most infamous people are also INFJ's, including Adolph Hitler and Osama Bin Laden (Gaille).

It comes as no surprise to me looking back now that even my decision to return to college was done in true INFJ fashion! I held the desire of returning to college deep within me, like a secret, contemplating it, mulling it over, overanalyzing it, setting it on the back burner more than a dozen times, and then at the oddest times the idea to return to college would catch fire again. But I always found a list of reasons why it was "not a good time" to go back to college; it just didn't feel right.

The years passed quickly from high school graduation to my forties, with my days filled with the routine demands associated with work, marriage, and family, and I was content with my life. So, it was quite surprising to me when, on a beautiful summer afternoon, while watching my young daughters swim and play at the community pool, I began daydreaming about college again. It startled me how strong the desire to return was this time! I was super happy with my life, yet this time there came an unbelievable surge of excitement at the thought of going back to school!

Looking around me on that hot summer afternoon, the pool seemed to be filled with toddlers and pregnant thirty-something moms, and in that instant, I felt something shift inside of me. Like a cog in a wheel that slips and then reseats itself, I felt my attitude and perceptions change not only about my present day but about my future years. My girls were in middle school, my husband and

I were getting older, and the future, although not frightening, felt foreboding in some ways. I wondered again if I would regret in my senior years not going back to college, and the answer came back decidedly loud and clear: "Go for it!" It was so loud in fact that I thought everyone splashing in the pool must have heard it too!

As I lay there, lounging in my bleached-out bikini, it was as if I was looking at myself from above, and I saw myself getting older and feeling that no matter how long my life might be, my time for college was running out. I sensed more intensely than ever before that it was time to stop thinking about it and commit myself to returning to college, and the sooner the better.

It was exhilarating to make the decision...decisively! Suddenly, the idea of achieving a college degree became part of my present and my future story, and this time I did not dismiss it or allow any negative thoughts to dissuade me, including my usual excuse of intellectual inadequacy, i.e., test anxiety. I went to work immediately, making my list of things to do, talked to my husband and daughters that evening and received their blessings, and enrolled in classes the next day.

My first night of class brought out all of my INFJ tendencies. I arrived early, sat quietly towards the back of the room, taking in everyone and everything before class started, giving a welcome smile when someone made eye contact with me or looked to take the seat next to me. I took notice of everything and everyone, enjoying the newness of it all.

I found the class fascinating and I loved it, but when it was time to go, I felt exhausted and wondered if I would be able to sustain the level of energy that would be needed to do well in my classes.

What I learned from reading *Type Talk at Work* is I am quiet but not shy, careful to conserve my energy but am willing to be impulsive and adventuresome. I focus deeply, on what is beyond the apparent, which does not make me a slow learner. I feel empathy when making observations, which causes me to run the gamut of emotions, but I am not a cry baby. And I am timely and organized–not, as I thought of myself, annoyingly predictable and overthinking in my decision making.

My whole life I had been comparing myself to others and putting myself down for personality characteristics that I could not change and that were actually a good balance to others who were different from me. Instead of being happy with myself for who I am, I put myself down, and that hurt me. I lacked confidence to assert myself, which made it difficult to love myself, let alone like myself. All of the things about myself that I thought were wrong with me were actually things I needed to honor and find the goodness in me (as, unbeknownst to me, others did)–to not reject or hide from my unique qualities but celebrate them and celebrate me.

Being an INFJ is a gift that God has given to me so that I may contribute to the world as no other can do. I am one of a kind, as are we all. God loves me as I am; he loves all of us exactly as we are.

As an Introvert, everything I do and say seems louder to me than it actually is, so when I was first asked to direct my choir at church, I recoiled inside, followed by nervous butterflies, followed by anxiety and fear. Knowing I would have to stand apart, extending my arms and hands beyond the sides of my body in large, demonstrative motions made my stomach drop thinking about it, but my pastor and my choir believed in me, and I quickly came out of my tightly closed shell and extended my arms and hands to bring forth beautiful music from both choir and congregation.

As an iNtuitive, my senses send information to my brain to be processed, and it is this sixth intuitive "sense" that waits on the sidelines to help me process more deeply in my conscious and subconscious all that I see, smell, taste, touch, and hear. I know it sounds silly, and it is really hard to explain, but I feel very blessed to have this gift. When I was young, I thought I was weird. It made me feel like an outsider and that I was "dumb"; now I just think I have something special that helps me in all areas of my life. This is especially true in my music ministry when choosing music that is beautiful, supportive, and spiritual for worship and praise. I feel a fullness of love and spirit rise in me as I read the scripture and my intuitive gift helps me match songs to the messages of the Old and New Testament readings, all to the glory of God.

The intuitive part of me is a blessing, but it has also been a cross to bear, as it brings clarity to sudden thoughts that are very sad, as was the case when my brother and my husband had undiagnosed cancers. I think they already knew there was something seriously wrong within their bodies, and my intuitive sense picked up on their unspoken anxiety. As we hugged and looked into each other's eyes, instantly I knew they had cancer, and within a month of these premonitions, each was diagnosed with their cancer.

But I cannot ignore the blessing of safety and caution my intuitive sense has given to me, as it has kept me out of trouble and safe from harm when I listened to the whisper of caution in my ear. Some people call this conscience; I call it a deeper voice inside of me that speaks to my heart, from God.

It is not surprising to me that I am a Feeling personality type, as I am very empathetic. This is probably the most dominant part of my personality and can be to my detriment in highly emotional situations involving family or friends, especially when conflict arises. I wish I could think clearly when I am hit with a difficult situation, but my feelings are strong, and sometimes they overtake my ability to problem-solve quickly. My adrenaline rushes through my body, my heart races, making my head throb, and my brain stops thinking. I become mute, having difficulty making words when trying to answer questions or articulate solutions. Every thought takes effort as I regain my composure.

I envy people who can "work a problem" by thinking clearly, logically, and unemotionally in real time; but knowing now that my emotional reaction to problems is natural to my personality type, I am able take deep breaths, stay in the moment, and silently say prayers for help in recovering from the initial anxiety and panic I feel.

The Judging aspect of my personality, which sounds really bad, has in fact been a great tool for me in keeping my life from spinning out of control. It's not about passing judgment on others, but rather discerning through a logical, list-making process for gathering information and timeliness. This has benefited me greatly when coordinating important events, especially when timing out critical actions and delegating. I am great at organizing and floating lots of balls in the air, but this is stressful, so learning how to balance my need for order with expectations for myself and others has helped me create successful events.

I truly value the Judging aspect of my personality, possibly the most, because it has helped me build a career and a good reputation as a trustworthy parent, student, wife, music director, team member, coworker, and silent auction coordinator!

If I had not completed the personality typing, I don't know if I would have had the confidence to attempt and complete four years of night classes to earn my bachelor's degree. Before typing myself, I did not have a good self-image. I put myself down for the things I viewed as problems or flaws. I didn't understand why I ran low on energy in social gatherings. I was indecisive and quiet when I needed to be assertive and more outspoken. After typing myself, I learned that everything about myself is exactly as it should be, and that each part of my personality is a gift. Personality typing myself has helped me to stay in the game and not be a quitter.

God led me to return to college. He knew all the reasons I had for putting it off, and even though I felt inadequate and afraid of failing, he pushed me forward and surrounded me with good people who encouraged me and believed in me, because he knew I had much to accomplish in this world, in His name. And on my graduation day, I stood tall with my classmates, and God stood with me, too, while my late husband and my daughters, along with my mom and dad, cheered for me as my name was called out, and I walked across the stage and received my diploma.

God gave me a vision for a bright future, a lovely daydream on a sunny afternoon. He understood my heart and he knew more than I knew myself how very much I yearned for knowledge and truth in my life. He knew my questions and where I would find my answers.

Thank you, God, for enlightening my mind to return to college. You knew I would mull it over until the day I died, forever feeling dissatisfied with myself had I not returned! You helped me set a course for completion, and you took me through to the end, and I am forever grateful for the experience! How very appropriate for me to attend two universities with mottos that strike at the heart of my INFJ personality and my purpose:

"To contemplate truth and to share with others the fruits of this contemplation": Ohio Dominican University, Columbus Ohio; Associate of Science, 2005.

"To Seek to Learn is to Seek to Serve": Mount Vernon Nazarene University, Mount Vernon, Ohio; Bachelor 's Degree, 2007.

God knows me completely, from my head to my toes, forward and backward, inside and out. He knows my insecurities and my peculiarities. He looks at me and smiles, loving everything about me, seeing me as perfect in every way. I am created in his image and likeness, a created reflection of his love.

Understanding who I am and why I am the way I am has brought me into a closer, more intimate relationship with God, because God is love, and once I was able to love myself as he loves me, I was able to be the image and likeness of God, unique in my own way, serving him, in his image, a reflection of his love.

Jesus

Now Saul, still breathing murderous threats against the disciples of the Lord, went to the high priest and asked him for letters to the synagogues in Damascus, that, if he should find any men or women who belonged to the Way, he might bring them back to Jerusalem in chains. On his journey to Damascus, a light from the sky suddenly flashed around him. He fell to the ground and heard a voice saying to him. "Saul, Saul, why are you persecuting me?"

He said, "Who are you, sir?"

The reply came, "I am Jesus, whom you are persecuting. Now get up and go into the city and you will be told what you must do."

The men who were traveling with him stood speechless, for they heard the voice but could see no one. Saul got up from the ground, but when he opened his eyes, he could see nothing; so they led him by the hand and brought him to Damascus. For three days he was unable to see, and he neither ate nor drank.

He stayed some days with the disciples in Damascus, and he began at once to proclaim Jesus in the synagogues, that he is the Son of God. (Acts 9:1-9; 19-20)

Neither Jesus nor anyone else has forced me to believe that he is the Son of God. The choice to accept him or reject him is mine, and I do so willingly, receiving his friendship, praising him for his sacrifice, and opening my heart to his love.

Jesus has me. After a lifetime of searching for answers and questioning the research, I have evolved and progressed in my faith, until I can say now that I firmly believe in Jesus Christ as Son of God, the promised Messiah, Emmanuel. Come what may, through all the horrors and tragedies that befall mankind, I believe. I may appear naïve or childlike in my belief, and I'm okay with that. I wish all believed, but I am realistic, and I know it may never come to pass that all believe in Jesus Christ.

I understand unbelief; it is hard to believe the extraordinary accounts of Jesus' miracles, the directness of his teachings, the sacrifice of his life. The people who could testify to what they saw or heard are long gone, and the opportunity to cross-examine or refute their claims has passed. There were no cell phone recordings or videos of Jesus as he traveled around the Middle East, there was no YouTube, no selfies with the King of Kings. All we have are the eyewitness accounts of people who lived it, who experienced the extraordinary interactions with Jesus, and who told and retold *their* stories until they or someone else wrote them down—which, when compiled, became the New Testament.

That Jesus fulfilled what is written in the Old Testament prophecies of Isaiah regarding the Lamb of God is verified by those who lived with Jesus, as described in the Gospels of Matthew, Mark, Luke, and John, followed by the Acts of the Apostles. Jesus lived, Jesus died, and Jesus rose from the dead. His life, death, and resurrection are both ordinary and extraordinary, human and divine, and I agree, absolutely hard to believe! Jesus' most faithful followers and his most vicious enemies knew what they saw and experienced, from his birth in Bethlehem to his crucifixion on Golgotha, and they knew the role they played in Jesus' life, ministry, death, and the formation of the Church as it is described in the Bible.

Jesus is a historical figure, a controversial figure, and he made his mark, yet his existence two thousand years ago continues to be debated today, some referring to Jesus as "an idea."

Jesus is not an idea. He was a living, breathing human being. He had a wonderful family life; he was known throughout his village as the son of Joseph, the carpenter. I can imagine Jesus working side by side with Joseph in the woodshed, striking his thumb with the hammer, and under his breath, saying, "Oh my God, that hurts!" I believe Jesus had a pretty normal childhood. He loved his family and relatives very dearly, and if I know boys, he probably got into mischief from time to time, too. I believe Jesus knew and understood he was human, with the perceived limitations of man, and he accepted all as a blessing.

Yes, there are people who do not want to know Jesus, who deny he existed, and work to prevent others from knowing Jesus. They vehemently dispute and question the rationale and validity of faith in Jesus and God. They are loud and boisterous and sometimes angry, while others are condescending and rude. They dismiss my argument for Jesus altogether. They shout me down and ridicule me when I profess to believe, demanding a sign from heaven, much in the same way as was done to Jesus and his followers in their day (Matthew 16:1-4).

Jesus asked people—nay, commanded people—to love God and to love one another. He preached the restoration of the Kingdom of God, the "New Jerusalem": a place of peace and prosperity, of equality and goodwill, without jealousy or envy, without war, only love (Mark 12:29-34). How could anyone want to deny Jesus Christ, the messenger of equality, justice, and love for the world?

Jesus knew and understood that the human heart is fickle and memories are short, as are the residual effects of promises made, and miracles seen last only so long. And he knew ultimately he would have to carry the weight of the sins of the world upon his shoulders, willingly, suffering a violent death at the hands of men in order to bring about the New Jerusalem on earth and in heaven.

What Jesus endured on the last day of his life would have killed me to experience. When I think about the brutality he suffered, I am sickened to my core. The skin and muscle of his back were bruised and shredded from the beating and whipping he endured from the Roman soldiers. I shudder when I think of the blinding pain from the crown of thorns stabbing into his skull while blood dripped into his eyes, stinging and blurring his vision. The woven fibers from his garments, donned for the laborious trudge up to Golgotha, must have felt like a hundred knife cuts as the weight of the cross pressed into his back. At the end of his journey, scabs and fabric tore from his body as his garment was pulled from his body. Hopefully by then he was so delirious with pain that when he was dropped down onto the wooden beams of the cross, he did not feel his hands and feet being nailed to the cross to hold him in place for the crucifixion.

The irony of the carpenter's son being nailed to a wooden cross is not lost on me.

The rugged cross was raised and dropped into a hole in the ground and gravity pulled Jesus' body forward, leaning down towards the ground. He had difficulty breathing. When he could no longer keep death from taking him, Jesus cried out in a loud voice,

"Into your hands I commend my spirit," and he exhaled his last breath (Luke 23:46).

The Lamb of God, a man without sin, became a sacrifice for me and for all, taking my sin and the sins of the world with him to the cross. His mother and most beloved friends watched as his agony consumed his life and the curse of sin died with him.

Sin died on the cross and love was resurrected on the third day. Jesus rose from the dead as he promised he would, and through the eyewitness accounts of Mary Magdalene and others, the tomb that Jesus was buried in was found empty and Jesus was alive (John 20:1-23)!

Yes, this is a very unbelievable story! It is natural that there are doubters, then and now. Thomas, one of Jesus' closest friends, refused to believe Jesus was alive, ghost or in the flesh, until he put his finger in the nail holes and touched Jesus' side where the lance pierced him. Jesus shared multiple meals with his followers post-resurrection; he revealed himself "in the breaking of the bread." Jesus' friends watched as he ate and drank real food and real drink (John 20:24-21:25). I know for the unbeliever it sounds like a fantastic work of fiction, but for me, it is true.

I believe Jesus is the Son of God, my savior, my redeemer, my friend, present now and for all time. He is not a figment of my imagination. He is not "an idea." I know what Jesus looks like. All I need to do is close my eyes and Jesus is with me. I can see him, I can hear his voice, I can feel his calming presence. He smiles and laughs with me, and he cries with me, too. Sometimes we just sit together and share a beautiful moment. For now, this is my New Jerusalem, a place of peace and prosperity, of equality and goodwill, without jealousy or envy, without war, only love.

Oh, yes, Jesus has me. For now, and for eternity.

Perspective

"My soul, be at rest in God alone, from whom comes my hope. God alone is my rock and my salvation, my secure height; I shall not fall. My safety and glory are with God, my strong rock of refuge. Trust God at all times, my people! Pour out your hearts to God our refuge!" Psalm 62:6-9

Have you ever wondered what it would be like to fly? I have! I have flown in my dreams, and it is exhilarating, scary, and fun, and it always leaves me wanting more! I never want to come down, but as dreams go, I always come back to earth and wake up to reality.

I would love to be able to see the world from God's perspective, from every angle, to know what is actually happening in and around me when activities in my life are challenging or seem out of control. On the other hand, if I saw everything from God's perspective I might not like what I see, and it would no doubt be too much for me to handle. He is, after all, God, and I am only an earth-bound, gravity-limited human.

With the constant feed of opinions, arguments, points of view, and information streaming from social media, the internet, texting, and email, I think this gives me some idea of what God sees and hears around the clock and around the world every day from his children here on Earth. The activity and noise must be deafening! I am just one person, so I can only imagine what it would be like multiplied by billions of people. And the amount of patience he must have! Oh my goodness! It gives new meaning to "the patience of Job!" And forgiveness? Even with the very minimal amount of media I use for information, I easily become irritable, overstimulated, and set on edge, waiting for the next headline drama to shock, anger, or scare me. Honestly, is every news story "Breaking News"?!

Nevertheless, technology is here to stay, and it has proven to be a very useful tool in keeping things real for me. When things turn upside down and tensions rise, my emotions can override logic and I lose perspective. And when loved ones are involved, my objectivity flies out the window and situations become larger than they are in reality. With the internet I am able to research and gather information instantly that helps me manage expectations, find solutions, and make plans for resolution and, in many cases, reconcile differences of opinion. Everything seems to demand immediate attention and there is no room for error. At these times, the internet has proven to be an invaluable tool!

My husband reminds me that attitude is altitude, and I need to fly above the trees to gain a better perspective. Instead of looking at things directly in front of me, I need to "zoom in and zoom out" to a Google Earth vantage point so that I can remain calm while taking things in, either at a granular level or expanded out to a world view.

When I was a young girl, I loved climbing trees. I loved the exertion of the climb as I moved from branch to branch, higher and higher towards the sky, placing my foot carefully while testing each limb for sturdiness, finding the right ones to place my full weight on. As I pulled myself to the top of the tree, squirrels dropped from limb to limb and birds flew away as I intruded on their sacred space. From twenty to thirty feet above the ground, I could see far and wide as I hid in plain sight from everyone down below. I felt triumphant as my strong arms and legs carried me to the very top of the tree. I felt completely in control of the moment.

Everything appeared very ordered and manageable from high above, and although it was quiet up there, voices and machinery and road noise and barking dogs were amplified by wind and space, and I could hear far-off conversations that carried on the summer breeze so clearly that I could have sworn the people were speaking from directly below.

I had clarity and vision from my perch on high, and it felt good.

Sitting there swaying in the wind, I learned that when I view things from a distance, I gain a new and different perspective. My concentration and focus are heightened (no pun intended) and my uninterrupted thoughts, full of questions and answers, are amplified. Problems and difficulties that once seemed so big are suddenly smaller and more manageable. The distance made me feel calm despite life and its continuous tumult and strife.

Now as a grown woman, my days of climbing trees are well behind me. I have had to learn other ways to keep my perspective fresh and relevant, and prayer is number one. Like climbing a tree, when I escape in prayer, I feel stronger in my mind, body, and spirit. Often, Jesus "would withdraw to deserted places to pray" (Luke 5:16), I think for the same reason. Prayer calms me down and secures my steps. I trust God as I move from one situation to the next, testing the sturdiness of my faith from a clear vantage point and looking at a situation from different perspectives. Prayer helps me "let go and let God" guide my climb and direct my steps, so that I am able to rise and meet the challenges of each new day. With God's help, I am able to change my perspective from a singular, limited position so that more than one "right answer" can be found. The power of prayer is not limited by my nearsightedness; God's truth brings solutions into focus, and I see with clear vision a way forward.

Even though I pray every day, it is difficult to keep my perspective in difficult situations, especially as a mom. When my daughter calls from 1,500 miles away, crying and not making much sense other than to say, "Mom...I need help," my emotions and worry as a mother kick in and it takes me a second to remember to stop, think, and remind myself to "fly above the trees" so that I get this right! I ask her to slow down and speak clearly about her problem, and once things are explained more calmly, I am better able to ask the right questions in order to give good advice and plan a course for possible solutions. It is not easy, but once I am calm, I am much more able to adjust my "altitude" and look at things more objectively.

Another area of opportunity for gaining perspective–literally–is overcoming my fear of bridges. My phobia has caused me to have terrible panic attacks on bridges, as both passenger and driver. It is a horrible and helpless feeling that started in my late twenties and still continues to this day. I don't know why, but I feel like I am going to drive right off the end or over the edge of the bridge and die. My heart pounds, I feel lightheaded, and sometimes I lose strength in my hands and feet as my panic causes my extremities to turn to lead, the way my legs feel after a long-distance run. One time, I was so overcome with panic that, once I was safely across the bridge, I let someone else drive the rest of the trip. The ordeal scared me and everyone in the car. It was very upsetting. I vowed then to get a handle of my fear!

So it seems absurd to use my husband's suggestion to go up thirty thousand feet–figuratively–to find a way to overcome my fear of bridges (and of heights, and mountain precipices, and airplanes), but that is exactly what I did!

When I travel, Step One is praying to God for safety and travel mercies. I love the words from the song, "Jesus, take the wheel" by Carrie Underwood because they have been my prayer for a long time! In Step Two I imagine coming to a bridge, and I breathe deeply and evenly (like Lamaze breathing) and send fresh oxygen to my brain and extremities. I practice this so that when I come upon a real bridge at any time, I can remain focused on driving (or riding) across it, not looking over the edge the entire time believing I'm going over. Step Three is to zoom way out in my mind and visualize myself traveling along the road and coming upon a scary bridge and driving safely across. I tell myself that thousands and thousands of travelers cross bridges every day, safely and without incident, and I can, too!

I know that when I am surprised by the unexpected, I panic, so planning my route ahead of time helps me prepare for what is to come, and I feel more in control of what I can and cannot do. It is easiest on familiar roads in familiar places, but the reality is if I am going to travel by car there will be bridges to cross and challenges to overcome. Therefore, I use internet maps to take a look at my route and I zoom in and out to see what I may encounter. And as a backup, I always have my United States Atlas in my car just in case GPS doesn't work!

Of course, no plan is failsafe, which I learned all too well on a trip to New Mexico with my daughters. We were heading back to Denver from Taos when my oldest informed me there was a detour on our route. I did not take this information well and I became highly agitated. I had been up since six a.m. that morning due to a trip to the emergency room, and it was well past lunchtime when the three of us got on our way. I was hungry and shaky, and my calm reserves were gone. I had planned the trip ahead of time, city to city, and this detour was hitting me all wrong! Alarm bells were going off in my ears and the ringing was deafening. I felt like I could pass out. I was definitely losing control. I burst out in short phrases to Meghan, "Get your phone! Google the road! Find the road, find the road! Is there a gorge? Look for the gorge…is there a bridge? Is there a gorge and a bridge?!"

A detour right at that moment was putting me over the edge.

I told the girls if I had to drive over the "big gorge bridge," we would die. My daughters looked at each other as if I had lost my mind and then looked at me and told me I was overreacting. Wrong thing to say! They knew I panicked on bridges! How could they say that? My whole reason for mapping out our route was to stay in control and avoid panic! I had never been to the southwest part of the country before, so everything was new and unfamiliar. Of course, we would be going across mountains and rivers; it was the Rocky Mountains for crying out loud! That is why I made sure there were no surprises!

So Meghan graciously offered to do the driving; she obviously did not understand I would neither drive nor ride into the unknown. I told her, "No way in h---!" (which is about where I felt I was at that moment).

Sitting in the rental car (not my own) at the red light in Taos (traffic everywhere) with my girls waiting for the blood to return to my face, all I could think of was that bridge and how it was ruining everything! I had researched ahead of time to create an easy, peaceful ride through the Rockies and located the one and only bridge in the vicinity of our travels that I would not, could not cross: the Rio Grande Gorge Bridge, nicknamed "High Bridge "and standing roughly six hundred feet above the Rio Grande–the tenth-highest bridge in the United States. My plans had been perfect! The thought of crossing it made my ears ring, made my stomach queasy, my face tingly, and my palms sweaty and weak. I knew I was panicking and not in control of my emotions. I had lost all perspective and I wanted to go home! The only thing I knew at that moment was that we were to avoid the bridge no matter what. No if, ands, or buts about it. I would crawl on my hands and knees and swim across the river before I would drive or ride across that bridge.

I prayed to God urgently, rushed and panicked, that he please help me find a new route before the light turned green. Praying helped my sense of control return and I began to calm down. God was with me. This is my faith. My vision widened and I held the steering wheel a little less fiercely. As I prayed, God gave me a fresh perspective, a new way of looking at my situation. With my panic abating I realized that even if the detour took me to the Rio Grande Gorge Bridge, I need only stop, turn the car around, and take a different route back to Denver, even if it was hundreds of miles out of the way!

And then after all of that unnecessary drama, Meghan told me the detour did not include crossing the Gorge Bridge! Hallelujah! (Thank you, cell phones and internet!) I cannot describe my relief, other than to say I felt lightheaded and giddy. For an instant I was young again, feeling triumphant at the top of the tree, back in control of the moment, swaying in the breeze, vulnerable yet secure, with faith and trust in my sturdy branch, supporting my weight, keeping me from falling to the ground.

My only disappointment in myself that day is I wish I had prayed first when I felt the panic rushing in. I could have pulled into a parking lot and taken the time needed to gain my perspective without all of the anxiety crashing through my body. Not a good look for my daughters to see, either; they were right, I was overreacting! I just needed God and a fresh perspective!

It is cliché but true: the road of life has many detours that I cannot plan for, try as I may. But by placing my trust in God I have learned to stay calm–most of the time–and to relax–most of the time–in the midst of the impossible. It is a saving grace that Jesus is always present and ready to assist me. Just like a flight attendant instructs parents when flying with children to save the child before themselves, Jesus always puts my oxygen mask on me first before he puts on his own.

I am still living into each situation, but now I have the wisdom of experience and better timing and preparation. My emotions play out in real time–I can't help it–but from a higher vantage point, I see that Jesus takes the wheel, secures my way, and calms my fears, and my attitude is changed by God's good perspective.

Surrender 1

"Your will be done" Jesus, in teaching his disciples the Lord's Prayer
Lord, my heart is not proud;
Nor are my eyes haughty;
I do not busy myself with great matters
with things too sublime for me.

Rather, I have stilled my soul,
Hushed it like a weaned child.
Like a weaned child on its mother's lap,
so is my soul within me.

Israel, hope in the LORD,
now and forever.
Psalm 131:1-3

Not my will, Lord, but yours be done.
Easy words to say but not easy words to live by.
It has taken my entire lifetime to understand how beautiful life can be when I surrender my will to God. It has also taken my entire lifetime to actually accept my understanding of what surrender requires. I am proud, and it is not easy to accept my limitations and put into practice relinquishing control and surrendering all to God.

When a child climbs into her mother's lap, there is something so gentle and innocent that occurs; it is sweet surrender. The child is not giving up or giving in, struggling against her mother. She is surrendering to the love and comfort that her mother provides. The child retains her will and trusts that her mother's will is to give her love in that moment of surrender!

This is how I wish to trust and surrender to God, like a child. But unlike the child, I cannot see or touch God, I cannot climb up into his lap, but I believe that come what may–good or bad–God is holding me securely because he loves me, and his will is being done in every moment of my surrender. It is not good for me to hold out and manage my problems in my rushed, immediate, and clumsy timing. I need to have blind faith and live in surrender of my will so that his will becomes my will. Then when I place my broken "stuff" in God's lap, I trust he will take care of it in his perfect will and his perfect timing.

"I surrender it all to You to be disposed of according to Your will. Give me only Your love and Your grace; with these I will be rich enough and will desire nothing more" (St. Ignatius of Loyola).

Through trial and error, I have learned when and how to surrender. If I wait too long, my failure is my witness. When the truth of a situation is clear and I need help, that is the time to allow the One who knows all, sees all, and can do all to rescue me. When my "Battery Low" alert comes on my computer, if I ignore it and do not plug it in, I risk losing everything that I have not saved. Panic ensues, and haste is the mode of response! I have to stop and plug my computer into its power source. The same thing applies with surrender! If I see the warning signs in my life and I do not stop and ask for God's help—If I do not stop and surrender to my limitations—I could lose everything I have been working on. I must accept when I cannot go it alone anymore and need to plug back into God, the power source of love and living.

The act of surrender has been painful, no two ways about it! It is terribly difficult for me to surrender when I see no concrete or well-defined solution, "no end in sight," and the light of hope is dim.

My deliberate act of surrender is extremely difficult in the midst of chaos and strife. I pray to God for help, not knowing where else to turn, looking to my Lord Jesus for wisdom. I surrender, yet still I can't help myself: I interfere, interjecting and imposing my control instead of easing out of the way. I am shortsighted and stubborn, relying solely on myself, wanting to get all the credit and pat myself on the back. Instead of digging in and finding only darkness, I should allow God to help me dig out and find light! Denying love, power, and aid in my life has been foolish, and when I have faltered and failed all I have to show for my efforts is a handful of dust and ashes.

Surrender is not about giving up or giving in; it is about *giving to:* giving to God and relinquishing my control—over a person, over a situation, over my ego—and living in expectation and acceptance that all things now and forever are a result of God's will. My surrender requires me to believe that all things happening in my life, once surrendered to God's care, are God's will. My life becomes my surrender.

Admittedly, it is a whole lot easier and less troublesome to surrender when I see a way clearly, when things are going my way, when I am "living large and in charge"; then it's easy to say, "Okay, Lord, I've gotten us this far, now you take the ball and run with it!" God is not my sidekick! I should not be so arrogant and absurd as to treat him so!

Surrender is tough. Denying this only prolongs the inevitable. I can choose frustration and fear over contentment and confidence. In the light of day, life goes on and I keep functioning, but in the night, the truth keeps me awake and I lie with my knees pulled up to my chest, hugging myself close in the loneliness of self-sufficiency. The dark is full of shadows, and I hide and cover my head with my blanket to avoid looking at the monster of unresolved issues lurking at the door. I hold out as long as I can, but I know I cannot face the dark on my own forever, and I relent, I weaken and soften, and I give my will to God and surrender.

Like a small child, I close my eyes and pray, pleading to Jesus in a plaintive whisper for all the badness to stop, for my problems to be solved, and for safety and security to return.

I plead in the night to be saved from things beyond my control.

And in my vulnerability, I receive his sure help, guidance, and protection; humility melts my pride, and I am free to receive his will, ready for his grace. I relinquish my control, turning over my life to God yet again, and only then am I able to come out from under the covers and into the light of faith, hope, and love shining in the darkness.

I surrender. Amen, amen, amen...I surrender all and I put my hope and trust in God.

Grace

"Merciful and gracious is the Lord, slow to anger, abounding in kindness" Psalm 103:8

I am a sinner.

I have done wrong in my life.

I have tried to hide from my sin, but it follows me wherever I go.

Over and over again I make excuses and justifications, and fool myself into believing that I am on the right side of truth and that everything is fine.

Even so, my conscience is relentless and deep down, I still know I have done wrong.

My sins weigh heavily on my entire being.

I know when I have sinned, and this knowledge gnaws at my bones, eats away at my peace, panics me to wakefulness in the night, makes me angry and bitter and shallow.

Rather than look at my sins and examine their consequences, I avert my eyes and refuse to see the damage my sins may have caused.

I withdraw and burrow away in shame.

But the truth always bubbles to the surface, and it cannot be denied.

I need to make amends, offer apologies, but this is a huge risk.

Whom can I trust?

Who will accept me in my nakedness?

Who will gently pull me out of the weeds and return me to the garden?

Who will forgive me?

I am a sinner.

Yes, I acknowledge I am a sinner, but by the grace of God I know I have been redeemed and saved from my sins. Over and over again, since my first scolding as a child when I was made aware of the difference between right and wrong, good and bad, I have been shaped and reshaped by my sin, and through the corrective guidance of others and my own acts of contrition I have remained on the right path for a joyful life.

My sins are both simple and complex, and God knows them all. I do not like it when I sin, and I do not like the way I feel when I know I have done wrong. I feel bad and out of sync with my life, especially if the rift is between myself and someone I know—or worse, someone I love. It does not sit well with me; it nags at me, bringing bile and stomach acid up into my mouth and causing my throat to constrict with raw emotion every time I think about the unresolved complaint. I need to feel right and whole in my relationships, not bitter and angry and resentful.

I need to be humble. I need to let go of grudges. I need to stop excusing myself and lying to myself and instead confess to God, but I resist because I know my confession will require a reconciling action on my part, and my pride is too strong, creating more conflicted feelings in me, and I continue to sin.

I am a sinner, but God is patient and His love is ever-present in my life, and his forgiveness is available anytime and anywhere.

My faith instructs me that by the grace of God I am saved, and I honestly believe this with my whole heart. From the day of my birth until the day that I die, no matter what I do, "there is nothing that can separate [me] from the love of God" (Romans 8:38). I know this to be true. God knows me, God loves me, and God has forgiven me yesterday, today, and tomorrow.

Why then do I continue to sin? God knows my heart, a heart that desires goodness and peace and love, free of immorality and hate. A heart that desires friendship with all people, free of jealousy and envy and lust. A heart that desires honesty, not deceit. A heart that desires a holy relationship with Jesus, open and honest and free, for he knows all and sees all, and he has placed these desires on my heart so that I may live a life that improves the world, not adds to its ruin.

But I am human, and it is hard to hold back on desire, with my pleasure, whims, and ego ever-present and central in every aspect of my life. My self-centeredness has created countless opportunities for sin to slither into my life and lead me into trouble. My desire for control and my willfulness have been driving forces over choices and decisions I have made, but thankfully—yes, thankfully—my unhappiness with the end results has made living my extravagant—prodigal—lifestyle embarrassing and shameful and wanting change.

I can no longer dismiss my bad behavior with a wink and a nod, writing feel-good checks to charitable causes, or blaming my peers for constantly raising the prosperity bar. I am responsible for my actions and inactions, and no disrespect to Flip Wilson, but "the devil made me do it" is an excuse that pushes the freedom of grace to the side, creating a wide space for darkness and loneliness to overtake me. Where joy and abundance of life in Jesus should be found, sin and joylessness prevail.

I have done things that I am accountable for. I have said things that only I can take back. I have bent rules and only I see the real results of a bad plan. I have caused my own misery and lack of fulfillment. I am responsible for me.

During my most wretched, sinful times, my wayward heart longed for guidance and mercy. Brought to my knees, I raised my eyes toward heaven, searching for God in the silence, baring my soul, asking for answers, asking for help, pleading for forgiveness and trusting him to deliver me from the pain and anguish of my guilt.

God's grace is never-ending, and each day I turn to God and in prayer and confess my sins of imperfection, and in doing so I am renewed in my spirit and purpose, and for a short while I am made pure and holy, resting comfortably in the arms of Jesus, my Savior.

God's grace is a perpetual gift that I humbly receive and abide in each day and through my surrender of will. By God's grace, I have known love and joy in the good times and the not-so-good times of my life.

I am a sinner, but I am no longer ashamed, nor am I afraid to say this about myself. It is my human condition. I alone cannot free myself from it, but I acknowledge it, and day by day I strive to live my life true to the commandments, true to my baptismal call, knowing that at any moment of the day or night I may find myself in the thick of it, trying to walk a fine line between right and wrong, good and evil.

At a glance, the Ten Commandments look like a list of dos and don'ts for people from another time and place, when in actuality, in God's wisdom, they were given to Moses to bring to me and all people for all times.

In prayer, I thank you, Lord God, for the Ten Commandments. They have been my aide in examining my behavior and they have guided my conscious decisions. They have been a perfect instruction for my parents and teachers and business leaders in guiding me in your ways, choosing right and wrong behavior from my childhood to adulthood, as daughter, student, and employee.

The commandments have been a tangible guidance to grace for me.

Exodus, Chapter 20

Then God delivered all these commandments:

"I, the LORD, am your God, who brought you out of the land of Egypt, that place of slavery.

You shall not have other gods besides me.

You shall not carve idols for yourselves in the shape of anything in the sky above or on the earth below or in the waters beneath the earth;

you shall not bow down before them or worship them. For I, the LORD, your God, am a jealous God, inflicting punishment for their fathers' wickedness on the children of those who hate me, down to the third and fourth generation;

but bestowing mercy down to the thousandth generation, on the children of those who love me and keep my commandments.

You shall not take the name of the LORD, your God, in vain. For the LORD will not leave unpunished [anyone] who takes his name in vain.

Remember to keep holy the sabbath day.

Six days you may labor and do all your work, but the seventh day is a sabbath of the LORD, your God. No work may be done then either by you, or your son or your daughter, or your male or female slave, or your beast, or by the alien who lives with you.

In six days the LORDmade the heavens and the earth, the sea and all that is in them; but on the seventh day he rested. That is why the LORD has blessed the sabbath day and made it holy.

Honor your father and your mother, that you may have a long life in the land which the LORD, your God, is giving you.

You shall not kill.

You shall not commit adultery.

You shall not steal.

You shall not bear false witness against your neighbor.

You shall not covet your neighbor's house. You shall not covet your neighbor's wife, nor his male or female slave, nor his ox or ass, nor anything that belongs to [your neighbor]." Exodus 20:1-17

Looking over this list and rereading each commandment, I am reminded that I have sinned many, many times, but by God's grace, along with his abundant love and presence in my life, I know I am forgiven and am released from the bonds of guilt and shame that my sins once produced in me.

"Let the one among you who is without sin be the first to throw a stone at her."

Then Jesus straightened up and said to her, "Woman, where are they? Has no one condemned you?"

She replied, "No one, sir."

Then Jesus said, "Neither do I condemn you. Go, [and] from now on do not sin anymore." (John 8:7, 10-11)

Before Jesus challenged the vengeful crowd, he knew their hearts, and by his grace the people in crowd and the woman were saved that day; and he knows my answer, too, that when each time I reach for the stones of self-righteousness, judgment, and countless other sins, by his grace of self-examination I drop the stone and walk away. Praise God for the pause in my anger and indignation before I strike a blow with words or bad deeds against my sister or brother that have consequences for my soul.

Admittedly, I am ashamed by my easy temptation to sin, but even in this moment I feel the grace of God rise up and surround me as my admission to sin frees me to receive God's absolution and his command to sin no more.

I acknowledge my constant temptation to sin, and I repel it, claiming the tablets of God as my armor and shield against sin and its power of corruption over my soul.

I confess I am not perfect, and I am grateful that by the grace of God and the sacrifice of Jesus Christ, the one and only perfect human being ever to walk the earth, I am not expected to be perfect. Jesus' love was so great for me, a sinner, that he suffered and died on the cross so that nothing would keep me from living eternally with him in heaven.

Through my darkest days, God's love sustains me, and his grace carries me through.

By his grace I try to live each day as a hopeful, joyful servant. I return to him in prayer at the beginning, middle and end of the day, acknowledging my sins and receiving his gift of grace with gratitude. And so blessed, I feel purified in heart to be a worthy servant of the Gospel of love.

Thank you, Jesus, thank you, yesterday, today, and tomorrow!

Serve

Paper Route

"There is dignity in all work." Senator Tim Scott, South Carolina

Times were changing fast at the beginning of the 1970s, and for girls like me that was exciting news! Although I was only ten years old, in my young life I had felt the sting of comments related to my gender, about not being strong enough to do "men's work," and it made me mad. I was not going to accept that as the final word. Opportunities were opening up for females to work in what were traditionally male-dominated jobs, and I was determined to prove myself equal to any boy!

Boys had always delivered the neighborhood newspaper, and up until I knew differently, I had never questioned why it was just boys. When I turned eleven, I found out girls were applying for paper routes, and I knew I wanted to win a route over a boy! Even if it meant being harassed and teased by everyone I knew, I told my mom I wanted to get a paper route! She was doubtful I could handle the responsibility of such a big job, but she told me to check with my brother, David, since he was experienced delivering newspapers up and down our street and he would know how to get started.

David was tired of delivering newspapers and he wanted to quit, and I was hopeful I would be assigned his route. I had helped him a few times delivering his newspapers, so it seemed like a good fit. Unfortunately, another boy was already in line to get David's route, so I had to wait for one to become available. I knew I could handle any assignment, even though I was a girl; I just wanted to be given the chance!

I cannot tell you how many times I heard, "Girls aren't strong enough, girls aren't fast enough, girls won't last." And the sideways looks I would get when I told people I wanted to be a papergirl (to this day I still receive looks of skepticism when I tell people I had a paper route)! Well, those comments and looks only fueled my determination more than ever to get a paper route so that I could prove them wrong and be the best papergirl ever.

I applied and waited, and after a few weeks, I got the call from the newspaper distribution manager. I think he was skeptical, too, because he made sure my parents were onboard before he would give me my delivery instructions; they had to assure him they would help me deliver and guarantee the circulation invoice would be paid. After that, nothing could stop me, and I began delivering the following Sunday! The route I received was about six blocks from my house, and it was a pretty big route for a girl of eleven, but I was up to the challenge, and I was determined to prove I was equal to any boy. I had fifty-nine daily papers and seventy-four Sunday papers to deliver, and for anyone who has never had a paper route, this was a big route…especially in a big city!

My favorite delivery day was Saturday because I could make record time, delivering all fifty-nine newspapers in less than an hour. The newspapers were pencil thin and I could carry all of them under my left arm while steering my bike with my right hand, and even if I hit a bump on the road, I did not lose my balance and fall off into the street. (That could have been a real problem on a windy day!)

The day I liked least was Sunday because what took me an hour to do on Saturday typically took me two hours on Sunday! The newspapers were about an inch and a half thick, and they weighed a lot. When the weather was bad my mom or dad helped me load my newspapers into the station wagon to drive me to my route, but most days I was able to pull my newspapers to my route in our red, wood-sided "Radio Flyer" wagon. It was hard work, but I have to say those were the days of fun and happiness for me!

I loved being a newspaper carrier. I felt grown up and free. My route was in a very safe neighborhood and not too far from home, but like so many paper carriers before me, I was initiated on my first day of delivery with a nasty bite on my ankle by a little chihuahua, a.k.a. "Ankle Biter." She bit me hard and I yelped, and if I had been afraid of dogs, this could have done me in on the very first day, "being a girl and all!" But it wasn't that bad, and the owner was very apologetic, and he promised it would never happen again, and it never did. Even still, I was always on the lookout when I delivered at that house…even after that family moved away!

I liked delivering newspapers, and it was fun when my buddy, my basset hound, Mickie, was with me. She was small and agile, and her short legs kept pace with mine. Like me, she loved the freedom to run fast, and as she ran beside me it was so amusing to watch her long ears flap wildly from side to side, and when she turned to look up at me it looked like she was smiling. I loved her companionship and she loved mine. We were quite a pair, and people always waved and laughed when they saw us coming and going, especially when Mickie rode in the wagon on the way home from our Sunday delivery.

When the weather was bad, especially during winter, Mickie stayed home, and my dad was my buddy. It was not often that I had dad all to myself, especially on weekends, and it made me feel special and important when he helped me. On Sundays we got up early waiting for the center of the newspaper, called "stuffers," to drop. It was really quiet and dark outside at four in the morning, especially in the winter. We could hear the delivery truck two blocks away, tossing bundles of stuffers to the ground at neighboring carriers' homes. The dead weight made a loud "thud!", breaking the silence and bringing me back fully awake.

As soon my stuffers dropped, Dad and I would bundle up, hurry out, and haul them back to the garage, hefting them onto the tailgate of the station wagon where we would quickly begin stuffing the advertisements into the rest of the newspapers. Once the papers were ready and loaded, Dad would drive me to my route and wait in the car while I went right to work delivering the newspapers.

I was careful to make sure they were kept clean and dry for my customers, as much as was possible. It was important that my customers knew I cared about them and their satisfaction. My extra care took extra time, but my customers appreciated the effort I took, and they told me so, saying this set me apart from the boys, who just threw the newspapers in the general vicinity of the front door!

I took great satisfaction in my work, and I strived to do my best.

There were so many personal rewards from being a newspaper carrier, and I loved the opportunity to serve the public in this way. In the year and a half that I had my route, I met lots of nice people who helped build up my self-confidence. When I collected payment, I was polite and courteous and always said thank you, and although a lot of them–like my mom and the dispatcher–were skeptical at first about a girl being capable of delivering newspapers, they soon began to warm up to me.

I could tell they liked me by their reciprocated smiles and relaxed manner. I looked forward to our conversations and I could tell many of them did, too. At an incredibly young age I was blessed to meet many people from different cultures, ethnicities, and walks of life. Every house and apartment was different, with unique smells and noise and home decor. No two were alike. That was neat, and the impression was indelible. I can still recall their smiling faces and the homes that they lived in.

I "owned" my newspaper business, and although at the time I did not know words or phrases like "customer service" and "integrity" and "conscientious," these values drove me to always do my best, and people appreciated the extra care, and they showed their appreciation when I collected their payment.

Collecting each week became routine, but one time stands out vividly from all the rest. It was July, and a lot of my customers were not home. I was frustrated and ready to go home but thought I would try one more house, and when I rang the bell, the man of the house swung open the door wildly and exclaimed, "My wife is having a baby! My wife is having a baby!" I was so startled and surprised; at eleven years old, I had not noticed his wife was pregnant! He was so out of his mind with excitement he fumbled around in his wallet and tossed a five-dollar bill at me for an eighty-cent collection (that was a lot of money then)! That new daddy laughed out loud and told me to keep the change! I tried to give it back, but he would not take it and then he turned and ran back into his house, leaving me on the front porch staring at a five-dollar bill.

I laughed all the way home, and the next week while I was out collecting, I tried to give the money back to him, but he would not take it. He told me he had forgotten all about it, and he was just so happy and proud of his new baby boy.

And then Christmas time came, and it was like every customer was having a baby! I did not know about Christmas tips, and I was overjoyed by the generosity and extra tipping from my customers! But more than the money, it was their spirit of giving that meant so much; people were so kind and thankful for my personal touch! I still have a hand-made felt ornament in the shape of a Christmas tree made by one of my senior customers. She told me she made the ornament especially for me. Later that day when I was putting the ornament on my family's Christmas tree, I discovered two one-dollar bills tucked into the back of it. Her thoughtfulness really touched my heart.

After that Christmas I realized the relationships and friendships I was forming with my customers were very important to me. I was gaining confidence as well as my own identity. At eleven years old, I was appreciated for my good work. I had a desire in my heart to do good, to be my best, and to be kind and bring joy to others. Over time I noticed that not all of my customers lived in houses with big families; some were widows and single people who needed human contact and love. I brought a familial connection to these lovely people, and it made me feel right and well.

"Do nothing out of selfishness or out of vainglory; rather, humbly regard others as more important than yourselves, each looking out not for his own interests, but [also] everyone for those of others" (Philippians 2: 3-4).

Before I started my newspaper business venture, I had no idea how much my young life would be enriched by it. Each day I fulfilled my responsibility, and I did it well. I was not too prideful to accept help from others, and I learned I could trust my mom and dad when I needed their help. At a time when jobs traditionally held by boys and men were opening up to girls, I took the chance to step outside the box, and despite all the skeptics, I proved that hard work and dedication along with the heart of a humble servant can bring success and dignity to work.

Teaching

"Everything that he undertook, for the service of the house of God or for the law and the commandments, was to do the will of his God. He did this wholeheartedly, and he prospered." 2 Chronicles 31:21

I loved teaching religious education at my parish, especially fifth graders! Their sweet, innocent, and enthusiastic responses to learning gave me hopeful optimism for their futures, and their positive energy flowed through our class time. It warmed my heart to welcome the children each week to class, knowing we would be learning about Jesus together. Although at times I am sure it was awkward having Mom for a teacher, I loved having my daughters in my class when they were each in fifth grade. They were helpful to me before, during, and after class and this meant a lot to me! We had a good time together, and to this day we still reminisce about things we enjoyed doing together in class.

The ten- and eleven-year-old boys and girls were the perfect age for being creative and thinking outside the box, and since they arrived for class right after their regular school day ended, it was up to me to grab and hold their attention. So I designed a journaling project that would settle them down in their seats and engage their imaginations and creativity.

After our introductions during the first class, the children put together their journal booklets, using colored construction paper folded in half for the outer cover, with plain white paper inserted in the center for writing their journal entries. The first question I gave them to journal about was intended to be easy and help them become familiar with the journaling activity.

The first question was personal, it was relatable, and it was relevant. I knew they all could answer it and there were no wrong answers, so it was a pretty safe bet they would all answer correctly!

The question was:

"What do you want to be when you grow up?"

Some students, including my daughters, knew right away what they wanted to be when they grew up and they wrote down their answers very quickly. Some of the kids puzzled over the question. They had never thought about it before. I had to ask a few probing questions about what they liked, what their interests were, what their parents and relatives did for a living, what their friends said they were good at doing, what they thought they were good at doing; but soon enough the light went on and they were joining in the fun, writing down their answers, too.

The answer I remember most was from a boy who knew exactly what he wanted to be when he grew up, but he was too shy to write about it, draw it on his cover, or say it out loud. He blushed and avoided answering when I would ask him about his progress, so I did not press him, but by the third class, after hearing all the different answers from his classmates, he felt safe enough to tell the class he wanted to forge steel swords when he grew up! What a fantastical, creative mind! I was floored by his answer! (Every time the commercial for the TV show *Forged in Fire* airs, I wonder if he is one of the contestants. Or even better, the creator of the show! Who would've thought it? With God, all things *are* possible!)

This was one job no one in class had ever thought of! After he shared his dream of forging steel swords, everyone encouraged him to realize his dream. Nobody made fun of him or tore down his dream, and this was very heart-warming.

Once the ice was broken and the kids were open to sharing, the class time flew by! The Holy Spirit was active in our class and the lessons brought forth many special insights from the students. Their views on religion, faith, God, Jesus and his family, school and friends, current events, the environment, sacraments, service, and so much more demonstrated they were wise beyond their years! Each class discussion broke down the complexities of faith and religion and revealed how God was calling each of them to use their spiritual gifts to make a difference in the world.

With each passing week the lessons taught the children how to be like Jesus, that we are all called to be kind, generous, thoughtful, and loving.

"For to this you have been called, because Christ also suffered for you, leaving you an example that you should follow in his footsteps" (1 Peter 2:21).

On All Saints Day the students chose a saint who is the patron of what they wanted to be when they grew up. Some chose St. Sebastian for Olympic athletes, St. Cecelia for rock stars, St. Luke for artists, and St. Blaise for veterinarians. After their research, the children made a presentation to the class about their saint's life, character, integrity, their heroic sacrifices, and the miracles attributed to the saint.

The children learned that, like them, saints were human, not mythical, fictitious, larger-than-life characters. Saints were ordinary people with ordinary jobs, homes, and families, people who like us might have doubted God, sinned, and lacked faith, but in the end triumphed in the name of the Lord God. For many students it was the first time they understood that saints were once living people with real lives who answered God's call to live courageously, who had visions from God that could not be refuted, and who served others where they could, suffering death for the betterment of others. It seemed far-fetched to them, but we are all saints in the making!

In 2018, years after I stopped teaching religious education, I watched with rapt attention the news coverage of the extraordinary dive rescue of twelve Thai soccer players and their coach who had been lost in a flooded cave. I thought, "This would be a story about saintly character that I would tell and retell over and over to my students to make the point that saints are real people living into sainthood!"

As I watched the drama unfold, I was reminded of the lesson on saints; I felt deep empathy for the families, realizing the boys were not much older than my sweet fifth-grade students. As the rescue mission unfolded, I sensed how much risk was involved and how impossible it appeared that the boys and their coach could be rescued before starvation or more flooding took their lives. Although a successful rescue was uncertain and the job was dangerous for all, the courageous divers were undeterred, and they suited up to wade in and swim through the dark waters in an effort to save the boys and their coach from the caves. They were already heroes in my eyes.

The route through the caves was perilous, but after a time the divers found the team and coach lying together in a space that was completely devoid of light and food, and after nine days they were still alive! The celebration was short, however, as there was much to be done to bring them out alive, and sadly one Thai Navy Seal, Petty Officer Saman Gunan, lost his life in the preliminary rescue work. He is a saint to me, giving his life to save those boys and their coach.

Master Sgt. Derek Anderson, who assisted with the rescue, declared, "God had His hand on this operation" (Van Veen).

God was with the rescuers through the perilous mission as they brought out one boy at a time through the murky waters. As was stated by "hero" diver Jim Warny, "It was a miracle everything worked" (Tobin).

Diver Chris Jewell was very fearful when he lost his grip on the guide rope, and I put forth that it was a miracle that he was able to recapture the rope in the dark, disorienting waters, and then continue on to bring the sedated boy he was carrying to safety.

At the end of the rescue mission, thank God, all twelve boys and their coach were rescued!

St. Brendan the Navigator, Patron Saint of Divers, thank you for guiding the rescuers' efforts to success!

This rescue anecdote is a beautiful lesson on the tremendous, courageous, self-sacrificing love found in humanity, all around the world. Although there were no life-saving heroics in my classroom, the students were heroes in my eyes when they helped each other and participated in class, when they brought snacks to share with one another, when they collected toiletries to donate to those in need. They made a difference in our learning and in growing our faith together.

I continue to pray that my former students seek the lofty ideals of their dreams, and I ask the saints to aid them in their pursuits. I hope my former students aspire to be like Jesus in their self-sacrificing actions. In all work and life situations, I pray the lessons learned in and out of our classroom will guide them to do the right thing and to say "yes" to challenges presented, great and small.

Dear Jesus, I pray that my former students know, love, and serve you with saintly yearnings, forged in Truth by the fire of your love. Amen.

Perpetual Work

"The Lord God then took the man and settled him in the garden of Eden, to cultivate and care for it." Genesis 2:15

It's hard to imagine life without work.

Some days I wistfully say I would like to try, but if I am honest, I like work, and as my mom has said, "You would be bored out of your mind doing nothing!"

From my earliest years I have kept myself busy with one type of work or another. There were small chores I would find around the house, and although they were sometimes a little more than a child of six could manage, they paid generously in praise and self-worth. Then bigger chores were given that paid an allowance and proved my worth to the family; and then when I was old enough, I worked a job that paid an hourly rate, and my conscientious diligence brought value to the customers and company. It was quite natural for me to look for a job, and my parents expected it, so I traded in lawn mowing and snow shoveling for a steady job and a paycheck.

I cannot deny it, praise for a job well done and watching the balance in my bank account increase with each deposited paycheck has given me great satisfaction and pride in the work I have performed and the rewards I have received.

"For I know well the plans I have in mind for you, says the Lord, plans for your welfare, not for woe! Plans to give you a future full of hope" (Jeremiah 29:11).

When Tim and I married, I left my banking job in New Jersey and moved to Cape Cod where Tim was stationed in the Air Force. We knew he would be discharged six weeks later, and we likely would not stay on the Cape, so I held off looking for work until our future was settled. Tim was hired by a company in Dayton, Ohio, and we were ecstatic to go back to a familiar place, one that Tim called home and where I had once had a home with my family!

Two weeks after Tim's discharge we were living in a hotel, provided to us through the company relocation package, while we looked for a permanent home.

Living in a hotel became very comfortable very quickly and I was in no hurry to change my situation. I loved sleeping in without an alarm jarring me awake. It was nice to eat my breakfast without gulping it down. And it was really nice not having to fight rush hour traffic. Contrary to my mom's warning, I was not bored out of my mind. It was the first time in my life that I was not in school or working, and it felt really good.

I enjoyed "the life of Riley," lounging by the pool, reading romance novels, and receiving maid service every day. As my brother David would say, I was "living large and in charge!"

But my husband was not at all amused, and soon he lost patience with me for not looking for a job, and rightfully so.

I remember the day he came home from work and told me he had enough of my laziness. I had been enjoying another day at the pool, wondering where he would take me for dinner that evening. He came into our hotel room, tired from working all day, and took one look at me in my bikini, and said,

"You need to get a job."

I tried to persuade him that I needed just a little more time, but he was right, it was time. He had been carrying all the weight working and providing for us, and I was reverting back to behaving like a teenager living with my parents.

I realized I might be free to do as I wished, but I wasn't contributing at all, and this made me feel guilty. I was almost twenty, with endless possibilities ahead of me. It was time to start fresh with my new husband and begin contributing to our life together. Like it or not, it was time for me to grow up!

And truthfully, my mom was right. I was getting bored, and something else was happening that I didn't recognize at the time: I was getting depressed. My life had just changed dramatically from living with my mom and dad my entire life to getting married and moving not once, but twice to places where I had no friends; I knew no one but Tim. I was withdrawing and getting much too comfortable with being alone during the day. It wasn't good for me.

God did not create me for sloth; he created me to tend this magnificent garden, tilling and planting and cultivating beauty in all the places I go.

I could find no good reason for lounging around the pool another day. I was young and healthy and capable. I needed to reengage in productive work and reconnect with people.

The vacation was over.

I went to work.

I found a job using my experience in banking, and over the years I enjoyed serving my customers and making friendships with my coworkers! There were promotions, raises, recognition, and awards for my work, but the highlight came when I was invited to sing at the corporate Christmas party. The experience was exhilarating, and from the comments I received from my coworkers, there was a deep need in them and their families to reclaim the true meaning of Christmas, Jesus' birth. I was surprised at how much I enjoyed sharing my love of Jesus through music, using my gifts and talents without the expectation of getting anything in return, all to God's glory.

It felt so good and right, and the feeling stayed with me long after the evening was over. I felt as though I had a new calling serving through music.

"If there is any encouragement in Christ, any solace in love, any participation in the Spirit, any compassion and mercy, complete my joy by being of the same mind, with the same love, united in heart, thinking one thing" (Philippians 2:1-2).

A few months after that special night, I received the thrilling news I was expecting a baby again, and when Meghan was born, I became a stay-at-home mom, the greatest work of my life. A year and a half later, Lauren was born, and my work at home doubled in joy and reward. After the girls were both in school full time I returned to work, but I chose a new career path in music ministry at my church and at the Catholic school in my town. It was fun using my talents–singing and playing my guitar–and sharing my knowledge of music and liturgy, honing my skills in teaching, organizing, and understanding scripture. I was blessed beyond words to become a peer to the devoted teachers and administrators and a beloved choir director to the students and church choir members. My love of Jesus and the desire to serve others became cemented in my soul during those years.

Overlapping this time in music ministry, I found part-time work in the Parks & Recreation Department in the city where I lived. I utilized my education from my university coursework to indulge in my green, "good-steward-of-the-earth" interests with people who were like-minded. It was a dream job. The work was so grand and altruistic and service oriented, and I worked with some of the best people I have ever known. Generous, loving, kind, and oh so good and compassionate to me and my family.

All to God's glory....

I refer to these years of my life as my "Camelot" years. I was so happy making music, and my work for the city was pure joy. I was growing through my work experience, my faith, and my talents, and I was receiving great recognition for my efforts. My daughters were excelling in their studies and extracurricular activities, and my husband was becoming extremely successful in his professional life. I felt like we were making a difference and making strides in our individual lives, as well as enriching our family experience.

More and more I realized I wanted to be a better person and to make a positive impact wherever I worked, in whatever capacity I could. I was excited for each new day and had big dreams! I was living the new and improved "life of Riley"!

And then, without any warning, the trajectory of my life changed dramatically when, just after my fiftieth birthday, my husband of thirty years was diagnosed with stage-four lung cancer. We were shocked and deeply saddened by this terrible diagnosis. In an instant our dreams and aspirations stopped. It was only by the grace of God and the love of family, friends, and coworkers that we continued to press on. Tim worked to the very last day, striving for perfection and fulfillment in performing his work at the highest level while squeezing out every bit of energy from his healthy cells. I continued to work in my many capacities, and the girls continued their work at school.

There was no time off for cancer. In fact, work gave each of us purpose for living each day. Tim worked valiantly, and he fought hard for his life, dying on his terms a year after his diagnosis, after days of "quality, not quantity."

Suddenly, work and job and career became an overwhelming, joyless burden to me. What had always brought me great satisfaction became exhausting, dismal, and unfulfilling. My jobs were like a heavy weight pressing down on me, and knowing they could not support us financially, I had to look for full-time work. It was stressful and exhausting for my girls, too. We missed Tim so much. It was a struggle to make decisions in the midst of change, and the uncertainty of our future without Tim exacerbated our sadness and grief.

I lost my zest for living. I did not want to work.

I had no energy, there was no pleasure in things that before were fun and amusing, and my ambition was replaced with a constant desire to quit. Earning money no longer felt like a reward for a job well done but a means to an end, for paying my bills. Work was a drudgery, and I did not want to go. I wanted to lie in bed and do nothing.

And then at one of my lowest points, looking vacantly at myself in the bathroom mirror, crying and asking God for the umpteenth time, "Why?" I heard Tim's chastising voice from long ago again say to me, "You need to get a job."

"They that hope in the Lord will renew their strength, they will soar as with eagles' wings. They will run and not grow weary, walk, and not grow faint" (Isaiah 40:31).

The same little girl who wielded a broom twice her size to clean her daddy's garage, who bought her first doll with her own "hard-earned money," and who became a business-girl at the age of eleven as a newspaper carrier was still a part of me, and she looked back at me and told me it was time to put my big-girl pants on and start working on the next phase of her and her daughter's lives.

"And Jesus said to his disciples, 'Whoever wishes to come after me must deny himself, take up his cross, and follow me" (Matthew 16:24).

I was alone and afraid, and I prayed constantly for the right job to come to me. I relied on my friends to send me information about job opportunities, and I applied for a dozen or so jobs, receiving a number of good interviews, but nothing fit.

I was beginning to lose hope and becoming very disheartened when a choir member who worked for the Catholic hospital in the area told me about a Department Coordinator job in the chaplain's office of Spiritual Care Services. This made me anxious, knowing that the chaplain's work was to give spiritual aid and comfort to people suffering and dying. The job was located in the same hospital Tim had just died in, but I felt I must try if I was to continue to move forward.

I applied for the job and received an interview and driving home from the interview, I knew I had found the perfect job! The next day the Director called me and offered it to me. I knew many prayers had been answered, and I was reminded that God is never far from me, and He will always take care of me and my daughters.

This new job blessed me in more ways than I can count. My work brought me an abundance of peace and I witnessed in the chaplains' work a love that was unique: trusting, selfless, holy. They treated me with gentleness and kindness and helped me find my way through the heartache of Tim's death. They showed me we are all bearers of God's love, shining his light and his love with those we meet. We helped one another divide the work, listened compassionately, provided kindness, cried with empathy, and served with gladness.

It is in church, in music ministry that I continue my work for the Lord with people who make my work enjoyable, rewarding and fulfilling. Providing music for worship constantly renews my life's purpose and gives me self-worth to withstand the down times of my life. I love working for the Lord, for the community, for all who are present.

All to God's glory....

No matter my age, from just starting out to retirement and beyond, by my very existence, there has been and will always be work that needs to be done. The encouragement from those who know and love me, who help me be the best I can be, has been a lifeline to success. Their support has made me feel worthy to serve in the ways God planned for me, from the very beginning of my life.

I have always been drawn to the service industry, whether employed or as a volunteer, and I have appreciated equally dollars and cents and hugs and kisses. Both have compensated me and expressed appreciation for my good work, and I have been so privileged to be called to holy service for the Lord.

Eden is in the here and now and I know I have been led to work its fertile soil, cultivating it with love and music for the restoration of paradise on earth. Giving from my heart and serving my family, friends, coworkers, and community to the benefit of all, I thank God and I praise Him for His blessings upon all of my good and holy work.

"May the favor of the Lord our God be ours. Prosper the work of our hands! Prosper the work of our hands!" (Psalm 90:17).

Chaplains

"Are they not all ministering spirits sent to serve, for the sake of those who are to inherit salvation?" Hebrews 1:14

Working in Spiritual Cares Services at Mount Carmel Health System (MCHS) in Columbus, Ohio, was a wonderful and rewarding experience. It was demanding, challenging...lonely at times...but oh so worthwhile. My job supported the chaplains in all of the administrative areas of the department to allow for them to focus their energies on pastoral care and it provided me an outlet to grow in ministry.

The chaplains were fun and quirky, and they worked well together supporting one another, always ready to meet the needs of the patients and their families, at all hours of the day and night. They were serious and compassionate, knowing that they may be the last person a patient spent time with before they closed their eyes for the final time. In consultation with families, the chaplains' compassion and prayerful care could bring about hope in the darkest times.

My first interaction with the chaplains at MCHS came before I worked for the hospital, when my husband, Tim, was diagnosed with stage-four lung cancer. The chaplain assigned to Tim's floor came by and sat unobtrusively with us for a while, and at the end of the visit he asked if we needed anything, ending his visit with a prayer for us. It was not so much what he said but how he treated us and respected our need for time; we were in shock, and it was difficult to comprehend that something was terribly wrong in Tim's body. Before he left, he promised he would return to check on us regularly, and he was true to his word.

His presence and conversation normalized the situation a bit and by the time he ended his visit, I felt better and less fearful for what was to come, and Tim felt better, too.

Many times over the twelve months, the chaplains visited Tim to chat and check on his spiritual and mental health and the chaplain priests brought communion. They all talked to Tim as a living person, knowing he would die but treating as if he were not dying on the day of their visit. They talked to Tim in the here and now, encouraging Tim to talk about whatever was on his mind, and it was nice to walk into the hospital room to the sound of Tim laughing at one of their funny stories. The chaplains prayed with Tim, consoled him, cried with him, and towards the end they just sat with him. Looking back, I know through these very special people, Jesus was visiting Tim.

Little did I know then that Tim's chaplains and I would soon become professional coworkers and friends.

After Tim died, I needed a full-time job to support my girls and me. I was working two part-time jobs, but they were not enough. One of my friends told me that the hospital was hiring, and I should take a look at the available jobs. I was so hopeful when I found the Spiritual Care Services job open and I applied immediately. Shortly thereafter I received a call from HR to schedule an interview (reminiscent of my Music Coordinator job from heaven)!

I was so happy to get the call. As strange as it was, it made me feel that some parts of my life were getting back to normal. I was starting my life over after thirty-one years of marriage, with a fresh beginning, from death into life.

The question that weighed heavily on my mind was whether I could handle the administrative position, separating my own grief from the calls that would come into the department for patient and family support–after just watching my husband die in a bed four floors directly above the desk I would work from. It seemed impossible given my sadness; my grieving had zapped every cell in my body and my energy reserves were depleted, but this was the time to trust God, and if the job were meant to be, things would fall into place and my energy would be restored.

But I knew that God was with me and he would be with me, giving me strength. I thought of the many chaplains that ministered to us over the preceding year, and I remembered the exemplary treatment from the very first chaplain that visited Tim and me, and I agreed to meet for the interview.

206

For the first half of the interview, I kept my answers professional and my emotions and personal story to myself, thinking that if the three supervisors interviewing me knew I had just lost my husband, they would think me too fragile to meet the demands of the department. I told them about my work history and qualifications, my faith and love of music, and at one point the conversation came round to the times when I have questioned God's presence in my life.

It was then that the CPE instructor asked me a question, and in her eyes, I saw such empathy that when I answered, my heart broke open and all of my stories tumbled out. I could no longer withhold my secrets. I shared that I had lost a baby, a stillborn little girl named Mary Lyn. I shared that my husband had just died in Palliative Care, four floors above where we were interviewing, and I told them my brother, David, was gravely ill and close to the end of his life.

I shared that I was grieving, that my daughters were grieving, but we were strong and faithful and moving forward in our lives.

And then I cried…in my job interview. I cried.

The Director of Spiritual Care Services retrieved a box of tissues and offered it to me.

I accepted her kindness. As I wiped the tears from my eyes and blew my nose, I felt certain my candor had blown my chance at the job.

But to my surprise, they did not judge me unworthy of the position because of my losses but deemed me wise and experienced, and they believed me worthy to take on the responsibilities of the work with my eyes wide open. I had allowed myself to be vulnerable and to my surprise I was offered the job.

By the end of the interview, I felt again like I had been ministered to by three compassionate angels. They touched my heart more than they will ever know.

The Lord "heals the broken hearted, binds up their wounds" (Psalm 147:3).

Working in Spiritual Care Services was an absolute gift from heaven. It was a holy place where I was blanketed in love and protected from despair. I worked alongside truly remarkable, God-centered ministers. Although my sadness and grief could not be taken away–as I had to live through it–the chaplains in so many beautiful ways helped me heal in body, mind, and spirit.

Slowly, good, happy days began to outnumber sad, bad days, and I knew I was getting better.

My losses and sorrow and the depth of my pain brought forth my own pastoral instincts, and there were times when I was able to minister to the chaplains. These were special times of grace.

From those times I earned the unofficial title, "The Chaplains' Chaplain," for which I feel deeply humbled and honored.

Putting into words how wonderful my time in Spiritual Care Services was is really difficult. It was the best answer to my prayers at the worst time of my life. It was the last place I could have imagined working and the exact place I was intended to work. I loved working there, I belonged there, and when I reflect back on my time there, I can sum up my feelings this way: safe, warm, cozy, abundant life-giving love.

"Blessed are the poor in spirit, for theirs is the kingdom of heaven. Blessed are they who mourn, for they will be comforted. Blessed are the meek, for they will inherit the land" (Matthew 5:3-5).

Working with the chaplains in Spiritual Care Services gave me strength to see beyond my current situation and face my future. My courage came from the courage I saw in the many patients and family members that I came into contact in the halls and elevators, chapels and cafeteria, parking lots and offices of the hospitals I worked in. I found my peace in the very place that the chaos and devastation of cancer reigned for just under a year in my family's life.

From my first encounter I had with the Spiritual Care Services Department as a frightened wife of a terminally ill patient until my last day as a professional woman departing an extraordinary workplace, God's love and compassion were ever present to me, in and through the work of the chaplains.

Spiritual Care Services was a gift of love to me that I will keep forever in my heart.

Thank you, dear chaplains, dear friends in God and Christ, dear, sweet angels of mercy, thank you for your love and your time and your compassionate conversations. And most of all, thank you for the laughter in the midst of so much sadness. You helped me thrive and find my joy in the valley as well as on the mountaintop. Blessed be!

𝒦𝒾𝓃𝒹𝓃𝑒𝓈𝓈

"The quality of being friendly, generous, and considerate." *Oxford Languages*

"All bitterness, fury, anger, shouting, and reviling must be removed from you, along with all malice. And be kind to one another, compassionate, forgiving one another as God has forgiven you in Christ." Ephesians 4:31-32

I am only human. I don't say this often, but when I do it's usually because I have come up short being friendly, generous, or considerate and have overreacted in a negative way towards someone. Sometimes people, for reasons only they know, can be intent on hurting me and my response is less than nice, and in my defense, I shout out to God and anyone else within earshot, "I'm only human!"

I know it is just an excuse, but it makes me feel better and justified in having not-so-nice thoughts or using not-so-nice words.

So how does kindness work its way back into my heart when someone or something sets me off? How can I deescalate when I am in distress or when my hackles are up? Take five! Walk away! Ignore and keep silent! Choose kindness.

Every day I encounter people from different walks of life. People can be rude, insulting, and nasty, and when they are my human side takes over! My heart starts pounding, my hands start shaking, I clench my teeth together and set my jaw, and my shoulders rise up. Classic fight or flight, God-given, human reactions. I can't stand it when people attack first and then calm down. How about a little civility? How about a little kindness? How about that?!

But for every difficult person I come across, there are hundreds who have been lovely and kind and nice to me. I need to focus on these people and model my treatment of others after their behavior. This is choosing kindness. I can be a grouch, or I can be friendly. I can be selfish, or I can be generous. I can be thoughtless, or I can be considerate. I can be spiteful, or I can be kind.

I am only human, and God knows this. I can't be perfect all the time, but I can be perfectly honest with him and myself and admit that I can do better, much better. I need more patience and less anger. I need to check my emotions at the door and not engage in a battle of wills. I need to exhibit compassion and kindness. I need to be friendly, generous, and considerate.

I am only human. Please Jesus, help me do better, because I can do better. I just have to try a little kindness. It is the right thing to do.

Try A Little Kindness
(written by Curt Sapaugh and Bobby Austin,
first recorded by Glen Campbell)

If you see your brother standing by the road
With a heavy load from the seeds he sowed
And if you see your sister falling by the way
Just stop and say you're going the wrong way

You've got to try a little kindness
Yes, show a little kindness
Shine your light for everyone to see
And if you'll try a little kindness
then you'll overlook the blindness
Of the narrow minded people on the narrow minded streets

Don't walk around the down and out,
lend a helping hand instead of doubt
And the kindness that you show every day
will help someone along their way

Donna Braidic

Mercy

There was a scholar of the law who stood up to test [Jesus] and asked, "Teacher," he asked, "what must I do to inherit eternal life?"

Jesus said to him, "What is written in the Law? How do you read it?"

He said in reply, "You shall love the Lord, your God, with all your heart, and with all your being, with all your strength, and with all your mind, and your neighbor as yourself."

He replied to him, "You have answered correctly; do this and you will live."

But he wished to justify himself, he said to Jesus, "And who is my neighbor?"

A good question, a sincere question, a challenging question, and depending on the manner in which the question was asked, the response might be different–customized to the moment and to the person asking the question. Given the circumstances of life and the many people I encounter along the way, surely there must be provisos about who my neighbor is....

I can imagine so clearly the "scholar of the law," so smart and worldly, cross-examining Jesus: "And who is my neighbor?"

The educated man, a scribe, believing he is steps ahead of Jesus, underestimates who he is trying to match wits with. As if in a chess match, he narrows his eyes, looking down his nose and jutting his chin as if pleased with his latest move. He leans forward in smug silence waiting for Jesus' answer. I can also picture the curious bystanders gathered round; their interest piqued by the debate getting underway. And I can see me, standing towards the back of the crowd, on the outer edges of the scene, feeling very curious and full of myself, thinking I already know the answer.

As we wait for Jesus to respond, I begin thinking of the people in my life who are my neighbor, starting with the ones whom I have loved most and who are closest to me, working my way down the list to those who have been most challenging. I hope the evidence

212

of my treatment of others will in fact be judged as loving and good, worthy of walking through the gates of heaven at the end of my life....

Finally, Jesus speaks, and I along with the scholar of the law and all those gathered round lean in a little more to hear. True to Jesus' form, his answer is not cut and dry. Jesus tells a parable, the story of the Good Samaritan, and through his lesson he turns the question of who my neighbor is back on the religious scribe and all of us. Jesus, knowing so well the motivation for the scholar's questioning, sets up a violent crime scene that calls into question the strongly adhered-to religious practices concerning cleanliness and the justification of the behavior of religious people.

There are perpetrators of the crime, robbers. There is a victim who is beaten, bloodied, stripped, and left for dead. There are three people who come upon this man. A priest first, who sees him and crosses to the other side of the road. Then a Levite, who does the same. Neither of these men want to get involved or to break the law by becoming soiled by the blood of the man. Then comes the Samaritan, a man despised by the Jews; he is the one who ignores the rules of Judaism, concerned only for the man's well-being and survival. Through gentle care and financial assistance, the Samaritan provides aid to the victim until he is well and back on his feet.

By the end of the story, the answer to "who is my neighbor?" is obvious for all who care and have compassion for humanity: my neighbor is the one who shows mercy.

Mercy.

I am brought back to the original scene with Jesus and the scholar of the law squaring off, and I look around at those standing by me, and they look at me, and we all feel a little uncomfortable, knowing we have not always shown mercy to those who have needed it most and whom we determined needed it the least. It is a moment of honesty, and it bruises my mind and heart.

And like the scholar of the law, I seek to justify myself: I know I should not look away, turn away, hide from those in need, but I have good reason to do so. Jesus, I want you to say, "Donna, it's okay, you are right to make excuses."

In my life my actions have not always checked the "merciful" box, and my love for others has come up short, not being sufficient in the moment, full of judgment and bias.

The scholar's answer rings true: "The one who showed mercy," and I feel it weigh heavily on my mind, and I hear Jesus' closing statement: "Go and do likewise."

Not that you *should have done* likewise. No, present tense: *Go and do* likewise. Start over. Change your attitude. Make a fresh start. And in his lesson Jesus himself shows mercy. He does not scold, he does not berate or embarrass, he forgives every shortcoming and shows mercy. Go and do likewise.

I am not a saint, but if I truly know, love, and serve God, I should not be afraid to treat all people with love, without distinction of a perceived worthiness for receiving mercy. I should aspire to be like Mother Teresa, who was the living embodiment of mercy. Whether the "greatest or the least," I must remember that we all bleed when cut, and we all die–physically and/or emotionally–when hurt or neglected, especially in times of need. Jesus' parable has forced me to take a personal inventory of how I treat people *in all circumstances,* how I love people and how I show mercy to them.

As much as I am distracted by hot pink and purple hair, tattoos, and piercings, I am called to see past the outer appearance of people and instead seek to know the person on the inside. A lack of personal hygiene can stop me dead in my tracks, yet I must not assume the offending person is aware of their neglected appearance or can do anything about it. I have been told many times to "stay away" from homeless people, that they can be unpredictable and dangerous. But in staying away, I avoid coming into contact with their plight and their pain.

I cannot always change the circumstances of a person, but I can change how I respond.

Jesus' parable calls me to put away my conventions and see the person, recognize their need, and show mercy. Do I show mercy, leaving prejudice and bias at the side of the road and meeting people where they are, regardless of where they come from, what their background is or their "pedigree"?

Jesus asks me to see all human beings as my neighbor–to treat everyone equally, with respect, and without prejudice, with pure, merciful love. Jesus plucks the strings of my compassionate heart and draws upon my desire to love first and set aside judgment and see every human being as a child of God.

Jesus finished telling the parable, and when the scholar of the law once again asked Jesus, "And who is my neighbor?"

Jesus said to him, "Which of these three, in your opinion, was neighbor to the robber's victim?"

He answered, "The one who treated him with mercy."

Jesus said to him, "Go and do likewise" (Luke 10:25-37).

I can imagine the scholar of the law, scratching his head while walking away, knowing he had been "schooled"; he tried to face off with the Master, and left the debate hat in hand. There must have been others in the crowd, too, who heard Jesus' lesson and walked away a little less sure of themselves in their treatment of their neighbor. I feel disappointment in myself, knowing that I have judged people based on a certain standard and have been afraid to render aid in fear of "enabling" the very problems that have landed people in the situation they find themselves in.

But I shall not be discouraged by my shortcomings!

At times my attitude and spirit have been fearful and jaded, but Jesus and the Holy Spirit continually soften my heart and through my life I have given help when and where I have been able. It has been a privilege and an honor to give and serve with donations of time, talent, and treasure to organizations that have professionals trained to help others in time of need. With a merciful heart for giving, I have helped feed, clothe, house, gift, teach, and listen to many who are underserved, and I have written inspirational notes to men and women serving time in prison.

From a young age I learned about charitable giving through my parents' example when our church needed donations for a family who was struggling. It was winter in central Ohio and times were tough. My parents explained to me and my siblings that a family was in need, and we would be helping them. The father worked many hours, and the mother and children made his pay stretch, but sometimes there was nothing left when the bills came in; they were broke. From this act of charitable giving my eyes and heart were opened and I learned there is a part of society where men, women, and children struggle to make ends meet.

Children and teenagers in need have always pulled on my heartstrings the most. I go weak in the knees when I hear a call to serve the young. This is why I could not turn a deaf ear to a plea for adult mentors for juveniles in minimum security detention, nor could I look away from the news article that Big Sisters were needed at the Big Brother, Big Sister Organization, nor could I harden my heart when my workplace sent an invitation to volunteer to tutor elementary-aged children in a partnership with the city school district.

I could not turn away from any of these pleas for help, and especially not for children struggling to learn. My first hurdle to overcome in tutoring was the location of the school; it was in a really bad part of town, and my husband and friends worried about me traveling alone. At the orientation meeting, the program administrator of the tutoring program warned that the children were very disadvantaged, and they may not respond well, but what they needed most was love and attention which could lead to better outcomes in school. Many of the children did not have two parents in the home, drug and alcohol usage was prevalent, and it was difficult for the children to advance in their schoolwork when they were struggling with upheaval in the home. They oftentimes did not have brand new clothing to wear and most of the children were on a food subsidy program.

I was not deterred, and a week later I was tutoring five of the sweetest, most innocent, and appreciative children one could ask for. They each worked very hard to improve in their subjects, and when our twelve weeks ended, their smiles shined bright when they received their passing grades. This may not sound very extraordinary, but it was for Fred, who was on track to be held back in second grade for a second time until he had been successfully tutored in reading. Once he was able to read *the questions and answers* on his subject tests and choose the correct answers, he was able to demonstrate how intelligent he was and instead of advancing to third grade, he skipped past third and went straight to fourth, testing into the talented and gifted program! Oh, the smile he had on his face when he showed me his report card. It was a gift of a lifetime, something I have cherished and held dear in my heart. Oh, mercy, you should have seen him smile!

This marvelous lesson taught me to not be so shortsighted in the ways that mercy is given. Once I looked past the children's poorly laundered clothes, uncombed hair, dirty fingernails, and poor grammar, and looked closely at their need, my heart was melted by their acceptance and love of me. They and their teachers and their parents put their trust in me; my "neighbors" deserved the best I could give, to be shown the dignity that Jesus preached in his parable.

The robbery victim in the Good Samaritan story represents everyone. As I have studied the parable and prayed to receive its wisdom, I understand more fully that there are people everywhere who need assistance for one reason or another, who may have been "robbed" of their dignity; exploited for another's gain; "beaten" down with criticism; "abandoned" by family and friends; "left for dead" in the depths of depression, homelessness, mental illness, drug addiction, delinquency, illiteracy.

Instead of doing as Jesus instructs me to do—to love my neighbor and show mercy—there have been times when I have chosen to avoid or ignore the desperate needs of my neighbor, to cross to the other side of the road, and in those times, I have tried to justify my lack of action while seeking forgiveness from God. But there have also been times of beauty and grace when I have responded fully to the needs of my neighbor, and the mercy I have shown has come back to me double, and I find myself thanking and praising God for the opportunity to make a difference and serve.

It is my shame and disappointment in myself when I have fallen short and so I ask Jesus again, "And who is my neighbor?"

And Jesus says to me, "Which of these three, in your opinion, was neighbor to the robber's victim?"

And like the scholar of the law, I reply, "The one who treated him with mercy."

And Jesus says to me, "Go and do likewise."

So, who is my neighbor?

My neighbor is everyone, and Jesus simply asks me to love and show mercy to all.

My neighbor is my friend as well as my enemy.

My neighbors come from every walk of life, and they have the same measure of joys and sorrows in their lives as I have in mine; some more than me.

My neighbor lives next door and needs help mowing the lawn. My neighbor is in line with me at the grocery store, embarrassed and needing monetary assistance when their wallet has less in it than their final tally at the checkout. My neighbor travels by plane with me, needing directions to their gate. My neighbor sits in the car next to me in a traffic jam, needing desperately to merge into my lane to proceed home quickly to a grieving family. My neighbor worships beside me at church and delights in being given a hug at the sign of peace. My neighbor dines at my table, a stranger when the meal begins and a good friend by the time dessert is served. My neighbor needs me, and I need my neighbor. We walk our life journeys separately, but sometimes our paths overlap, and when I or they need help, it is good for us to walk together and show mercy as the moment dictates.

I take to heart Jesus' parable, knowing it is a lesson for me to live by, mirroring his greatest commandments: to love God and to love my neighbor. In showing mercy, I am loving God and my neighbor, giving and receiving God's merciful love.

I pray for a time when I give the same love and mercy to all as did the Good Samaritan to a broken and beaten man. I pray the Holy Spirit emboldens me to love first and to show mercy to all people in all circumstances. I can make a difference in a person's life. A smile, a wave, a kind word, a friendly "hello" and "thank you"–these neighborly gestures can change a person's heart to love, restore a person's dignity, lift a person from despair, and bring light where there is darkness.

My neighbor is the one who shows mercy. I must go and do likewise.

Love and mercy can heal a hurting world. Show mercy.

Forgiveness

"Therefore, if you bring your gift to the altar and there recall that your brother [or sister] has anything against you, leave your gift there at the altar, go first and be reconciled to [them] and then come and offer your gift." Matthew 5:23-24

Forgiveness is a two-way street, and there are two sides to every offense.

It is hard to admit, but if I'm honest, sometimes I wait for others to come to me first to apologize rather than me going to them first, if I believe them to have started the conflict. I avoid and delay the inevitable, possibly losing forever the opportunity to apologize to them. Unfortunately, I have gone for long periods with silence between me and my friend, making it harder to bridge the gap between hurt feelings and an admission of hurtful behavior, and we have grown distant. I realize there is still a lot of work to be done, because whether I am right or wrong, the guilt I feel is prolonged and unsettled.

It's hard to "face the music," but how can I be in "right relationship with God" when I have missed the mark in loving and forgiving "not seven times but seventy-seven times" (Matthew 18:22)? Apologies and reconciliation must come from me for the injustices I have done to another, against myself, and against God, and I also hope the olive branch is extended to me when hurts and injustices are done to me.

I know when I have done wrong, because I feel the tension in my throat as I withhold my apology and maintain my innocence. There is no getting around it! Family, friends, neighbors, co-workers are precious treasures, and I cannot hide in my house, or screen my calls, or stop going places because I know I will run into so-and-so. No! I have to make peace as much as I can and as often as I can, because without it, I cannot have peace in my heart until things are resolved; and whether the outcome is a handshake, a hug, or a parting of the ways, I will have done what I should do in the eyes of the Lord.

"If a house is divided against itself, that house cannot stand." Mark 3:25

In my family, in my neighborhood, in my workplace, in my church, if there are troubles that need attending to and forgiveness is the way to peace, it is imperative that I be an agent for reconciliation and peace. A small wedge between two people can grow into a wide chasm and families, businesses, worshiping communities, and even nations can slowly fall apart by the ripple effect of unresolved wrongs.

As a Christian, I am called to model the behavior of Christ, and whether I am receiving forgiveness or giving forgiveness I cannot be smug or stiff; I am called to have a humble and contrite heart. Anything else, and I feel like a hypocrite. As difficult as it has been at times to say, "I'm sorry," or accept another's apology to me, I have seen and experienced the transformational healing that occurs when newfound understanding occurs between me and another.

So, then, what's the big deal? Just apologize if it is so wonderful. What's stopping me? An admission that I was wrong? Maybe. Fear? Probably. Fear of what? That my apology is not enough, and I will lose someone dear to me. Then why did you hurt them in the first place? Because I had to be right. Oh.

When I was a child, I felt miserable when I misbehaved or did something I knew was wrong. I had trouble falling asleep and imagined monsters sneaking into my bedroom. I felt scared and insecure until I told my mom and dad what I had done wrong and apologized for it. It was hard to say, "I'm sorry," because I did not want to disappoint them or be punished, but I could not keep the guilt in my heart any longer; it hurt too much. Sometimes I went back to my room crying, but my apology and tears helped cleanse the guilt of my sin. The imaginary monsters left, too, and I felt safe and able to sleep peacefully again.

As I grew older, and my teenage "crimes" became riskier, it wasn't as easy to admit my wrongs and accept responsibility for my actions when I was caught. I lied and looked for ways to cover my sin, but eventually, just like when I was a child, the guilt would torment me, and the truth would eventually come out. And even though I ended up being grounded or given more chores to do around the house, in a way I welcomed the punishment to help alleviate my feelings of guilt.

Now, as an adult, when I "know better," things are murkier in the area of assigning or accepting guilt and blame. With my own children, friends and neighbors, workplace pals, my husband, it is natural to argue, disagree, and raise voices. Unfortunately, it does not always feel natural to apologize and admit I am wrong. Unfortunately, relationships unravel and grudges become like cement in my heart and all I have left to prove there was once something true are old photos, trinkets and baubles, and silly mementos filed away at the bottom of my dresser drawer.

When I spoke my wedding vows to Tim, I had stars in my eyes. Everything was sunshine and daffodils, and love ruled the day. I truly set my heart on the ideal of "to love and to cherish, from this day forward, until death do us part." But slowly shouting and harmful words, criticisms, a lack of support, and jealousy troubled our marriage and threatened our commitment, and I began to question my "I do." I was so naïve and in love on my wedding day, and I was blindsided by the power struggles and conflicts that beset us and fueled my desire at times to quit the marriage.

But God brought the two of us together, and our wedding promises to love each other through the good and the bad resonated through the years and called us to magnify the good and forgive the bad. I took a vow to love and through the power of this promise I was able to forgive the worst, and it made my imperfect marriage with my late husband endure until death did part us. Even after Tim's passing, there was still some hurt and blame I held against him. I knew it was not good for me to cling to past hurts, so I prayed to Jesus, forgiving Tim, and releasing him from his earthbound transgressions against me. It was right and just to do so.

There are unlimited wrongs, unlimited victims, unlimited apologies, and unlimited punishments for all offenses, some punishable by criminal law. Sometimes the bigger the offense, the harder the admission of wrongdoing. Even in the worst cases, when a person is truly repentant, peace and healing are possible.

Sometimes an apology will not come, but forgiveness can still be given. A number of years ago I attended a church function and the speaker, Rachel Muha, spoke about forgiveness. Her nineteen-year-old son, Brian, had been kidnapped from his college apartment along with his roommate, and the two young men were murdered. I was shocked and absolutely devastated for Mrs. Muha and her family. I couldn't understand how she could find the strength to speak in public about the tragic loss of her child. He was only ten years older than my daughters, and his murder at college shook me.

Mrs. Muha told the audience that Brian's life would matter. Her family was starting a foundation to help others in Brian's memory.

And then she said something I could not fathom: she said she forgave the men who murdered her son. I was astounded by this amazing act of love. Her response to an incomprehensible crime was to give incomprehensible forgiveness.

Mrs. Muha expanded to the outer limits the meaning of forgiveness. She was as close to being like Jesus Christ as I had ever known anyone to be.

"Rachel spoke at the sentencings of the men who'd killed her son. She told them that there was still time to change. They could turn to God and still have a happy life, even in prison. She is still waiting for the men, now 38 and 39 and each serving a life sentence, to reach out with an apology. If they ever do, she says, 'they'll find a friend in me'" (Morgan).

Jesus clearly demonstrated there is no limit to his love when he said, "Father, forgive them, they know not what they do" (Luke 23:34).

Forgive me, Father, for I *do know* what I have done wrong against my neighbor and what I still need to do to make things right again.

As long as there are people, there will be conflicts that need resolution. Words hurt. Abuse hurts. Fights hurt.

People have lied to me. And I to them.

They have broken promises. And so have I.

Some have falsely accused me of things I have not done, while others have been haughty and put on airs around me. Oops, me too.

People have physically assaulted me, been rude and mean to me, and yelled profanities in my face. I have no excuse; I have done the same to others.

People have denied knowing me when I needed them most. This one, so painful, cut my heart in two; how could I then do this even one time to another? Yet I have done this, too.

Some betrayals cut really deep, both ways. When I recall some abuses, they are as scary today as the day they occurred, and I have not been able to forgive for good. But I keep trying.

I am certainly not without my faults or debts against others.

I dare not "cast the first stone," or "throw a rock at my friend's glass house" when mine can just as easily shatter. And if my friend has a plank in their eye, I first need to remove the entire log from my own eye before judging or criticizing or regarding myself as superior in any way.

I confess, with humble heart, that I have done the same things against others that others have done against me, and most assuredly this has created bitterness towards me in the hearts of those I have offended. I have caused pain, and it will take time for those I have hurt to forgive me. I do hope for their forgiveness, and I pray that someday all will be made right and well between us.

Jesus said, "Father, forgive them, they know not what they do."

With outstretched arms, Jesus accepted every kind of abuse and forgave all who caused his suffering, including me. Jesus is my Savior, for he took upon himself the sins of humankind from the beginning to the end of time, and these sins died with him upon the cross.

As for me, I am still working on being like Jesus and Rachel Muha, forgiving transgressions whether apologized to or not.

Troubles weaken me and create uncertainty, yet all I have to do is express a conciliatory message: "I'm sorry," or "I forgive you," to my brother or sister and we turn a corner toward reconciliation. It is hard, but it is absolutely worth it. When my relationships are right, there is peace in my heart, and in subtle ways the world becomes more aligned with Jesus' ways, the way of peace, the way of hope, the way of love.

My last bit of Donna wisdom: Regret weighs heavily while an apology can prove to be a beautiful moment of grace—for the giver and the receiver.

Forgive me, Father, for I have not kept my word to you; I have sinned again. I ask for your guidance and acceptance and love despite my actions. I ask your forgiveness for all the sins of my body, my heart, my mind, and even those deep down in my soul. Please keep close to me always and help me stay on the path that you have set before me on my journey on this earth. Lead me, guide me in your ways. Holy Spirit, awaken me! Make me ready to serve all I meet with a spirit of love and forgiveness. Thank you, Lord, for your love that never ceases to amaze me! Lift me up and take me forward into this day. You are my Savior, my friend. I love you, Lord. Amen.

Motherhood

"[He] gives the childless wife a home, the joyful mother of children. Hallelujah!" Psalm 113:9

Motherhood and the gift of my daughters has been one of the most wonderful things to happen to me in my entire life. I never imagined how amazing a blessing it would be to be a mother or how much joy I would feel every day since their births. It has been an unbelievable privilege and great responsibility to be entrusted with raising my girls from infancy to adulthood, helping them learn and bringing them up to be responsible, mature adults. Every time I look at them, I burst with love and pride that they are my daughters!

My daughters are miracles, and I rejoice that I am their mom. From the moment I received the news that I was pregnant, I have never regretted one moment of motherhood. From cute and cuddly babies to awkward and prickly adolescents to loving and oh so unpredictable adults, my daughters are beautiful on the inside and out. It is a privilege to be their mom. They have changed me and made me kinder and more loving toward others, realizing we are all someone's child.

From the day I brought the girls home from the hospital, I knew the day would come when I would have to step back and let them find their way, with God to lead them and walk with them on the path that they would choose.

It is quite astonishing to me that from the moment I first held my daughters a space naturally opened up in my life for them. I did not mind at all waking for the four a.m. feedings; the hours slipped by so fast. In the stillness of the early morning, I held my infant daughter in my arms, nursing her and then slowly rocking her back to sleep as the moonlight rose and fell over my shoulder through the curtains. I would look at her precious form with wonder and awe, kissing each fingertip and memorizing each tiny feature on her face, as if taking a photograph in my mind, wanting my joy to last forever.

I was so blissfully happy, and although they were newly born, I pondered their futures, wondering who they would become and the places they would go. My heart overflowed with love and all I could think was, "Dear God, how blessed am I."

Their personalities did not take long to emerge, quite forcefully, and their strong and determined confidence emboldened them toward achievement through good progress and reward. Yet there was also the kindest, gentlest quality in their demeanors that made them vulnerable and timid when threatened or mistreated by others. And because the girls trusted me to necessarily guide and correct them, they sought out my approval, discipline, acceptance, and love, holding my hand tightly for safety and protection as they crossed into the unknown passages of their childhood.

The time has flown by quickly since my daughters were born, and many times I have wished I could do it all over again. From baby giggles and teething to laughter and braces, they have brought me immense joy. Even from baby's first haircut to teenagers' shocking pink and green and gothic black hairdos, I found something to take delight in with my girls. From their crib to middle-school sleepovers to dormitories and questionable living arrangements, every good, bad, and in-between experience has made memories that I cherish in my heart. As much as I wanted to hurry the days and months of potty-training, I equally tried to put off first dates and shopping for prom dresses and college orientations, as I knew my girls would be leaving me soon and I would be on my own again.

As adults, even though I know Meghan and Lauren are capable of taking care of themselves, I worry about them and for their safety, and I pray for them every day, knowing I have done my best and now it is up to God to help them along the rest of the way. With a sigh and a prayer, I ask only the very best for them, knowing that they were born for a beautiful purpose.

I have tried to be a good example for my daughters, making prayer and faith, family, friends, church community, and trust in God a part of all aspects of their lives. I knew difficult times would come along for Meghan and Lauren—it is only natural. As young people asserting their independence, moving away from parental oversight, mistakes have been made, hard lessons have been learned. But no matter the challenges my girls encounter, I hope they will always remember me saying, "God is with you, God loves you, and no matter what you do, nothing you do will make God go away from you."

"Nothing can separate us from the love of God" (Romans 8:38).

As the years passed my role as mom has changed, and with each step my daughters took towards independence I moved further and further into the backdrop of their lives. I had to let go and allow them to rely less on me, respecting their need to grow into the people they wanted to be. The time came to accept that my daughters were growing up and they did not need me in the same ways that they once needed me, as small children. I realized a big part of my journey of motherhood had come to an end.

It was time to practice what I preached and trust God to be with my daughters, to go before them, to put good people in their lives and help steer them down right paths.

It was time to let go of my control and let my daughters become the sole drivers on their individual life journeys.

This was a hard truth to accept, and it made me fearful for them. The world is wonderful, full of possibilities, but it is also a scary place. All roads may lead to home, but not all alleyways do.

To surrender to God my need to care for Meghan and Lauren has been difficult–gut-wrenching at times–but it is the right thing to do. I must let go. God loves them more than I can comprehend.

In my prayers for the girls, I picture myself taking Meghan and Lauren's soft, young hands and placing them into Jesus' strong but gentle hands. The girls look at me and then at Jesus, and without a word they turn to go, and they cross into their futures bravely trusting Jesus as I wave them on, believing with my whole heart that he will take care of them and lead them on right paths.

My dear daughters, "Are not two sparrows sold for a penny? Yet not one of them will fall to the ground outside your Father's care. And even the very hairs of your head are all numbered. So don't be afraid; you are worth more than many sparrows" (Matthew 10:29-31).

Meghan and Lauren are grown women now and my dreams and aspirations for their futures are the same now as when they held my hand so tightly in their childhood: for faith in the God of all goodness; for good people in their lives who will honor them, cherish them, and treat them with respect and dignity, never harming them or putting them in danger; for success professionally; for good health; for love to surround them and bless them in joy and in sorrow; for a happy home. My girls are so bright and intelligent and creative and lively, and God has given them these gifts so that they may achieve wonderful, limitless things in their lives.

Motherhood has changed me in ways I could not have imagined, and I am blessed. From the physical to the emotional, of pain giving birth to the fear of letting go; from heart-breaking disappointment and anger one day to unbelievable joy and tears of gratitude the next, the gift of motherhood is a miracle that I treasure from God always and forevermore.

Cherish time. Children are young only once, teenagers for but a long minute, and adults for the rest of their lives. The time with them is short and fleeting.

Love is...

"Let us greet him with a song of praise, joyfully sing out our psalms. For the Lord is the great God, the great king over all gods." Psalm 95:2-3

Upon returning from a church musicians convention late one summer, my creative juices were flowing, and I felt a renewed passion for my music ministry, and I wanted to share it with my choir. I wanted them to be as inspired as I had been and to be changed as I had been. I channeled my newfound energy and created an activity for my choir that I hoped would bring them closer to God and would invigorate their personal mission of spreading the Gospel of love through our music ministry.

I called it, "Love is...."

The activity was designed to provide time each week for my choir members to reflect on the different ways they have experienced God's love in the ordinary events of daily living and then share them at choir rehearsal for the benefit of the group. My intent was to heighten our awareness of God's love and blessings, to acknowledge these blessings, and through the gratitude felt by us collectively as "choir," transform our music into a blessing of love to the congregation to be taken out into the world.

My inspiration for "Love is..." came while singing a newly published song at the convention called "Love is the Touch" by Alison Robertson set to the Celtic hymn tune "Slane." I settled easily into the familiar tune and immersed myself in singing the moving text.

As I sang along with my friends and the music presenters, my inhibitions slipped away, and I allowed myself to feel the song and its message of love. The music and lyrics brought up emotions in me that I had been long suppressing, emotions that were fragile and raw from months of worry and anxiety over my husband Tim's health, and by midway through the song, I could no longer hold back my tears and my resolve collapsed from within. I let the tears flow and gave into the music and its message of love.

I felt vulnerable and embarrassed but okay feeling the way I did. I was surrounded by love.

The song did not leave me long in my sadness and unease, for the arrangement included interludes and dynamics that carried me over the bridge of my anticipated loss and set me down softly in hope and recovery, truth and security, "for God is of love." By the end of the song, my singing had become an offering of humble gratitude to my family, friends, neighbors, and community for their support and love during Tim's devastating illness.

As the song ended, I felt once again the gladness of my heart for God's love and his provisions, coming full circle from joy to sadness to joy again.

Love is...feeling the touch of God through a beautiful, simple song and wanting to share this love with my choir.

The lyrics of the song underscore the many blessings I receive from God, from the small and ordinary to the extraordinary and supernatural. They provide a powerful message of the tremendous love God has for all human beings, his children. With each singing of the song, my gratitude and praise and glory to God grew and the idea and expression of appreciation for God's blessings made the "Love is..." sharing a natural response.

My concept of "Love is..." was simple and fairly easy to implement, and although a few folks in the choir thought it was silly, possibly childish, most accepted my idea with an open mind and heart.

Jesus said, "Let the little children come to me, and do not hinder them, for the kingdom of heaven belongs to such as these" (Matthew 19:14).

The task was simple: each choir member took a small piece of paper from a basket when they arrived for rehearsal and wrote on it, "Love is...," and then they completed the phrase with whatever love was for them on that day. It could be something indulgent–"Love is...eating chocolate ice cream for breakfast"–or as simple as "Love is...irresistible," or "Love is...my tired husband doing the dishes after dinner," or it could be something more reverent–"Love is...my Lord Jesus dying on the cross for me."

When they finished writing their "Love is…," they dropped the piece of paper back in the basket, and at the end of each choir rehearsal the basket was passed around and each of us took one of the slips of paper out and during our prayer time we read aloud one another's "Love is…" declarations.

It was magical to hear what caused thirty or so people to feel loved, and also to read someone else's "Love is…" and reflect on it as if it were my own. These times were a blessing and I looked forward to this sharing each week. Choir night was special for me for so many reasons, and this simple sharing among friends about the ordinary and extraordinary things of life was a highlight for my life.

Love is…doing something silly out of love and trust, even though the value is not immediately apparent. When love is shared honestly, love grows in the hearts of people through greater awareness of God's blessings, and the transformative love experienced glorifies God, who is love.

Love is…in everything if I just take time to notice.

Love is…transformative.

Love is…a natural outflow of my gratitude in each moment lived.

Love is…God in me.

God Is Love

"Beloved, let us love one another, because love is of God; everyone who loves is begotten by God and knows God. Whoever is without love does not know God, for God is love. In this way the love of God was revealed to us: God sent his only Son into the world so that we might have life through him. In this is love: not that we have loved God, but that he loved us and sent his Son as expiation for our sins. Beloved, if God so loved us, we must also love one another. No one has ever seen God. Yet, if we love one another, God remains in us, and his love is brought to perfection in us" (1 John 4:7-12).

Donna Braidic

Freedom

"Now this is the message we have heard from him and proclaim to you: God is light; and in him there is no darkness at all." 1 John 1:5

"Be free, yet without using freedom as a pretext for evil, but as [servants] of God." 1 Peter 2:16

"No one has greater love than this, to lay down one's life for one's friends." John 15:13

"We the People of the United States, in Order to form a more perfect Union, establish Justice, ensure domestic Tranquility, provide for the common Defense, promote the general Welfare, and secure the Blessings of Liberty to ourselves and our Posterity, do ordain and establish this Constitution for the United States of America." Preamble of the United States Constitution

I love my country, the United States of America, the "land of the free and the home of the brave."

I thank God for my freedoms and the endless possibilities that living in a free country brings to me. I am able to dream and aspire to be anything I wish to be! Prosperity and success are achievable, every advantage has been afforded to me, and I feel very blessed! I wish this was the experience of all who call this country home, and I pray that with this and each new generation all people's freedoms are more secure.

When I look back over human history to the present day and examine the hardships endured by men, women, and children, and the brutal bondage imposed by tyrants and dictators and kings, taking profit and power from the forced labor and enslavement of people, my need for justice rises up in me. I can only imagine the fire burning in the hearts of people who said, "Enough!" and took steps to change the course of their lives and the lives of generations to come. They had extraordinary courage, intellect, and strength to fulfill their destiny, and a strong belief and faith in God carried many over the finish line.

I am humbled and grateful for the many sacrifices made and the courage exhibited by these change makers. They have made the difference in times of bondage, war, and strife, and through their faith and conviction of purpose they have proven to me that anything is possible with God.

Traveling back in time thousands of years ago, I can almost see Moses, standing on the edge of the Red Sea with his staff in his hand raised out over the sea, addressing the Israelites, "Fear not! Stand your ground, and you will see the victory the Lord will win for you today. These Egyptians whom you see today you will never see again. The Lord himself will fight for you; you have only to keep still" (Exodus 14: 13-14).

The power of God was with Moses, and he commanded the terrified Israelites to go forward through the dry passage where the Lord had parted the sea for their escape from Pharaoh's army. They would have to run between the walls of water to gain freedom. Walls of water.

The people had no choice. There was no more time; it was do or die: die in the wilderness or be free. As the army drove closer, the people chose to trust the Lord and Moses and they escaped on the dry path to freedom. When all had crossed, the waters flooded back in and the soldiers were "swept to the sea," and Moses and his family and his people who had been enslaved for generations rejoiced and praised the Lord for delivering them to freedom.

For centuries enslaved people have risen up and followed the voice in their heart that commands them to trust and be free.

When I watch the news and see the stories about people not able to live in freedom, I ask myself, "What would I do if my freedom were threatened or taken away; what would I do?"

I would pray for God's protection and for the spirit of the Lord to aid me in the fight (as I have seen happen with the brave people of Ukraine), to give me courage and the will to overcome evil, and with every ounce of my strength to defend freedom, restore it, and preserve it for future generations.

As a citizen of the United States of America, I enjoy the many blessings of freedom guaranteed under the law, contained in the Constitution of the United States. The Founding Fathers debated and argued and negotiated passionately with one another, representing many points of view, to draft a document with precise wording that could survive the scrutiny of legal minds and stand the test of time.

When finished, the Constitution contained Articles and Amendments of law that proved to be a thorough articulation of governmental oversight and protection of freedom, and it included supremely important checks and balances. Since its signing in 1776, numerous amendments have been made to the Constitution to reflect the changing times, attitudes, and social norms of the people of the country. There are many shining moments in my country's history when men and women have exercised their right to speak and peaceably assemble and march in protest to affect lasting change. As a woman, I am especially grateful to the Suffragette Movement for mobilizing women a century ago to secure the passage of the 19th Amendment, which gave all women the right to vote.

I can easily say that the Constitution–the law of the land–is as irreplaceable and as cherished by me as the Bible–the law of God– because they both assert the same guarantee: freedom!

Freedom on earth and freedom in heaven. Freedom to be me, to change and grow and prosper and live according to my purpose to know, love and serve God–where and when and how I choose! To sing and speak and praise God openly in my life. Freedom from darkness, freedom from sin! Freedom to hope and pray and walk in the light of Christ, the one who sacrificed his life to secure my freedom for all time.

In the totality of each work, written centuries apart, I believe there to be wise counsel, containing enduring laws for all people to ensure the continuity of love, peace, prosperity, and equality of persons for all time.

In studying the doctrines and living in accord with the decrees of each, within the boundaries of the laws, the unifying truth they communicate to me is this: Freedom dispels the darkness!

When I was fourteen years old, my parents grounded me for a month when they caught me breaking a major rule–no underage drinking–and they took my freedom away, confining me to the house and my room, with no friends allowed to visit. I felt like I was in exile. It made me really mad at the time! How could they take my freedom away for what seemed like *for-e-ver*?! It was my life! I felt powerless and I grumbled about the unfairness of it all. That month seemed like an eternity, dark and lonely and full of teenage drama. But when the month was finally over and I was able to reunite with my friends, I had a deeper appreciation for my role in losing or keeping my freedom, and for the fact that freedom means the world to me.

In my twenties, I read two books that taught me how precious and fragile freedom can be: *The Diary of Anne Frank* by Anne Frank and *Anne Frank Remembered* by Miep Gies, true stories by real heroes. Sadly, I knew how the stories ended; but I still read them as if my life and freedom depended on their outcome. Each heroine writes of her love and joy living in the light of freedom in the Netherlands before the Nazi invasion of their country, and of the unending misery and death inflicted upon the Jewish people by the Nazis, including Anne's family and friends in the ensuing dark years of World War II.

Both compelling stories gripped my heart and brought me to tears as I read about Anne Frank, a Dutch, thirteen-year-old Jewish girl and Miep Gies, a Dutch, thirty-three-year-old non-Jewish woman. Through each descriptive word I felt the suffocating darkness that shrouded the world after Anne's freedom was taken away. I recoiled at the obscene evilness of man as Anne and her family and friend,' whereabouts were betrayed to the Nazis and they were ripped from the protection of Miep and forced to endure the atrocities of the Holocaust in the concentration camps.

I was captivated by Anne and her resilience, and I laughed at her humor and spunkiness. I related to her honest feelings of resentment over her confinement and its unfairness. Her descriptions of life and hiding in the annex made my teenage grounding insignificant and my behavior embarrassing. I cannot imagine how constrained and frustrated she must have felt! She lost so much at such a young age! As a teenage girl blossoming into a young woman while under the constant scrutiny of others, she was denied the one thing teenagers crave: privacy.

Yet she did not give in to despair, freeing her thoughts and imaginings by writing them down in her diary. Even though she was confined, her freedom to think, to express herself in writing, and to worship her God could not be taken away from her. She wrote of her devotion to her Jewish faith, offering her prayers and keeping her joy and trust and faith in God. Anne's words were true and honest when writing about herself and her family, the Van Pels family, Fritz Pfeffer, and Miep, whose extraordinary resourcefulness provided nourishment and dignity for all hiding in the annex.

Miep, employed by Anne's father, was loyal and true, and she did not hesitate when Otto Frank asked her to help his family and his Jewish friends when options ran out for avoiding arrest and transport to the death camps. Miep hid the Frank family for two years and provided what they needed to survive during this time. Miep was so courageous, never abandoning her friends while placing herself and her husband at great risk and peril. In the face of injustice and evil, Miep was a true friend indeed, setting aside concern for her own freedom, safety, and survival so that her friends might avoid capture and someday live in the light of freedom again.

Harriet Tubman is another admirable woman who would not be refused her freedom. Harriet's determination and strong will cut down all obstacles and cleared the way to freedom from slavery for herself and others. Harriet was an extraordinary African American woman and devout Christian who was able to accomplish the impossible. Her audacity, strength, and conviction spurred her forward in her escape plans, and against all odds, she made it to Philadelphia where she was free!

But gaining freedom was not enough for Harriet! Once freedom was burning in her heart, she defied death and did the unthinkable, the unselfish, the most dangerous act of heroism: she returned to her enslaved family and friends in Maryland and brought seventy more to freedom! Harriett's trust in God's deliverance was absolute and ordained. Her faith in God was undeniable and her visions and intuition saved her countless times from being caught and killed. Harriet found freedom that dispelled the darkness of slavery from her life. Hallelujah! Hallelujah!

Time has passed and these larger-than-life role models have passed on, but their freedom stories continue to live on in my heart and throughout history. Their true stories of sacrifice for the glory of freedom, living life in joy and light, are a gift to humanity, and they have given me and many others the inspiration and courage to unite and say with one voice, "Let freedom ring!"

I believe at the heart of every person God has planted a mighty courage that rises up when freedom is threatened, when light is obscured by darkness, when people are sick and tired of being oppressed, and when people are told to be silent.

Every minute of every day there are people performing acts of bravery that protect me and my fellow Americans from tyranny and strife, oppression and discrimination, preserving freedom for the United States and its citizens, so that we may live securely in "the land of the free and the home of the brave."

I am reminded of Dr. Martin Luther King, Jr.'s often-quoted words describing that people will be judged by "the content of their character."

When I think of the American spirit and heroism and the content of one's character, I recall the passengers and crew on hijacked Flight 93. On September 11, 2001, terrorists hijacked Flight 93 with the intent to crash it into the Capitol Building of the United States of America. Although limited in their communication, passengers signaled with one another and agreed they would take back the airplane. Over western Pennsylvania, in an attempt to save the flight, to save the passengers, to save the people on the ground, and to wrestle freedom back from the hands of terrorists in the cockpit, Todd Beamer's last valiant words to his fellow conspirators were, "Are you guys ready? Let's roll!"

When terrorists attacked the United States on 9/11, I was shaken to my core. I was in shock, and I was not alone. Never before in my lifetime had such an act of war been carried out on United States soil, killing almost three thousand innocent people, God rest their souls. It would be hours, days, months, even years before I would understand the full extent of the human loss and the heroics associated with the events of that day "in the land of the free and the home of the brave."

I never felt so vulnerable in my life as in the days that followed 9/11, yet I carried on, knowing with certainty that my President and Commander-in-Chief, along with the brave men and women of the United States Armed Forces, would protect me and my family.

They would protect my freedom at any cost, and it would take me and everyone working together, united as one, to rise up from that day and bring the country and the world out of the darkness of evil.

I joined with my friends and neighbors for candlelight vigils and prayer circles asking for God's justice and peace. We gathered around flagpoles and sang the National Anthem with renewed gusto and purpose, sure of our trust in God, believing in freedom, freedom dispelling the darkness. Through these deliberate acts of faith, I felt the healing of the nation begin.

A few days after that terrible day, television networks all over the world broadcasted the President's call for justice. With hope in my heart, I watched as President George W. Bush stood upon the jagged rubble of the Twin Towers at the World Trade Center in New York City, resolute and strong. I listened to his words as he yelled into the bullhorn while brave rescue workers in the rubble below paused in their recovery efforts to hear his message:

Bush: Thank you all. I want you all to know (-- it [bullhorn] can't go any louder --) I want you all to know that America today, America today is on bended knee, in prayer for the people whose lives were lost here, for the workers who work here, for the families who mourn. The nation stands with the good people of New York City and New Jersey and Connecticut as we mourn the loss of thousands of our citizens.

Rescue Worker: I can't hear you!

President Bush: I can hear you! I can hear you! The rest of the world hears you! And the people -- and the people who knocked these buildings down will hear all of us soon!

Rescue Workers: [Chanting] U.S.A.! U.S.A.! U.S.A.! U.S.A.! U.S.A.! U.S.A.! U.S.A.! U.S.A.!

President Bush: The nation -- The nation sends its love and compassion --

Rescue Worker: God bless America!

President Bush: -- to everybody who is here. Thank you for your hard work. Thank you for makin' the nation proud, and may God bless America.

Rescue Workers: [Chanting] U.S.A.! U.S.A.! U.S.A.! U.S.A.! (Bush)

In the early days of Operation Enduring Freedom and Iraqi Freedom I saw many friends deploy to Iraq and Afghanistan, along with many others who signed up for the cause. My heart was so heavy, and I worried for their safety, and I prayed to God that all would return home soon. Unfortunately, as the war on terror continued for two decades, thousands of soldiers and civilians were injured and killed in the cause for freedom. Even in the last hours of the war, thirteen brave service members lost their lives trying to save thousands of civilians as time ran out on their freedom.

So many brave souls have made the ultimate sacrifice for me and for all in the cause of freedom. As I raise my hand to my heart for the Pledge of Allegiance or sing the National Anthem I am mindful of the cost of freedom. One of the highlights and honors of my life was performing the National Anthem with my daughters at the community fireworks display. Performing the anthem was my way of saying thank you. Thank you to all the men and women who have risked it all, like Anne and Miep and Harriet and Todd and President Bush and the many men and women who have served in the armed forces, here and abroad, in peace and in wartime, and used their gifts from God to answer the call to live an extraordinary life for themselves and for the sake of others.

In these moments of reflection on freedom, I cry tears of gratitude for the exceptional people who have preserved freedom. Their testimonials convey their love of life and country, the absolute urgency of their actions, and their selfless determination and will. I cannot listen to patriotic music without a big lump in my throat and pride brimming in my heart for all who serve. I am especially proud to honor my late husband's memory and his service in the United States Air Force, achieving the rank of Staff Sergeant while protecting our country during the Cold War. May God bless you, Tim, for answering the call to serve for the cause of freedom.

On anniversaries commemorating our service members and their contributions to freedom, we celebrate the continuity of freedom across time and space. From the young, newly enlisted soldier to the retired World War II veteran, I see a seamless changing of the guard from one generation to the next, from one century to the next, lighting the way for future generations.

A couple of months before the 75th Anniversary of D-Day, my husband Scott and I had the privilege of meeting one of the oldest surviving American World War II veterans, who was traveling through South Carolina on his way to Normandy, France, with his son and daughters on his "No Regrets Tour." In our meeting I felt very humbled by the enormity of his sacrifice and his survival. It was with genuine gratitude that I said to him, "Thank you, Sir, for fighting for my freedom."

Two months later, as old newsreels from World War II and the D-Day Invasion played simultaneously on my television screen, I understood how momentous the veterans' decisive life and death moments were. I felt like I was seeing centuries of sacrifice and bravery through the eyes of our veterans, through the eyes of Todd Beamer and Anne Frank and Miep Gies and Harriet Tubman and President Bush, the eyes of the Founding Fathers', through the eyes of Jesus.

At the end of the program, as the camera panned over Normandy American Cemetery and the acres and acres of white crosses, I knew in my mind and felt in my heart what God wanted me to know and understand: freedom is won at great human cost. People have died for my freedom, they have paid the ultimate price, and I should never take this for granted. God's spirit has invigorated and enlivened the minds and hearts of extraordinarily brave people, and they have won for me a most precious gift, a shining light dispelling the darkness of evil: freedom!

Many brave souls have heard the voice of freedom's call and they have fought in the battles of war to secure the fate and freedom of nations and their people.

Could that be the drum and the bugle and the patriot's battle cries echoing from the grave, leading a heavenly charge for freedom that I hear carried on the wind as I pay my respects at the grave of a long-ago soldier?

While others work to ensure my safety, I enjoy all the luxuries of life without fear and without pause in my routine: peaceful sleep, recreation, work, prayer and worship, school, vacation, hugs and kisses from my husband and children, and so much more. While others work tirelessly throughout the night without complaint to ensure my safety and freedom, I will live with a grateful heart, and rejoice in the unlimited possibilities found in freedom in the United States of America.

People have saved the world from chaos and cruelty for me. I will never, ever forget them.

Dear Lord, I feel so blessed to live in the United States of America. I am so grateful for my freedom. Thank you for inspiring wisdom in the Founding Fathers in writing the Constitution of the United States. Thank you for all people around the world, and I ask a special blessing for those who serve you in preserving freedom. Please give me courage to reject evil. I pray earnestly for freedom to continue to ring out in this land, dispelling darkness, and that we, your children, may all live in supreme gratitude for the gift. Thank you, Jesus. Thank you.

"In great deeds, something abides. On great fields, something stays. Forms change and pass; bodies disappear; but spirits linger, to consecrate ground for the vision-place of souls... generations that know us not and that we know not of, heart-drawn to see where and by whom great things were suffered and done for them, shall come to this deathless field, to ponder and dream; and lo! the shadow of a mighty presence shall wrap them in its bosom, and the power of the vision pass into their souls" (Joshua Lawrence Chamberlain).

Amen.

Donna Braidic

Strong Character

"No one had a bad word to say about [Judith], for she was a very *God-fearing woman*." Judith 8:8

"Joseph [Mary's] husband [...] was *a righteous man*." Matthew 1:19

"And they placed over his head the written charge against him: This is Jesus, *the King of the Jews*."   Matthew 27:37

"I commend to you Phoebe our sister, who is [also] *a minister of the church* at Cenchreae." Romans 16:1

Passing through an old cemetery in Charleston, South Carolina, curiosity about those buried beneath the ground causes me to pause for a moment and ponder the lives that have passed, reading the names, dates and different messages inscribed on the well-worn tombstones. The epitaphs of the deceased capture the essence of the person who lived and in a few brief words, whether by poem or statement; I feel like I know a little bit about the person's character and how they lived. With a brief sentence or phrase in remembrance of John or Mary or Edith or Tobias, I feel connected to the trails they blazed and the families they raised, of the battles they fought and the hardships they lived through. I am reminded again of the words of Dr. Martin Luther King, Jr., as I catch a glimpse of the character of each person laid to rest, and I wonder how I will be remembered when I am gone...will I be worthy to have these words spoken of me, "Well done, my good and faithful servant" (Matthew 25:21)?

Through music ministry I have been given the unique experience of providing music at many funerals and memorial services for deceased I have known and not known, in service to their family and friends. It is not an easy ministry, but it is a vitally important one. Funerals keep me humble and aware of life's beginning and end. Funerals keep me authentic and loving in presenting simple yet beautiful, heavenly music to honor the deceased while supporting family and friends gathered in their time of great sadness and sorrow. Throughout the years, songs such as "On Eagles Wings," "How Great Thou Art," "Amazing Grace," and "In the Garden" have given voice to the great compassion of God and his divine presence and promise of eternity. It is beautiful to see how people who are drawn together in sorrow can be uplifted by the words and music of these cherished songs.

It is a blessing to meet the bereaved and hear their affectionate comments about their loved one. There is a special intimacy and closeness in the confidences that they share, and there is a frailty of spirit among the grieving that necessitates sincerity in honoring the person who has died. There are tears and laughter as each person recalls the sad, funny, outrageous, and inspiring stories of their loved one's life, and the honesty and vulnerability of each are very heartwarming.

As they give witness to the many qualities that made their loved one so special, I cannot help wondering if I, too, share similar admirable qualities. I find myself hoping that I will be remembered in the same fond way, thinking of the people in my life whom I may have impacted positively, and I recommit myself to being the best person I can be. Funerals, as sad as they are, create powerful opportunities for bringing hope and change to my heart.

At my husband's funeral, many who knew Tim shared with me memories of him and the impact he made on their lives. They spoke warmly of Tim, and the compliments I heard most were "he loved his girls" and "he was a good man." Many more kind words were spoken, but I think these would have pleased Tim most, knowing that he had lived a life that evidenced to others that he loved his wife and daughters, and it showed in the way he conducted himself.

Since Tim's passing, I have remarried, and I could list dozens of good character traits about Scott that made me fall in love with him and that keep my heart dancing whenever I am with him. However, when sifted and refined, this is what I know to be true of Scott:

Scott is funny and he was born with a twinkle in his eye and a song in his heart. He is generous, loving, and kind. Scott gives his very best to God. Scott gives his very best to me, to my daughters, and to all who know him. Scott has a loving servant's heart.

I think a lot of people pass away without ever knowing the lasting impact they have had on another person's life, and this is regrettable.

Even when someone seems totally put-together, they may need affirming words, an epitaph, of how they are regarded in the here and now by those who know and love them:

"Son, you are highly spoken of"; "Father, you never met a problem you couldn't solve"; "Counselor, you listen well"; "Nurse, you are an angel"; "Child, you are talented"; "Daughter, you make me proud"; "Coworker, you are reliable"; "Boss, you are an amazing negotiator"; "Patriot, you are valiant and strong"; "Physician, you are a champion of the underserved"; "Woman, you are a pioneer"; "Mother, you never give up"; "Brother, you are a great leader"; "Sister, you are a genius"; "Wife, you are my perfect lover; "Daughter, you are an amazing artist"; "Pastor, you are humble"; "Husband, you are a good and loyal friend."

You are special. You are beautiful.

You are a good gal. You are a good guy.

Yesterday, today, tomorrow, and forever, I hope my final epitaph to be:

In all things, she did her best, to live with purpose, until final rest: to know, love and serve God.

Surrender 2

"The Lord is my shepherd;
 there is nothing I lack.
 In green pastures you let me graze;
 to safe waters you lead me;
 you restore my strength.
 You guide me along the right path for the sake of your name.
 Even when I walk through a dark valley,
 I fear no harm for you are at my side;
 Your rod and your staff give me courage.

 You set a table before me
 as my enemies watch;
 You anoint my head with oil,
 my cup overflows.
 Only goodness and love will pursue me
 all the days of my life;
 I will dwell in the house of the Lord
 for years to come." Psalm 23

"And the peace of God, that surpasses all understanding, will guard your hearts and your minds, in Christ Jesus." Philippians 4:7

Jesus is aware of everything that happens to me and to everyone. Even in the most difficult times, when no one understands what I am going through nor can they console me, Jesus, my friend, and brother, understands me and helps me through. When I am ready to admit defeat or am giving up on myself, I feel him push me and lead me forward by the power of the Holy Spirit. Despite not having a physical presence that I can see and touch and feel, I know and believe he is with me always. And because he shows no partiality in his love and care for his brothers and sisters, he helps me as he helps all, equally, so that in difficult situations, whether in conflict or in peace, all might live in harmony, goodwill, giving forgiveness, and restfulness.

"I think I can, I think I can..." is my statement of faith, convicting myself to God's divine help in bringing me through my daily challenges, penetrating the vast unknown of the future, giving me courage to remain resolute in my decisions. God has helped me overcome my tendency to second-guess myself and has given me confidence and courage where once I was insecure and fearful. He has placed in my life two husbands who have loved and supported me, amazing friends who have encouraged me and who have taught me how to be strong and stretch beyond my own limitations, and he has given me a family that has believed in me without question, and their confidence in my abilities is immeasurable. I have been very blessed!

Even so, at times of uncertainty I feel a tug of war inside of me, where one side stays strong, not giving in to my weaknesses, while on the other side I am weak and feel helpless, hiding away from my problems, conflicts, and losses. It is in these times that the Lord intervenes and sends my friends and family to the rescue.

My faith strengthens me so that I let go and let the Holy Spirit steer me in the right direction. With a firm grip on my heart and mind, God's divine presence assures me that nothing is impossible to bear, and when I surrender my control to Jesus and submit to His authority that is supreme and over all creation, I am ready to accept my life as it unfolds.

One rule, one truth that remains constant and never changing is that all life will come to an end somehow, somewhere, sometime, someday. Death is a rule of life that I cannot change nor appeal to a higher court for clemency. There is no hiding from it, and when a friend or loved one dies, it can render me speechless. It is sudden and swift, no matter how long it takes to occur. It can be cruel, especially when innocent lives are lost. It makes me angry. It doesn't seem fair, and it is final. Game over, with no instant replay or do-overs.

I can rail against death, plead with God, but the outcome is always the same. Life ends, one way or another, and it is difficult for me to surrender to this absolute truth. Despite my deep and abiding faith in God and in heaven, the thought of my own death is scary.

Jesus knew and understood this truth from a young age, and he trusted his Father in heaven even though he knew he would die a violent death, an innocent man. When Jesus was in the Garden of Gethsemane, his fear was so great he sweated blood, knowing he would go through unspeakable torture and betrayal in the last hours of his life. And although he asked God to spare him, he accepted his Father's will (Luke 22:41-44).

Jesus surrendered his will, living his last day in agonizing service to God and all of humanity, knowing in the end he would win everlasting life for himself and for all.

In the last days of Tim's life, he experienced his own agony of impending death. The day before he died, he was extremely agitated and needed to be medicated to calm him down. He was struggling mightily in his mind between his will to live and the reality that his body was failing fast. Tim was not ready to leave life when he was hitting his stride professionally. He was respected by his peers, and he was accomplishing so much, with still so much to do. He did not want to say his final goodbyes to me, or his daughters who were just entering adulthood, or his family or friends who were coming to say their final goodbyes to him. He did not want to die. He was angry and wanted to be left alone but was asking for prayers for the days ahead.

During his last night, I believe while he lay sleepless in the dark Tim talked to Jesus. I think they had a long conversation and when no more could be said, he asked for his life to be spared, but if he could not be healed, he would surrender and ready himself to meet God, face to face in heaven.

When I arrived at his hospital room the following day, his mood was very different. He did not indicate to me that anything happened, but he was changed; he had a peace and a glow about him that surpassed all understanding. Tim was calm, talkative, smiling, and good humored with everyone who visited, making me and everyone feel relaxed and at ease. When his Infectious Diseases doctor came by, Tim thanked him for his care, and they gave each other a knowing glance with a slight nod of the head in acknowledgment; they both knew they would not be seeing each other again. They wished each other well and said good-bye. Oddly, there was no fear on either of their faces. There was acceptance, peace, and friendship. Witnessing this moment between doctor and patient alleviated my fear and I began to accept what I knew was coming.

I surrendered because I witnessed Tim's surrender. He never gave up his hope and faith, never for a moment, but he knew it was time to go, and he was ready. I had to let him go. Tim and God were to be together by the end of that day.

"Amen, I say to you, today you will be with me in Paradise" (Luke 23:43).

I have learned surrender is not a weakness; it is an act of service to God and to others. Surrender is not giving up or giving in. It takes courage, it shows definitive action, and it requires a choice to trust God. Surrender is a sacrifice of will that leads to godly service. When I surrender my will to God's will, no matter how scary, I am taking a true leap of faith. It is hard to walk through the valley of unknowing and uncertainty, but I know that I am in the care of God as his will becomes my will.

Certainly, I have faltered many times and I have buried my head in the sand. I have come very close to giving up, too, and it has taken a supreme effort to persevere and ask God for his help and for his will to be done. With faith as the binding agent between me and God, I have continued moving forward.

Prayerfully and with trust God leads me and guides me, and when I truly let go, I know a peace that surpasses all understanding. When I surrender my will and my control and share my journey with Jesus, all my yesterdays, todays, and tomorrows play out in real time, and I am able to accept what happens more unquestioningly. It is with a grateful heart that I persevere and keep living, no matter the challenges to come.

My surrender is giving my life and will over to God so that my path, my service, follows closely and securely to what He has planned for me.

As a seeker of peace and calm in the storms of life, I believe that God is in control. I believe that God loves me and all of his children equally. I believe that God loves all of his creation beyond all telling. I believe there is life after death. I believe the power of his love is redemption. I believe in his peace that surpasses all understanding.

I believe in the power of surrender.

When I keep God at the center of my life, and choose his will over mine, I feel strength and power come to me, giving me courage to press on.

Donna Braidic

Purpose

Sports

"Do you not know that the runners in the stadium all run in the race, but only one wins the prize? Run so as to win. Every athlete exercises discipline in every way. They do it to win a perishable crown, but we for an imperishable one. Thus I do not run aimlessly; I do not fight as if I were shadowboxing. No, I drive my body and train it, for fear that, after having preached to others, I myself should be disqualified." 1 Corinthians 9:24-27

When I was a young girl and not quite a teenager yet, I loved being outdoors and playing until dark. It was not uncommon for my mom to call me in for dinner at least three, maybe four times before I would come running, sweaty and dirty and reeking from exertion. I was not a girl who liked wearing dresses and patent leather shoes and dainty bows in my hair; no, I liked wearing boys' hand-me-downs! They were a lot more comfortable and definitely easier to climb trees in without people looking up my dress!

Never once did I worry about losing a barrette or fancy bow from my hair while jumping on my neighbor's trampoline. It was hilarious watching my friend's hair fly all around her head as we bounced, bounced, BOUNCED to within reach of her second story bedroom window! And I cannot imagine how many times I would have scraped the finish off of the toe of a patent leather shoe had I been wearing them as I sped around the neighborhood on my brother's banana-seat bike. With that said, those shiny black patent leathers against the dazzling purple of the bike seat would have looked really cool today and would have added an extra layer of exhilaration to the ride!

I tried so hard to blend in with the boys for as long as I could. They let me be myself and we had fun in my front yard playing every sport you could think of. I couldn't understand why all the girls wanted to grow up so fast; developing into a young woman was the last thing I wanted to happen to my strong, active body.

I was lucky to have a mom who understood and encouraged my athleticism, telling me about sports that were finally being offered for girls' participation. She didn't have to tell me twice! I was usually one of the first girls in line, always ready to sign up and receive my hat and team shirt!

Recreational softball was the first organized sport I participated in. I was relieved that male-dominated sports were finally being offered with girls' leagues, even if they were just recreational leagues. Of course, I complained about the unfairness of "boys only" hardball and "girls only" softball; but honestly, as much as I believed in my ability to equal the boys in strength and agility, it would have been very dangerous for me or any girl to play hardball with the boys—then or now—without the proper conditioning and training, experience, and endurance!

At the time I didn't appreciate the hard-won victory for me and for all females to compete in sports. I just wanted to compete and prove myself! I vaguely paid attention to the news about women burning their bras and taking a stand for equality with men, but I heard what people said about the women and it wasn't nice. Even though the world was evolving, and the women's liberation movement was gaining members, I remained cautious in my excitement and passion for sports. Female athleticism was still a threat to the feminine ideal and not entirely mainstream, and society was resistant to women being strong and independent, evidenced by the flak I took from girls and guys for being lean and mean.

My unpopularity with the girls (and boys) grew even more after I won the Presidential Physical Fitness Award. The "blossoming" girls, who pretended weakness but primped and preened to maintain their soft edges like it was a competitive sport, made me feel like I was weird, "gay," and I admit, I wondered sometimes if I was more boy than girl. But this "gender confusion" only lasted about a year—that is, until my first crush and kiss with my very cute neighbor boy. Unfortunately, that kiss also ended my acceptance into the "boys' club" because, suddenly, with one 4th of July kiss under the big oak tree, I was no longer a flat-chested girl wearing boy's 12-slim blue jeans; I was a girl with long blonde hair, blue eyes, and newly developing "bumps," and curves that filled out my bikini!

Oh, well! So much for hanging with the boys! But I was okay with this change. I found a new group of girls who were girls just like me: feminine, athletic trailblazers who were competitive, spirited, strong-willed, and committed to competitive sport!

I think participating in sports was my happy place, and I know without a doubt it kept me busy and out of trouble. Whether in individual competition or in team sports, I loved the feeling of winning as my athletically intuitive body responded with accuracy when challenged. Each movement and rush of adrenaline honed my mind and heightened my concentration. On the field I was in my zone.

I loved the feeling of running fast and crossing the finish line first! It made me feel invincible, but it was the losses that, although discouraging at the time, helped build my character for life. Losing did not break my spirit, even though at times it felt that way. In fact, losing made me train harder, think more wisely, and listen and study more attentively, and the losses gave me a good dose of humility. I learned that Coach usually does know what's best for me and the team! On or off the field, the lessons learned for winning and graceful losing developed my character which has served me well throughout my life.

Sports helped me become a more well-rounded person through teamwork, negotiation, argument, debate, and compromise. I would not be as strong as I am mentally, physically, or spiritually if not for my early years of competition. I developed a winning, fighting spirit that has kept me going and not giving up even when it felt like life was a losing situation.

As a Christian I face off against the strongest opponent there is in this world, and it is not easy. Temptation and evil in all of its forms battle for my soul every day, and winning for Christ, for me, and for others requires great inner fortitude, protection, and strength. Negativity, depression, malicious behaviors, gossip, and lies have weakened my core like trash talk by an opponent, but when I keep my mind and actions focused on serving the Lord, I come out a winner in my heart every time.

But I am human, and I have been lazy and weak in my spirituality. I have lost my focus and quit training at times and become sedentary in my life. "Unsportsmanlike," unchristian behavior is a hurdle to overcome, placed in my life by the enemy. Satan knows all of my weaknesses and he exploits them for his gain. Ego, self-centeredness, judgmental and righteous thought, unfair words, and most of all hypocrisy are easy traps that lead me to spiritual death and loss of mission. Scoring points at another person's expense does not make me a winner; it makes me vindictive and hurtful, leading me only into darkness.

But God is good, and life is not a race that I run alone. I need and depend on God and others to help me persevere and maintain my fight and competitive spirit. I have conditioned and trained to build up strength and fortitude through bible study, church attendance, and prayer, and I have relied heavily on coaching and teamwork from my family and friends as they support me always and cheer me onward. They keep me accountable, realistic, and honest about my strengths and weaknesses. I have listened closely to the inspired messages preached by God's servants in pastoral ministry and through their rousing "gameday" enthusiastic speech, I have been pushed to new levels of determination and endurance for Christ.

Every day is "gameday" when competing in the world for Christ, and love is the ultimate X-factor necessary for winning against evil. I have faced my opponent on the field of good and evil, and winning against the devil is my goal. I have lost at times, I have forfeited at times, but most of the time, I hope I am judged to have won the day! I have learned from my mistakes and have studied my "game film" to improve my winning strategy and readiness for my next encounter with temptation and sin.

I do not know when this life of mine will end, but when it does, I plan to slide into Heaven's home plate and climb up onto the winner's podium wearing my well-worn "The Servants" uniform!

Then, Jesus himself will stand before me and place a garland of white lilies around my neck and present the gilded trophy of eternal freedom into my hands and proclaim, "Well done, good and faithful servant! Well done!"

And from the clouds all around me a choir of angels will be heard singing God's heavenly anthem as Christ's banner is raised high above my head, and tears of joy run will down my cheeks.

Until then…game on!

Faith 1

One of my favorite bible verses is Hebrews 11:1: "Faith is the realization of things hoped for and evidence of things not seen." I love this passage because it answers one of my greatest questions concerning faith: What is faith and how do I find it? It elicits a strong response within me–emotionally and logically–in my heart and in my mind, all the way to the core of my being. The verse is like a riddle that I think was deliberately written this way to capture the curiosity of the hearer, to elicit serious internal debate for and against accepting faith as a product of hopes realized while continuing to live in the real world where the unprovable nature of God is evidenced in the joys and sufferings of living!

I believe every human being is driven to seek, know, and then prove to themselves and others the mysteries of life and the universe. Is God real? Where can God be found? Why do I believe in a God that seems absent from the miseries of his so-called children? It's easy to believe in God when things are going well! What about when things are falling apart? What about then? Where is God then? Where is faith?

When I was a little girl of six years old, I did not know what it meant to feel the presence of God, but I thought I should feel something special at church that would say, "God is here." Yet all I felt was small and lonely sitting in the cold, wooden pews. The sanctuary was dimly lit and filled with ominous statues of dead people with eyes that stared, lifeless and piercing, into my soul. The altar was unwelcoming and unapproachable with its bright, golden goblets set out for only a select few to partake of. The smell of burnt incense hung in the air like death and the space felt joyless. I did not feel God. I did not feel love. I felt scared and guilty.

But as time went by, I observed the grown-ups sitting behind and in front of me, and I noticed something special and comforting as they participated in the Mass. They listened as one, they knelt as one, they prayed as one, and they spoke as one. I felt their faith as they sang hymns to God and as they processed to the altar to receive communion. There was in the sanctuary an essence of hope, of anticipation of healing and peace. I felt God in the people. I felt God in the space. I felt God's holy presence in the breaking of the bread.

I cannot pinpoint the exact moment I knew and believed in God, but this I am sure of: I believe and trust in the supernatural, divine nature of God, and I love him.

Some days, usually when something is very wrong in my life or in the world, I'm not sure what I believe, and it can be hard not to give up and give in to the temptation to shake my fist at God, to deny his existence, and tell him to get out of my life. Yes, I have been very weak in my faith, doubting that God cares about me, and it is in these times that I want the most concrete evidence of God's existence. I turn to prayer for answers, and I speak honestly to God, letting him know that it is hard to believe he is present in the silence. But I hold onto hope and the belief that my God is still listening, and this sustains my faith to see things through.

Like gold is to a pirate, finding the faith buried deep inside of me has been a lifelong quest, a treasure of greatest value, found in my joys and sufferings and the totality of my life. Its power over me has been unbreakable, and even at life's most challenging times, when it would have been oh so easy to quit the search for faith and let go of its incalculable riches, I have continued my pursuit and found the prize of faith to carry me along life's journey.

I cannot turn a blind eye to the lived and realized mountain of evidence that has accumulated over my lifetime proving that God is truly working in my life. This would, in fact, be a denial of all that I am, and I would be lost.

I have asked myself at times, "If God is so great and he loves me so much, why will he not show himself to me? Why won't he stand before me and prove his existence?"

Like so many, I would love to see God with my own eyes, to shake his hand and look into his eyes and see pure love shining back at me. Oh, to touch his face and see God's tears of joy as I exclaim, "Abba, Father!" To hear his kind voice reply, "Donna, I have loved you always. You are my precious child, and I have always been with you."

257

Imagine if this were to happen to people! People throughout the world would believe in God and his goodness and holiness! There would be healing and peace and love all around the world!

And then I remember he has already done this when he presented himself to Moses as flame in a burning bush on Mount Horeb and spoke the words, "I AM WHO AM." God spoke his word through the many holy prophets of the Old Testament: Isaiah, Jeremiah, Ezekiel, Daniel. He sang his songs of love and lamentation and wisdom from the lips of David, the Shepherd and King. God became Man in the human being of Jesus Christ, Emmanuel: God with us.

God came into the world like all babies throughout the world; Jesus was born from his mother, Mary. His body grew in height and strength, and he learned a trade from his earthly father, Joseph, allowing him to contribute to his family as he became a man. He increased his knowledge by listening to his elders and the rabbis in the synagogue, and when he reached maturity the Son of God, Jesus, embarked on his Messianic mission to teach the people about his merciful Father, God, and the kingdom of heaven.

God took on the physical nature of humankind and made himself available to all, wanting all to believe and to be saved.

Jesus–God–did everything he could to bring people to himself so that a new kingdom on earth, a new beginning, a new Eden, might be created. He performed so many miracles and still people did not believe he was the Son of God.

The people rejected Jesus, they rejected God, and they chose not to believe. Even though the evidence for God had been established in the living history and eye-witness accounts passed down through generations before Jesus' birth, still people did not believe. From the lowliest of servants who had very little to lose to the highest king who had all he could ever want, from the least educated to the foremost philosophers, from the Gentile witnesses to the most honored Rabbi and High Priest people heard but did not listen.

So, I ask myself, knowing all that I know and professing as strongly as I profess my faith in God, why do I still search for evidence of God when times get tough?

As I write this reflection, Russia has invaded and is waging war against Ukraine. I marvel at the strong faith of the Ukrainian people and the unfaltering hope they express when they say they will prevail against the evil of war raining down on their country. I am in awe of the valiant citizenry as they work together to save their country, their freedom, their democracy, their sovereignty, from tyranny. When the bombs drop on innocent people I wonder if they cry out to God, "Where are you in this awful place?!" And then I witness their faith as they stand in the rubble and pray together in solidarity and ask the world to pray for them, too.

"Faith is the realization of things hoped for and evidence of things not seen" (Hebrews 11:1).

Where is God when bad things happen? Where is he when an F-5 tornado hits in the middle of the night and an entire town is wiped out, or a hurricane demolishes the Gulf Coast panhandle of Florida? Where is God in the battles of war or in the hospital ICUs filled with COVID-19 patients fighting for their every breath? Where is God on the streets of our cities where teenagers are killing one another, and drug abuse and overdoses of the homeless are ignored, having become an accepted casualty of life on the streets? Where is God in all of this and so much more?

I understand the need for answers because I have asked these questions myself. I understand where this frustration comes from. I feel the anger and fury that comes from the need for justice, because I have felt them myself.

Even still, I know God is present in the most tragic, horrendous moments of life. I know it because I have seen him in the human spirit of hope and love. God is love, and he does not leave us. He welcomes the refugee with open arms and a warm meal. He cradles the drug addict in the rehab center. He sings a lullaby to the orphans crying in the night. He welcomes the grieving with courtesy and kindness in the halls of our funeral homes. He is present in all people and in all situations; God does not abandon us. Love is the evidence of God's presence in his children; hope believes and faith grows. God is listening and answering every question, every doubt, every need and want, in the spirit of love.

When I had my "epiphany" moment that Hebrews 11:1 must be a logic statement about faith in God and how it occurs in the human spirit, I called upon my math whiz friend and I asked her to write a logic statement for me. I explained to Mel that my intuition told me that the verse was a statement in and of itself that supports itself, but the catch is it relies on subjective assumptions and experiences rather than objective data and certain physical evidence.

My friend wrote this truly brilliant logic statement for me in September 2017:

Faith = f(things)*realization + evidence*(things*-1*seen).

Hebrews 11:1 is not only a valid logic statement to me, but I believe it is also the inspired Word of God put on the heart of the author of the Book of Hebrews. Eyes may not see all, ears may not hear all, and hands and fingers and toes may not touch and feel all, but that does not mean that what I hope for is not producing faith in me. My living and every part of my being proclaims belief in things I cannot see, including God.

When the rain falls from the sky and flows down the rivers and streams until it is pulled from the reservoir to my faucet for me to drink, I have faith that although I did not see the clouds form from the evaporation from the earth, it is water from the sky that I drink.

I hope all who see my faith will be inspired to trust in God and discover faith in themselves, because when I came to this extraordinary place of belief and faith, I knew a peace and trust and resilience that had eluded me.

I know there are those who lose hope, but please, still have faith. I know there are those who do not believe, yet still have hope, and this hope is not in vain.

Hope resides deep in my core where God hugs me and reassures me that he loves me, and I feel his presence from the inside out, and my faith grows. It is hard to believe, but I know he is there, even in the most tragic, horrendous moments of life. I know it because I have seen him in the human spirit of hope and love. God is love, and he does not leave us, even if we do not know to ask him to stay. Love is evidence of faith, which is the result of hope, which is a response for living each day. God is listening and answering every question, every doubt, every need and want, in the spirit of love.

Hold onto hope and live in joy, for the suffering in life produces evidence of God's love each and every moment of our faith-filled lives.

Faith 2

What a perplexing joy, the relationship between me and the Trinity. Father, Son, and Holy Spirit.

There is something so much greater than myself at work in my life that over time, through my prayer, study, service, adversities, and relationships, its origin has been revealed to me: it is God, creator of all things, who is my "higher power," my Sovereign Lord, my Father in heaven.

God put it on my heart and in my mind to tell my story of faith because he knows his children on earth are searching for answers about who God is and how to find him in the minutia of their lives, people just like me. He gave me the gumption and perseverance to write my thoughts and feelings down, and it is for this reason and by his power that this book has come to be. God speaks his love, his presence, his power through my story. This I know.

God created me, as he created everything and everyone upon the earth and in the heavens. It is difficult for me to comprehend the vastness of God, yet when I look up at the blue skies or upon a snow-covered mountain range or down a crowded city street or into the cradle of a newborn baby, I see with my own eyes in the smallest details God's hand in creation.

God is always in my life. I cannot hide from him, nor do I want to. I am unique and wonderfully made.

God understands me. "He gets me!"

God created Jesus, his Divine presence, his very own son, to live in this world. Jesus also was unique and wonderfully made, and he too lived as I have lived in this world, a human being. Jesus and I are alike, and I call him my brother, my friend. Jesus was always under the watchful eye of God, and I imagine this was a great comfort to him, as it has been to me; because no matter who you are, life can be very difficult, and especially so for someone who carried the salvation of the world on his shoulders as Jesus did.

Whether on top of a mountain praying to God or calming a storm on the sea of Galilee, in a cave at night sleeping with a rock for a pillow or traipsing through the desert with worn-out sandals, at home with his mom or in the synagogue with the high priests, or just hanging out with friends over a cook fire, Jesus knew God was with him.

And like all humans Jesus was not spared adversity or death; in fact, he went through more emotional, physical, spiritual, social, and political challenges than me or anyone I know. Jesus was abandoned, interrogated, shamed, brutally tortured, and nailed to a cross at his hands and feet, left to suffocate until he died with just his mom and a few others looking on at the base of the cross, loving, loyal and true (Matthew 27:45-56).

Jesus gave his life for me. Jesus died for me, and I shall live with him in eternity.

God created the Holy Spirit to be a lasting presence in the world, and I have chosen to receive the Holy Spirit into my life to guide me and to reveal to me the source of all life. I have opened myself up, surrendered my will to delve deeply, inwardly within myself to find the source of life. It has not been easy, it has not always been a joyful experience, but it has always been an experience of love, growth, and understanding.

Veni Sancte Spiritus! Come Holy Spirit!

God created this beautiful world. It is not an accident. It is an amazing result of God's love and grace exploding into something so miraculous and awesome that my mind and logic cannot grasp the totality of its origin, and try as I may to trace back to its beginning, I cannot. That the world still exists today is a sign of God's love and presence in creation, in human suffering, and in human ingenuity. Life truly is fragile and complex, in constant flux and change, and I believe God never takes his eyes off of me or any of us, regardless of the calamities and crimes of the universe.

God loves me. God loves us all. I believe this. This is my faith.

"Come, Holy Spirit, fill the hearts of your faithful and kindle in them the fire of your love. Send forth your spirit, and they shall be created. And you shall renew the face of the earth."

Stability, Security, Success, Self-Actualization

"Do not conform yourself to this age but be transformed by the renewal of your mind, that you may discern what is the will of God, what is good and pleasing and perfect." Romans 12:2

In this book, I have written simple yet very personal reflections about people, places, and things that have influenced me and have helped me find God, pushing me to live my purpose, one day to the next. Does each reflection have "Donna's Purpose" inscribed above the title? No. But each "living without" reflection is underwritten, "Donna's Purpose Discovered." I could not, would not, should not be who I am if I had lived without any one of the blessings that I have reflected on in this book.

Each and every one of us on this earth lives in purpose—realized or not—and I believe all God asks of me is to do my best for him in my relationships, my work, and in my devotion to him. I have been called in different ways, but I know without a doubt my highest calling has been as a mother to my daughters. It has challenged me greatly and it has helped me know great love, sacrifice, suffering, and joy. I am blessed to be called to motherhood and it . is my duty to teach my daughters in word and deed that we are meant to live in love, not hate; peace, not war; faith, not atheism; hope, not pessimism; generosity, not self-serving; good stewardship, not wasteful destruction; one human being among many, existing to make a difference, with purpose.

When I look back, I realize there are three primary areas that have been most important for helping me develop at each stage of my life to become the person that I am. Since my birth I have been influenced by and grown from my personal, professional, and spiritual interactions, which have impacted my development and have moved me in ways that on my own I could not have imagined. Brought to realization by the light of love emanating from each, showing me the way, I discovered my purpose.

Generally speaking, God's purpose for me in raising my daughters seemed very clear-cut when they were little. It was just me (and their dad) with God leading the way. No boyfriends, no cell phones, no social media, no jobs, no school to influence their lives: just me and their father and that was just fine. I believed with my whole heart that my parental duty until they reached adulthood was to guide them, provide for them, teach them, protect them, and model for them the characteristics and virtues of a good citizen, as well as a good Christian, in the same way that others had modeled these for me. Then my job would be done, and my daughters would continue forward, doing for themselves. The only error in my thinking was that I thought my job was finite. In truth, being a parent never ends; it just changes.

One of the hardest things I have had to do as a parent is step aside and allow my girls to learn their own life lessons, make their own mistakes, celebrate their own successes, and turn to God in faith for direction, healing, and assistance on their individual journeys. They have had great successes and learned from terrible mistakes; they have moved two steps forward and fallen one step back; they have received praise and have also been rebuked. Most importantly they have gained wisdom and by their choices they have charted a course for their futures, progressively discerning their purpose in life.

I treasure forever the bonded relationship I have with my daughters and the depth of love we share. Since their births, I have delighted every day in the miracle that they are, and I thank God for blessing me so wonderfully. I have seen them do so many amazing things in their lifetimes and I burst with pride when I think of them! Of course, there have also been times when they hurt me, when their behavior made me pull back in despair and challenged me to set limits as they defied my will. But I would not change a thing, because good and bad, these times have formed my daughters into beautiful adult women.

One of my greatest joys and responsibilities is being a mother.

From the moment I learned I was expecting a baby, the love in my heart began to expand and grow in ways I never thought possible, and my concern for my child's life, success, and well-being became paramount in my mind.

I couldn't wait for each month of pregnancy to pass into the next; I still marvel at the changes my body went through as they grew! I welcomed their life-affirming kicks and head butts as they reminded me of the little person growing inside of me. To see their tiny foot pressed against the side of my abdomen or feel their strong elbow of resistance push back on my side was amazing and still makes me smile with a giggle, because even before they were born, they were exerting their will and determination upon me and on an invisible world!

During those nine months, the nursery was prepared and the house was childproofed in anticipation of the little one's arrival. All the hazards inside and outside the house, once ignored, became apparent and I was on constant alert, removing every object that could inflict injury and pain on my child. Before their births everything was sunshine and rainbows, but once I had them home, I realized there were many hazards that the girls could harm themselves on.

I prayed daily to God and to their guardian angels to protect them and keep them safe, and to provide for their prosperity and happiness.

It is impossible to measure my joy when they were delivered into the world or the pure enjoyment of bonding through all of the special interactions of mother and child: nursing and swaddling, learning to crawl and walk and run, reading, cuddling, singing, playing, drawing, and painting outside the lines. Love encircled us in our time together.

Of course, boundaries were tested and there was plenty of misbehaving that required me to be wise in my discipline and instill in the girls a proper sense of parental authority; I had to teach them right from wrong. I had to be firm so that they would not end up being "spoiled, unmanageable children," as their father warned would happen if I lost control.

Proverbs 13:24 says, "He who spares his rod hates his son, but he who loves him takes care to chastise him." The same goes for mothers and daughters.

Although "a good spanking" was an acceptable punishment when I grew up (trust me, I know), in the 1990s spanking was frowned upon. If I spanked the girls, my hand was viewed as a weapon of abuse, so I had to learn on the job that a stern tone, a time out, or taking favorite toys away would grab the girls' attention and change their behavior. Even so, some of these "loving corrections" had an adverse effect and I ended up hurting my girls' feelings much more than if I had just given them a quick swat on the bottom and sent them to their room, as my parents had done with me!

As a new mom, I believed my greatest responsibilities in raising my children were to teach them to be respectful to mommy and daddy and to their elders; to know about God and Jesus; to be good, unselfish people, kind and loving to others; to teach them to love and be good sisters to one another.

The girls learned to be best sisters, spending many hours a day playing on the family room floor together, learning how to share and how to keep secrets. Often, they were mistaken for twins, only seventeen months apart and looking very much alike. They melted many hearts with their sweet smiles and unique personalities. They seldom had temper tantrums or cried to get their way, but they could be stubborn and strong-willed like their dad, and many times they had no filter on what they said.

I will never forget the time when Lauren, a mere three years old, looked up with her big blue eyes and said to my parents' elderly Italian friend as he finished his very speedy dinner prayer, "Hey, Carmen, this is grace, not a race!" We all held our breath until this sweet man paused, looked straight at Lauren, tilted his head and with a twinkle in his eye, began to laugh loudly at himself and the brutal honesty of a small child. He had tears in his eyes when he said to Lauren, "You are right, little one; it is grace, but I'm a hungry old man and I want to eat!"

As the girls continued to grow, I loved seeing my daughters' gifts and talents develop, both artistically and intellectually. They shared many qualities that strengthened their bond and also endeared them to others: generosity, hospitality, humor, and helpfulness. There is no denying they are sisters, but they are also unique and completely different in so many ways!

I have always believed in their unlimited potential, and at times I have pressured them and imposed my high expectations on them, and as a result they have resisted me, resented me, or completely ignored me and my guidance. I did my best when I sent my girls outside to play, when I told them to do their homework, when I made them do their chores and clean up after their pets and practice their music, when I taught them about God and Jesus and the Holy Spirit, when I praised them for good grades and when I disciplined them for breaking rules. We did not have video games or social media, but we spent time outdoors "Camping with Christ" and looking up at the stars, roasting marshmallows over a cook fire and making fond memories with friends.

Certainly, we have had our share of mother/daughter confrontations from childhood into adulthood: arguments, resentments, and silences which caused rifts in our relationship and even caused one or the other to leave the security of home. We have cried and sulked and barely spoken a word to each other until love intervened and we found forgiveness.

When my daughters transitioned from teenagers to adults it was hard for me to keep pace. I wanted to keep them under my keen eye and living by my rules, but they wanted their grown-up lives, separate and independent. As free-thinking adults, they changed a great deal, and I saw these changes manifest in their social activities, friends, homes, clothing, religious practices, eating habits, vocabulary, hair color, etc.–things that I did not always approve of. We were going in different directions, where once we moved in tandem.

It seemed that in the blink of an eye my family of four shrank back down to two and then down to one when my husband died, and I felt like I had lost everyone and a big part of myself. I lost my identity as a mom and as a wife, and it hurt deep in my core. It felt like my heart was tearing.

I felt like I lost my purpose.

It was a terribly emotional time of grieving for my girls, too; the loss of their dad was almost too much to bear. Their lives were forever changed; their optimism for a bright future was replaced with grieving the loss of their dad. They were living one day at a time, and although we were bonded in grief, I never felt farther from them than I did at that time.

The girls escaped back to their different colleges, spending more and more time away at school and in town with friends, all of us living separate lives and with different lifestyles. Their intermittent drop-ins at my house with strangers created a lot of stress for me, and I did not always approve of who they brought home. Although I was still mom to the girls, I was slowly adjusting to being just Donna again, and these unplanned visits were unfair to me. As much as I dreaded it, it was clear to me the girls needed to move out on their own and I was to become an empty nester.

I prayed to Jesus for guidance and direction with this decision and asked how I would present to the girls that which was clear to me. A year and a half after their dad's passing, I told the girls I thought it was time for them to take the next step toward further independence and find an apartment to move to. Four months later, they were both living in their new homes.

This was by far the hardest thing I would do as a parent–that is until two years later when I moved away to a new home next door to my mom and dad in a new state with my new husband, leaving my girls to live their adult lives on their own terms and in their own way.

It was with this history of motherhood and the baggage of life that I found myself in a highly charged conversation with my parents and husband one afternoon about "young people today" and what they are doing with their lives. My daughters, although in their late twenties by this time, were included in the category–young people today–and as their mother I immediately felt defensive, on the alert, and everything that was said I took personally.

I bristled with feelings of guilt, and I blamed myself for the direction my daughters' lives were taking. I was frustrated with my daughters because I could not control their adult choices, and I believed they were making choices that were negatively impacting their lives and didn't bode well for their futures.

In a flash, I second-guessed every decision I had made as a parent. Should I have spanked the girls when they were little and done away with the time-out chair? Spent more time with them? Less time with them? How did I fail them? Where did I go wrong?

Our conversation continued with a general theme of blaming young people for their lack of direction, lack of responsibility, poor decision-making, questionable financial security, and uncertain career paths, thus removing any blame or responsibility from parents and upbringing. If I allowed myself to accept this as truth,

I could never look at myself in the mirror again, because I knew as a parent it was my responsibility to bring my girls up in a way that set them up for success. Blaming young people entirely for their actions or lack thereof was not right; it was part of it, but I felt responsible, too, as a parent.

I wondered if it was my fault when the girls slid backwards, falling out of step with their own needs to achieve their full potential and, ultimately, self-actualization as described by Abraham Maslow in his Hierarchy of Needs. I believed their father and I had provided their basic needs, but it was up to them to meet their psychological and self-fulfillment needs.

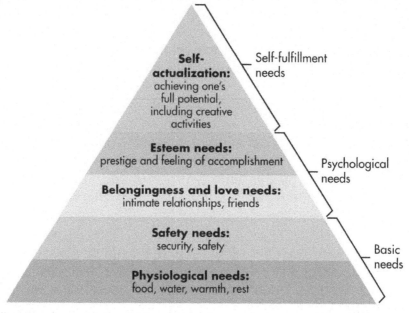

(Image from McLeod.)

As the conversation with my parents and husband continued, I became more and more perturbed that fault and blame were being placed entirely on young people for their lack of direction and motivation, and I blurted out, "It's not just the kids' fault that they are the way they are. It's the parents, too, who have in one way or another influenced their behavior. Our kids are given everything. They struggle for nothing!"

But this was just a quick, petulant answer for a very concerning problem.

And it passed judgment unfairly on kids and adults alike. Yes, it absolutely did.

And it was a false generalization, lumping all kids and parents together and concluding that everyone has an equal share in money and power and advantage. It implied all kids have it easy, all parents care too much, shelter their kids and never let them struggle, and this is flat-out wrong.

But in that moment my guilt and defensiveness rose up, and although it was shocking, it opened up a conversation about the challenges parents face, that I have faced, and that my daughters have faced: challenges all youth and adults face today from all walks of life. Yes, the truth is, my daughters were given everything they needed, as much as was possible, and in the end I over-indulged them, over-protected them, and in so doing, supplanted their struggle to succeed on their own.

I confess I have made mistakes as a mom. When I told my girls they needed to move out, I believed it was for them, but it was for me, too. I was tired and depressed, and I didn't know how to control them anymore. Scott was in my life, giving me love and support, and I truly believed the girls moving out would impel them towards being independent, mature young women.

The house was not the same after their dad died; it felt spacious and hollow. I genuinely felt my daughters were struggling against their own grief, trying to maintain some normalcy while going through the motions of living. I thought their feelings of guilt over leaving me alone might be preventing them from taking their next step towards independence; in essence I was holding them back. In telling them to move out I believed I was releasing them from their "old life" and any feelings of responsibility they had toward me. I didn't take into consideration that I might be dropping the bottom right out from under them, leaving them feeling alone, free-falling.

I have since learned that this was very hard for my girls; it hurt them, and some hurts are hard to mend completely, on both sides. But we continue to mend them over time because we forgive, and we love each other.

There is no perfect human answer for solving the woes of our youth or the consternation of our elders, but God knows all of our challenges. Although I have made mistakes as a parent, I have been a good mom, too, and I cannot beat myself up.

I gave good guidance; I gave good love.

Possibly the lesson I have learned is that in all times and generations there are drastic societal changes that are not evident until each generation lives late into their years. It may sound old-fashioned, but I believe in the traditions that I was raised in and that I have passed on to my daughters. It has been incumbent upon us to adapt but not abandon what is right and just. Maybe this is what God is teaching me. If so, God, please help me to be the best parent I can be in these changing times, and help me to continue to promote all of the good, sustainable things of youth as I live and fulfill my purpose as a human, a woman, a wife, and a mom.

God created me for this purpose. God created my daughters for a purpose, and he is helping me help them find their way. That is my purpose as their parent, and I rejoice in it!

Purpose: "The One"

"God freely created us so that we might know, love, and serve him in this life and be happy with him forever. God's purpose in creating us is to draw forth from us a response of love and service here on earth, so that we may attain our goal of everlasting happiness with him in heaven.

All the things in this world are gifts of God, created for us, to be the means by which we can come to know him better, love him more surely, and serve him more faithfully.

As a result, we ought to appreciate and use these gifts of God insofar as they help us toward our goal of loving service and union with God. But insofar as any created things hinder our progress toward our goal, we ought to let them go." St. Ignatius of Loyola

The words of St. Ignatius of Loyola have changed me. Like an epiphany, I see with new eyes the gift of wisdom that he imparts. Read again the second sentence, "God's purpose in creating us." *God's* purpose. God's *purpose*? God's purpose!

The saint's words, "*God's purpose*," are so subtle that I didn't see his important message right away. It was so quick that I nearly missed it! Then suddenly, like a Magic Eye picture, once seen it's the only thing I can see! God had a purpose in creating me and all of humanity. I didn't just happen; I don't just exist! I was born to fulfill God's purpose here on earth. The picture of my life, once distorted and blurred by the events in it, is clearer now and I see God's planned purpose for my life.

By virtue of St. Ignatius' calling to know, love, and serve God, he tells us we are part of God's story, God's beginning, middle, and end.

My earthly life, from my birth to my death, one day to the next–good and bad–is part of God's amazing plan for the world while I live, until eternity. God created me intentionally, for a reason, with purpose, to love and serve while I live.

"For I know well the plans I have in mind for you, says the Lord; plans for your welfare, not for woe! Plans to give you a future full of hope. When you call me, when you go to pray to me, I will listen to you. When you look for me, you will find me. Yes, when you seek me with all your heart, you will find me with you, says the Lord, and I will change your lot; I will gather you together from all the nations and all the places to which I have banished you, says the Lord, and bring you back to the place from which I have exiled you." Jeremiah 29: 11-14

Life is unpredictable, as many of my experiences and stories attest to, and I would assume this is true for everyone. And through it all, I thank God for my life because it is by and through all that I have experienced that I have come to know, love, and serve God, personally and uniquely on my journey. Looking back, I see how my purpose in its early days was shallow and me-driven. Even so, with all of my ups and downs, highs and lows, as far back as I can remember, I have been fulfilling my purpose, whether I have realized it or not, and I will continue to devote my life to its purposeful fulfillment.

I have learned that knowing, loving, and serving God is not a one-size-fits-all undertaking. How can it be when "I am fearfully and wonderfully made" (Psalm 139:14), created by God to live my unique and wonderful life on the path he has laid before me? I am not here to imitate someone else's life. I am here to live my life, authentically and intentionally. Foolishly, at times I have made the mistake of comparing my journey to someone else's wise and discerned journey, judging my lack of understanding for my own as my downfall and weakness, and thus stumbling into insecurity and Satan's Lane of lies, malice, and ego.

It was during these times that I did not like myself or the direction my life was taking, and I sought greater spiritual exploration. I asked the Holy Spirit to guide me, inspire me, be with me in my daily living so that I might know God intimately, because as much as I was told God would never reject me, I still had some hurdles to overcome; I did not quite feel worthy of his love. I felt flawed and irredeemable as a result of my selfish choices, and the sting of shame still burned on my cheeks when I remembered the emotional and physical abuses I had endured. As a result, I had created barriers of protection around my spiritual life and around my heart.

I asked God to penetrate these barriers and heal me, and he began his work in me right away. In allowing God to remove my feelings of unworthiness and damage, I changed from the inside out. I let go of my pride and I replaced it with humility and chose love of self, of family, of life.

In time, relationships were mended, advice was received, and I accepted my limitations. The Holy Spirit was working within the parameters of my life to convert me to a deeper life of service.

This was a very transformative time for me personally, spiritually, and in my faith. I became joyful, forgiving, and more loving of myself and towards others. The Holy Spirit led me to a greater commitment to parish life in music ministry where I used my voice, my guitar, my intuition for choosing music, and my ability to direct others to make beautiful music. It was astonishing to answer God's call and feel so alive in doing so. Music ministry became a new pathway for my spiritual growth, giving way to the divine and a secure connection to God.

Music ministry is truly a labor of love, undergirded by my purpose to know, love, and serve God, the impetus for my actions. Performing music is one way I am able to communicate God's peace, joy, and love to the world. I have seen the same approach by others in their own professions, realizing the same fulfillment of love and purpose; as actors and athletes, restauranteurs and healthcare professionals, moms and dads, husbands and wives, artists and ministers; truly, in more walks of life than I can list, people realize their purpose in blessing the world!

My sister is an actor and I have seen her purpose come to life, on stage through her character portrayals and behind the scenes through her generous mentoring of fellow actors. Veteran actors and new talent alike, directors and crew members, have been graced by her theatrical strengths and expertise so that a production comes to life for the audience! This was surely what I witnessed at the performance of *The Curious Incident of the Dog in the Night-time* by Mark Haddon. My sister's performance was brilliant, as was that of the entire cast. I witnessed an undeniable love that went beyond the characters they portrayed, beyond the story they told. The entire crew shared a love and a bond with one another and the audience that I concluded was a result of their love of purpose, their craft undergirded by their knowledge, love, and service to God. It is what I felt, it is what I experienced, and it is what moved me to tears at the end of the performance, and still does. Bravo!

In this same way I hope that people who come to church experience God's love through the music and the work of liturgy.

It is said that when a choir or a group of people sing together, their hearts sync up and beat in unison (Haensch). I believe this is absolutely true as I have experienced firsthand my own heart beating in time to the music, creating positive energy with others as we sing together for a singular purpose, connecting hearts, minds, and souls, until all hearts are beating as one. In modern language, synergy! In faith language, the unity of the Holy Spirit!

Through the energy and spirit of music at worship, God is present, and over the years many people have extended their gratitude to me in person and in written notes for the love and grace they have felt. One very memorable thank you note was sent to me by a visitor at church. She said the beautiful music of the choir touched her heart, and her lovely words in turn touched mine. Her words brought to mind the times on my own journey when I attended Mass and felt alone, needing to be touched deeply rather than on the surface, needing a reason for faith, begging to feel loved, searching for God and answers to "Why?", and how one beautiful song at Mass, or at a concert or Broadway show or on the radio, found its way into my heart and soul and brought me back to love.

I shared the thank you note with my choir, and everyone was smiles and giggles, hearing that their music had touched someone so thoroughly. I highlighted to them that whether they are aware of it or not, their hard work and commitment make a difference, and people feel God come alive in their souls through music.

The choir gave a great gift, a beautiful duty of bringing Christ to others.

It was with a heart of empathy and grace that the idea of "The One" came to me years after receiving the thank you note, understanding more completely with each passing year that there is one person in every congregation or grocery line or classroom or audience who, like me at times, needs to be touched by the love of others, the love of God.

"The One" is everyone, sons and daughters of God, born to live fully in fulfillment of God's purpose while searching for the meaning and purpose of life.

"The One" is everywhere. They come to church and may sit just a few pews away from me, hoping to experience God's love and acceptance in the holy sacraments. Or they may sit next to me at work, underpaid, harried, feeling inadequate and needing affirmation as they try to manage their life and their kids' lives. They may sit at my dining table, hair combed down into their shaded eyes, barely present, uttering three words: "hello," "nothin'," and "goodbye."

"The One" sits across the aisle from me on the bus and shares an armrest with me on the airplane. They walk by on the street, barely noticing me, earbuds shutting me and the rest of the world out. "The One" rides in strollers with drool running down their chins, an iPad in their chubby hands serving as a surrogate caregiver. They are police on patrol, and millionaires in executive suites. "The One" is everyone, from every walk of life, waiting for a blessed tonic, a song of love to be sung into their heart, a light for their soul.

"The One" helps me accomplish my purpose in music ministry, bringing forth a real desire in me to inspire and touch lives through music. "The One" reminds me of my higher purpose to glorify God in my music and in my life. God put this on my heart, and I am responding to his call and fulfilling my purpose.

I pray that all ears will hear, and all eyes will see, and all hearts will be moved and roused from spiritual slumber so that all will perceive more clearly God's purpose for his sons and daughters, a beautiful, purposeful life. God's purpose.

At the end of St. Ignatius' message, "to know, love and serve God" is the hope of fulfillment to enjoy everlasting happiness with God in heaven. The journey of my entire life has been unfolding each day, and as I have walked and wandered, I have gained wisdom of purpose. As long as I stay focused on God's plan for my life, my path will be clear and straight, and I will never walk alone while I love and serve the Lord.

Donna Braidic

Isaiah 49, Carey Landry
I will never forget you, My people
I have carved you on the palm of My hand
I will never forget you
I will not leave you orphaned
I will never forget My own

Does a mother forget her baby?
Or a woman the child within her womb?
Yet even if these forget,
Yes, even if these forget,
I will never forget my own

I will never forget you, My people
I have carved you on the palm of My hand
I will never forget you
I will not leave you orphaned
I will never forget My own

Enlightenment

Purpose 1

"Necessity is the mother of invention." Plato

What came first: the chicken or the egg?

It's certainly debatable!

Everyone has an opinion about what came first, and I daresay my answers are similar to everyone else's ever since the first time Aristotle posed this question more than two thousand years ago: certainly the egg was first to become a chicken…yes, but a chicken had to exist first to lay the egg…God created two chickens, a male and a female, and the female laid the egg, and therefore the chicken came first! No…God must have placed an egg in a nest where it hatched and grew into a chicken! Yes, but there needs to be two eggs, then…. And so on and so forth.

Aristotle's question is very interesting and perplexing because in essence he is asking what the origin of all living things is, which is indeed the greatest unsolved mystery of the universe! In spite of scientific and technological advancements we still ponder and explore explanations for life. The best assumption I can make for human existence is based on a very limited amount of class time on the subject, television documentaries and magazine articles, and many, many visits to museums across the country, visiting the amazing Natural History exhibits created by anthropologists and other curators dedicated to discovering and understanding the origins of human beings.

I find it very fascinating that millions and millions of years ago something fantastic and wonderful happened on this planet and human life came into existence in its most primitive form. The Book of Genesis provides an amazing overview of the creation story, including chapter 2:7 when the Lord God formed man, and chapter 2:22 when the Lord God formed woman, and I accept this story as true. Just as my family has passed down its stories from my elders' earliest recollections and records, I believe Genesis provides an oral history from the earliest forms of communication, passed down for hundreds of thousands of years describing human emergence that was well preserved and recorded lest the history be forgotten.

Evolving over the millennia, human intelligence and IQ increased, emotional and physical competencies evolved, spiritual enlightenment and reliance on God became normative, and faith in the supernatural became something to seek and find. Civilizations grew more sophisticated and developed an understanding of engineering, physics, and logic. Ultimately through these advancements, people became more self-reliant and more independent, and a desire for greater satisfaction in life arose in the human spirit. The quest for adventure, the pursuit of dreams, and a realization of purpose became a necessity for a fulfilling life.

Which leads me to wonder if Aristotle ever looked up to the skies and with hands shaking up to heaven asked, "Why am I here? What is my purpose?" This is the greater mystery to me!

Just like the chicken and the first human, I was born. I happened! I am here. That is a given! Now what?

Knowing why I am here, why we are all here, is of much greater importance and relevance to me. I know *how* I came to be; I want to know *why* I came to be. And taking it a step further, which came first: me or my purpose?

I used to wonder if my purpose was predetermined by God before I was born, "when I was still in my mother's womb" (Psalm 139:13), planted deeply and firmly in my soul to be revealed to me once I reached the age of maturity by the Holy Spirit—or if it would be a product of my living, revealed to me organically as I adapted and grew through real-life experiences. Now I think it is both, and by the grace of God, I have been piecing my purpose together one day at a time, like a jigsaw puzzle, through each interaction and connection I make with people, places, and things. With each piece of life experience fitting together I feel a new excitement, satisfaction, and joy as the bigger picture of my life and purpose is revealed.

God put my purpose in me.

I compare it to the "kernel" in a computer which is programmed at the computer's creation. It is "the core of a computer's operating system, with complete control over everything in the system" (Moltzau). It is "present and alive" throughout the life of the computer, whether the computer is in the factory, in a box on a warehouse shelf, on a desk in my home, or stored away in the attic. It does not matter if the computer is powered on or off, the kernel is always ready and waiting to operate the computer hardware and software components. As I type these words the kernel in my computer is performing its function quietly in the system software.

At my conception God was present and I was formed with both physical and spiritual "components," body and soul. Within my soul was my purpose, my kernel, which was ready and waiting to be born. When I left my mother's womb and gasped my first breath of life, my purpose spontaneously started to influence my needs and wants for finding fulfillment and satisfaction! Immediately, my brain and heart and soul synced up, forming a conduit between me and God and all things in my life. God is a part of all I am and all I do, my memories, my experiences, my dreams and aspirations, my drive, my ambition, my waking, my resting, my loving...everything!

God is the master engineer of me and every soul on earth. His design is perfect, and God does not make mistakes! He has pre-installed his perpetual "kernel" in each and every one of us to ensure that our inmost being is on standby, ready to light up and engage with him the moment the search for purpose begins.

In my infancy my reliance on my parents was primary, mirroring a reliance on God, yet once I was able to say "yes" and "no," my will emerged, and I opposed my parents' will. I began to test and verify the boundaries of good and bad choices, and as I grew older, my self-centered interests and whims ignored my parents' will, as well as God's commandments—God's law—and I did shamefully stupid things!

As I grew and matured from infancy into a toddler into a teenager and finally into an adult, I stopped relying so heavily on my parents and teachers for good guidance and direction, preferring to depend on myself. I became self-reliant, self-confident, self-aware, self-disciplined, all in an effort to develop a self-image that would support my self-purpose.

When I claimed my "self's" independence, I slipped quietly from my dependence on God, leaving him almost completely out of the picture. Yet, God, like a mother who has just given birth to her baby, knew me before I was born. God knew what I was destined to accomplish, and he also knew my human heart and its desires; he knew what would entice me to stray and go it alone, and he waited on the edges of my life.

At the time I did not grasp how much I needed God the Father, Jesus, and the Holy Spirit to guide me. I did not understand what "opening my inmost being" meant, and I did not allow myself to be vulnerable to ask for help in my ignorance and naivete. Before I gained clarity of purpose, my life was confusing, shallow, lacking relevance, and needing direction. It was I who left God out of my life, and more than once I suffered for my arrogance.

At my very lowest times, I asked why a loving Father would allow so many bad things to happen. Why would a loving Father not prevent or change all of the terrible outcomes? Does he hear me? Why don't things change?

In answer, I heard a voice deep in my soul say to me, "I love you. These things cannot be changed, but you can change how you respond to them."

I am only human; I am not perfect. I make mistakes, and I can change. Thus humbled, I needed only to ask the Holy Spirit to reveal to me who I am, why I am, and what I am here for.

In my surrender I recognized the underlying desire in me to be more, to know more, to love more, to serve more. Through hardship and joy, I became open to enlightenment, and I recognized the soulful yearning to perceive with clear vision my place and purpose in this world. God's purpose for my life was not to be thwarted; it was planted deeply and firmly in my soul.

It has been in these betwixt and between times that Jesus has refined me and helped me become who I am created to be. In my struggles and in my celebrations, he tunes my heart to his perfect pitch, to his perfect purpose for my life:

To know, love and serve God who strengthens my resolve to remain faithful in all circumstances, surrendering my will for His will, so that I might bring happiness, joy and solace to all I meet, through the sharing of God's love and faithfulness in all aspects of my life; through the music I sing and play, in the work I do and the interactions I have with others while at home and in the workplace, in the sharing times of conversation, relaxation and times of the leisure. (St. Ignatius of Loyola)

I believe finding one's purpose is a basic necessity of life and once discovered it invigorates, enlarges, and sustains every reason for living. Purpose builds up instead of tearing down. Purpose is a fountain, not a drain. Purpose greases the wheels of progress instead of creating friction that grinds things to a halt. Purpose undergirds everything I endeavor to do and everything I want to be in my life.

We all have a purpose.

"Therefore, I tell you, whatever you ask for in prayer, believe that you have received it, and it will be yours" (Mark 11:24).

In prayer I have asked God to reveal to me my purpose. I have contemplated from deep within, from my inmost being, what God wants me to know of my purpose. And in my living and loving and suffering and yes, my mistakes, God has spoken in my heart that my purpose is and always will be in every season and circumstance to know, love, and serve him. In doing this I am at peace.

My life is fuller and more joyful and more purposeful now that I "rely on God for my understanding" (Proverbs 3:4-5).

Through my continuing prayer life, I respond differently to challenges and hardships in life and in how I perceive God's part in it all. In my need to understand why I am here I have chosen to know, love, and serve God, and in so doing, I have received all I have ever needed.

Living without God the Father, and Jesus, and the Holy Spirit hurts too much. Living without love hurts too much. Living without purpose and serving hurts too much. I choose soul and spirit and purpose, my "kernel," to guide my path and choose rightly, to "plan my course and direct my steps" (Proverbs 16:9).

God loves me, and he but asks me to open my heart and my mind and my soul to his love. God wants me to trust him and accept life no matter what happens, to pray and keep open the channels of communication between him and me and to keep them open, come what may. God seeks in every corner of my heart for the hurts and wrongs that I have stored away, and he wants to heal those places so that I may be joyful in my living.

What is my purpose?

My purpose remains the same, a live current within me, awake in every circumstance and in every dilemma and personal crisis— at times fraying on the edges, stretched to the limit, yet never breaking, tearing, or severing from the spiritual lifeline that is between me and my God: a lifeline for all humans since the beginning of time.

My purpose has not changed; I have changed. I now know that my purpose is knowing, loving, and serving God. It is at the core of my being, the heart and soul of my purpose. It undergirds every aspect of my living and working and playing. It sustains me. It is intentional. It is the springboard for the work of my life.

"I can do all things through Christ who strengthens me" (Philippians 4:13).

Purpose 2

"No turning back, no turning back!" (Simon Marak, "I Have Decided to Follow Jesus")

As the years have passed, I clearly see the true measure of my faith in the trust I have conveyed when opening my heart to love and letting go and letting God direct my life. Yet at times of great consequential decisions, it has been quite frightening to throw my hopes and dreams like confetti up into the sky and watch the wind carry my prayers to a God I cannot see. I have waited for answers with the belief that God and his angels will answer my prayers before my own impatience and the passage of time, like a black hole, consumes the light of my dreams.

This was the case when I decided to step back from directing my choir, a choir I loved beyond words for its people who loved me and my family–a choir whose members' love for each other and love of their church and God inspired many to a deeper faith and belief in God, a choir that I for many years poured my spiritual energies into through my service to the Lord, a choir that produced extraordinary music. I felt like I was leaving my child–a child that had grown into an adult, a child ready to stand on their own after years of formation, a child that I was not ready to let go of but must.

Leaving the choir was the last thing I wanted to do, but it was a decision formed from a need to move forward after my late husband's death. The demands on my energy in the midst of grieving and change in career, along with supporting my grown daughters, zapped my strength and my ability to perform my choir duties at the level I had set for myself for so long. I was on my knees, no longer able to perform with the same desire and energy I had once taken for granted.

It was time for me to let go and let God. I prayed he would provide the choir a new director that would continue the work that he had begun in me. I prayed that I would find peace in the midst of this difficult time of darkness in my life:

Lord, help me be like Jesus. Please help me to decrease in my ministry as choir director while the new choir director comes to light and increases in their service to you and to the choir. Help me decrease as he/she increases. Amen

As time passed and I increased my work in service to others in my new job in Spiritual Care Services, and as my feeling of loss decreased along with my grip on my choir–really, God's choir–I bid my farewell and passed the baton on to my replacement with great love and desire for her success.

It was not me that changed the direction of my life; it was the events of my life, and when I felt powerless and rudderless in my future vision for myself, God was there watching and listening and providing a way for me to go forward in joy. He knew my heart was breaking and he never left my side.

And God continued to answer my prayers.

God has been so good to me.

I ask myself, do I say God is so good to me because, come what may, I have prayed my will be his will, giving over my power to determine the direction of my life and my dreams, and what I have prayed for has turned out well? Or do I say it because all along God has been so good to me, making his plans for my life what I have lived, and the dreams of my heart have been within my reach and in God's perfect timing? The answer is both.

Thomas Merton expressed it best for me in his *Prayer of Abandonment*:

My Lord God, I have no idea where I am going. I do not see the road ahead of me. I cannot know for certain where it will end. Nor do I really know myself, and the fact that I think I am following your will does mean that I am actually doing so. But I believe the desire to please you does in fact please you. And I hope I have that desire in all that I am doing. I hope that I will never do anything apart from that desire. And I know that, if I do this, you will lead me by the right road, though I may know nothing about it. Therefore I will trust you always though I may seem to be lost and in the shadow of death. I will not fear, for you are ever with me, and You will never leave me to face my perils alone (Merton).

God has blessed me with time for peace and respite from my sorrows and he has turned my grieving into joy. He waited with me and when he heard me ask, "What next?", he led me and my family forward to a new life, a new community, a new ministry, while at the same time preserving and invigorating what I had left behind.

Since leaving my beloved choir, my life has changed dramatically, with many consequential questions answered and joyful celebrations brought forth from unknown, unanticipated dreams come true! I have remarried and begun a new life with my husband in South Carolina. My lifestyle has become more leisurely, and my time is stretched between family, travel, and yes, church ministry, as I answer the call again to lead. God knew the restlessness of my spirit and he has spread before me a banquet of not one but two parish music ministries! The choirs are small but mighty, and the spirit of the Lord is strong within the ministries.

God has called me to increase my service in church ministry as he has made a way for me to decrease my work and involvement in other areas. God's light shines brightly over my home, and I am at peace in my decisions. This is my story now. I cannot see into my future, but I know that whatever darkness may cast a shadow over my shoulder while I journey along life's path, the light of God shines in front of me, and I need only follow it to eternity.

"And do not get drunk on wine, in which lies debauchery, but be filled with the Spirit, addressing one another [in] psalms and hymns and spiritual songs, singing and playing to the Lord in your hearts, giving thanks always and for everything in the name of our Lord Jesus Christ to God the Father" (Ephesians 5:18-20).

God is good, all the time. All the time, God is good.

Purpose 3

"I waited, waited for the LORD;
  Who bent down and heard my cry.
  Drew me out of the pit of destruction,
  out of the mud of the swamp,
  Set my feet upon rock,
  steadied my step,.
  And put a new song in my mouth,
  a hymn to our God.
  Many shall look on in awe
  and they shall trust in the LORD." Psalm 40:1-4

God is Father, Jesus, and the Holy Spirit–the Trinity–three in one, and I call upon each in different ways for different reasons.

The Father is omnipotent, a great voice from heaven, ever watchful, protective, merciful, always giving second chances. God is merciful, God is kind and compassionate, God is love.

Jesus is quiet, strong, shrewd, and he speaks directly, his fierce dark eyes piercing yet kind. In my mind he is taller than me, but I don't feel inferior to him; I feel equal and respected by him.

The Holy Spirit is a white and blue wind, with a red and orange flame swirling through the center unhindered by space or time, energizing me and all it touches, transforming prayers and ideas into action for the Lord.

Verses 1-4 of Psalm 40 are some of my favorite verses in the entire Bible because in four sentences the psalmist goes from the pit of despair to elation and feeling transformed again because he trusted God!

In the first verse, the psalmist feels alone and abandoned, stuck in a bad situation, waiting for God to come to his aid. He waits patiently for the Lord, not questioning why the Lord is delayed in coming to the rescue. He knows God will get there when he gets there, in his perfect timing! He remains faithful and although he does not know how long it will take, he knows that God in his mercy will come to his aid.

Oh, how I pray to God for this same patience and trust during difficult times, when I am stuck in a difficult situation that I see no way out of.

I imagine Jesus leaning over a pit and reaching his strong carpenter's hand down for me to grasp onto. I look up and grasp his hand and hold on tightly, and looking into my eyes, he asks, "Do you trust me?" I squeeze a little harder and respond, "Yes, Jesus, I trust you. Please pull me to your safety and protection. Please bring me to your love." With that, Jesus pulls me effortlessly out of the pit as if I have the weight of a feather. He sets me down easily at his side and I collapse into his arms. I am safe and secure in his presence again.

Jesus forgives me and my sinfulness. He frees me from the pit of destruction and despair, and I no longer feel abandoned or afraid. It is an overwhelming experience. All is well, peace prevails, and my joy is complete.

And with that, the Holy Spirit takes my joy and multiplies it. He enlivens my soul, he puts "a new song in my mouth," and all will see the transformation of my being and will trust and believe in God.

Like the psalmist, once rescued and standing on firm rock, solid ground, I am able to walk with steady feet to my purpose, and my desire to know, love, and serve God more completely is renewed, brought to life in my deliverance.

"Jesus loves me unconditionally, and there is nothing I can do that will ever separate me from his love" (Romans 8:38).

Every moment of every day, regardless of what I do or don't do, Jesus loves me. He is a hair's-breadth away, with one hand steadily guiding me and the other ready to pull me back to him. His compassion flows over me like a cool breeze on a warm summer's day. Jesus is always in my life, and because of him I love more, laugh more, give more, forgive more, and enjoy life to the fullest, avoiding a fall into the pit of destruction again.

Jesus has blessed me with wonderful gifts in order to bless others, and he has set my feet firmly where they need to be so that

I can thrive and fulfill my purpose to know, love, and serve him wherever life takes me.

Purpose 4: Music

"To sing is to pray twice." St. Cecelia

We all have gifts to share, talents to discover and use, and opportunities for planting seeds of goodness and love. Peace is possible; healing is possible; heaven on earth is possible.

I am grateful for the gift of music and am in awe of the powerful goodness it produces in me and others. Music makes me stronger in my faith and unafraid when my nerves try to steal my confidence.

The words and melody of songs from all genres shape my mood, and when I close my eyes and listen, my imagination begins to ponder and dream, creating art in my mind. The instruments, words, and voice(s) have great power, evoking memories of high emotion and movement of my body, mind, heart, and soul. Music, dance, and singing move me to wakefulness when nothing else can, causing a myriad of emotions to spill over from its beauty.

Even at my angriest, most unagreeable times, my heart has softened against my will when I prayerfully listen to or perform songs of both secular and religious origin. Even my hardest heart and stiffest neck take a pause when music is playing. And when a song like "What a Wonderful World" comes on the radio and Louis Armstrong's rich voice fills the room, my heart melts and tears roll down my cheeks. Like a plow breaking through frozen ground during a spring thaw, words and melody can cut like a plowshare through my stubborn thoughts of hurt and anger. Once my surface resistance has broken, my heart is opened, and the seeds of forgiveness find fertile soil to grow, and the fruits of love begin to grow like notes on a staff waiting to be sung.

There are many people in pain–physically, emotionally, mentally, and spiritually–and I can't fix them or change their situation, but by its very nature, music prays twice the needs of people to heaven, and so I sing and pray for them.

Love is in music; love is the message of Christ. Love tears down walls built on human emotion, releasing stubborn, righteous energy that separates people. Love unites people in Christ and music brings harmony to all.

When I sing, I pray twice: I sing a prayer of hope and faith and love. I sing a prayer of hope and faith and love. Amen.

Purpose 5: God is love

God is love.

This was true before I knew God, before I loved God, before I served God.

God has always been in plain view everywhere I have been, and he will continue to be in plain view everywhere I go. God has pushed me forward and God has pulled me back. God has shaken me, and God has soothed me. God has winked at me, God has plopped right down in my lap, God has run behind me and before me. God has let me go and God has held me up. God has waited for me, and God has run ahead of me.

It wasn't until I went looking for God, searching for truth—his Truth—that I acknowledged I did not really know him, love him, or serve him in all aspects of my life. I created boundaries and set limitations on his love.

I knew God and I knew how I wanted God to know me.

I loved God and I knew how I wanted God to love me.

I served God and I knew how I wanted God to serve me. Me, me, me.

It wasn't until I went looking for God that I realized my ignorance in my approach to knowing, loving, and serving God. It wasn't until I searched for God that I realized the flaw in my thinking that God is made by my design. I see now God is not an idea, a fiction, a large and looming mystery of the past. God is not a figment of my imagination, God is not "on demand," paid for monthly like a cable bill.

God is an actual presence in my life, God exists in my being. God is real, as real as me. God is all things and is in all things. God is in pain, in suffering, in war, in death. God does not force these things. They are a continuation of human activity since the beginning of time.

Out of fear and avoidance of unpleasant things, I did not search for God in hurtful, painful things. I did not search for love in my troubles. Why would God be found in what I do not love? I have preferred living unhappily rather than facing what makes me unhappy in my human, worldly life. I have chosen to suffer pain for years rather than experience peace through the reconciling love of God. I have suffered without God when I could have suffered in the comfort of God's love.

It wasn't until I understood that my perception of God being absent in bad, evil, wrongful deeds was wrong that I was able to look for the real evidence of God's presence in bad, evil, wrongful deeds. When I stopped turning away from God and resisting his care, I stopped living without him. Gradually, over time, I realized I was living without God at the times I needed him most. Bad things happen. Accidents happen. People do really bad things. Hate and evil exist. Cancer kills. People die. When I stopped living without God, I found acceptance that life is not always as I would have it be. When I stopped living without God, I found love. When I stopped living without God, I found healing and a reason for my life. When I stopped living without God, I found me.

I have seen God, I have heard God, I have smelled God, I have tasted God, I have touched God.

I have loved God.

I have served God.

When I stopped living without God, my purpose became clear.

Stop living without God and be loved.

God is love.

Love.

Donna Braidic

Bibliography

Beaton, Becky. "The Chambered Nautilus." *Dr. Becky Beaton, LLC*, 2013. https://www.drbeckybeaton.com/the-nautilus.html.

"The Bible Numerology Code Number 7." Astrovera. Accessed November 1, /2019. http://www.astrovera.com/bible-religion/176-bible-number-7.html.

Bush, George W. "Bullhorn Address to Ground Zero Rescue Workers." September 14, 2001, New York City. Transcribed on *American Rhetoric*. https://www.americanrhetoric.com/speeches/gwbush911groundzerobullhorn.htm.

Gaille, Brandon. "73 Most Famous People with INFJ Myers Briggs Personality Type." *Brandon Gaille*, June 27, 2013. https://brandongaille.com/73-most-famous-people-with-infj-myers-briggs-personality-type/.

Haensch, Anna. "When Choirs Sing, Many Hearts Beat As One." *NPR*, July 10, 2013. https://www.npr.org/sections/health-shots/2013/07/09/200390454/when-choirs-sing-many-hearts-beat-as-one.

"Kindness." *Oxford Languages*. Accessed September 27, 2022. https://languages.oup.com/google-dictionary-en/.

Kristenson, Sarah. "55 Famous People & Celebrities with ESTP Personality Type." *Happier Human*, April 15, 2022. https://www.happierhuman.com/estp-famous-people/.

Kroeger, Otto, and Janet M. Thuesen. *Type Talk at Work*. New York, N.Y: Dell Pub., 1993.

Landry, Carey. "Isaiah 49." Oregon Catholic Press, 1975.

Merton, Thomas. Prayer of Abandonment. *Thoughts in Solitude*. New York, N.Y: Farrar, Straus, & Cudahy, 1958.

McLeod, Saul. "Maslow's Hierarchy of Needs." *Simply Psychology*, April 4, 2022. https://www.simplypsychology.org/maslow.html.

Morgan, Kate. "How A Mother Turned Her Grief Into Goodness." *Woman's Day*, December 8, 2019.

https://www.womansday.com/life/inspirational-stories/a29833029/brian-muha-foundation-info-rachel-muha/.

Moltzau, Alex. "What is the Kernel?" *Towards Data Science*, September 27, 2019. https://towardsdatascience.com/what-is-a-kernel-7c532d5d3e56.

Norbet, Gregory. "Hosea." Oregon Catholic Press, n.d

"Peace." *Oxford Languages*. Accessed September 27, 2022. https://languages.oup.com/google-dictionary-en/.

Rilke, Rainer Maria. *Letters to a Young Poet*. Qtd. in *Quotes by Elise*. Accessed May 26, 2029. www.elise.com/quotes/rainer_maria_rilke_-_live_the_questions_now.

Tobin, Olivia. "Thai cave rescue news: Hero diver says it was a 'miracle' everyone got of Tham Luang alive." *Evening Strand*, July 17, 2018. https://www.standard.co.uk/news/world/thai-cave-rescue-hero-diver-says-it-was-a-miracle-everyone-got-of-tham-luang-alive-a3888791.html.

Van Veen, Dan. "Thai Soccer Team Rescue a True Miracle." *Assemblies of God*, August 7, 2018. https://news.ag.org/features/thai-soccer-team-rescue-a-true-miracle.

Cover art

Driftwood Beach: Epiphany. Lauren Shea, artist. So much love and gratitude for the beauty of Lauren's work and her ability to capture the soul of me seeing into my life through the loving and kind eyes of God.

"The chambered nautilus is one of the oldest creatures known to survive in the earth's oceans. It is a symbol of nature's grace in growth, expansion, and renewal. It is also a symbol of order amidst chaos as reflected in its spiral precision" (Beaton).

On a beautiful winter afternoon on Driftwood Beach, Jekyll Island, Georgia, I wandered about the beach investigating the many and varied remnants of trees. Standing stark and rigid against the clear, blue sky and rising up out of the soft, flowing sands, the gray, dead trees formed gnarled, bent, contorted shapes, with some resembling serpents slithering in and out of the ground. Despite years of battering from storms and surf and the intensity of the hot, southern sun the trees continue to stand. The scene defies logic, a true masterpiece of God's amazing imagination.

I walked along by myself for quite a while, barely noticing the other people on the beach who also marveled at the natural beauty all around us. I took dozens of pictures on my cell phone camera, hoping to capture the beauty of this alien place, when I turned to my right and saw a flash of red in my peripheral vision. I looked more closely and saw a little way off a young woman dressed more for June than January. I moved on, but my curiosity drew me back to her. Standing barefoot in the crazy, chaotic shadows of the trees, she made me think of a nymph. The random beauty of her youth and innocence against the stark permanence of death struck me.

The beach, part of the Georgia coastline since the continents broke apart, and the trees, dead for years, remind me that the world has been evolving and changing and adapting since the beginning of time, and God has been present through it all.

Elements of the Painting:

The nautilus in the painting symbolizes the life I have lived. Its chambers represent my growth as a child of God, and that each ending connects to a new beginning. Through my many "living withouts"–good and bad–I have continuously grown and enlarged my presence in the world. My life: colorful, mysterious, hidden until held up to the light.

The young woman figure wears a red swimsuit and a white, flowing button-down tunic, colors representative of the presence of the Holy Spirit. When I met Emma on the beach she was pure joy and spirit, beaming with love as she smiled for my camera. I will never forget the moment when I snapped the picture and realized our meeting was not happenstance; I was looking into the face of God.

The beach–Driftwood Beach, Jekyll Island, Georgia–primitive, dead, stark, naked. Jesus died on wood, planks hewn from trees. God in the midst of chaos, turmoil and strife, God present in death.

Water: Jesus called his disciples to follow him while walking along the beach, living water.

About the Author

Donna Braidic lives in South Carolina with her husband Scott.

Donna found peace and God's healing presence on the calm waters of Lake Greenwood, and soon enough the nudges of friends and family to write down her words of inspiration found their mark. Through years of study and worship and music the words of her heart flowed, and this book was born.

About the Artist

Lauren M. Shea is a classically trained painter with a Bachelor of Fine Arts from Columbus College of Art & Design. Lauren lives in Columbus, Ohio.